A SECRET MAP OF IRELAND

Rosita Boland was born in Clare. She has
published two books of poetry, *Dissecting the
Heart* (Gallery Press, 2003) and *Muscle Creek*
(Raven Arts Press, 1991), and the non-fiction
*Sea Legs – Hitch-hiking the Coast of Ireland
Alone* (New Island Books, 1992). Her poems
are in several anthologies, including *The Field
Day Anthology of Irish Literature*, and are on
the new 2005 Leaving Certificate English
poetry syllabus. She won the *Sunday Tribune/
Hennessy* First Fiction Award in 1997. She
has travelled widely and is a staff journalist
with *The Irish Times*.

A version of the Armagh chapter was
published in the Spring 2005 edition of *The
Dublin Review*.

A SECRET MAP

~ OF ~

IRELAND

ROSITA BOLAND

NEW
ISLAND

A Secret Map of Ireland
First published 2005
by New Island
2 Brookside
Dundrum Road
Dublin 14
www.newisland.ie

isbn 1 904301 78 9

British Library Cataloguing in Publication Data. A CIP catalogue record for this book is available from the British Library.

Typeset by New Island
Cover design by Anú Design
Printed in the UK by CPD, Ebbw Vale, Wales

New Island received financial assistance from The Arts Council
(An Chomhairle Ealaíon), Dublin, Ireland

10 9 8 7 6 5 4 3 2 1

For my brothers and sister,
Arthur, David and Cáitríona Boland,
with love and friendship

And in memory of our dear uncle, Gerald Bruen

CONT

ENTS

"What began it all was the bright bone of a
dream I could hardly hold onto."
From *Running in the Family*, Michael Ondaatje

COUNTIES OF IRELAND

INTRODUCTION

The first map I ever owned was *The Educational School Map of Ireland*, which we all had to buy in fourth class when I was nine. I think it cost sixpence. The counties were different colours – pink, green, yellow, orange – the various colours assigned to counties seemingly at random. I never worked out why the counties were the colours they were. They were not, for instance, colour-coded by province. Armagh was green, but so too were Limerick, Roscommon, Waterford, Dublin and Carlow. Clare, my own county, was yellow.

I studied the map constantly, utterly fascinated by it. For a small map, it packed in a lot of detail. A thick red line showed the railways. Crossed swords showed the sites of battles: *Vinegar Hill, Cnocnanos, Ballineety, Aughrim, Carrickshok, Clontibret.* Small crosses marked historical sites: *Ardmore, Clonfert, Gartan, Bunratty, Monasterboice.* Names and heights of mountains were printed in tiny black type: *Carntuohill 3414, Devils Bit 1583, Lognacoille 3047, Cruagh Patrick 2518, Sl Donard 2790.* There were no roads marked on it at all. Instead, there were rivers snaking everywhere: *R Liffey, R Blackwater, R Bann, R Robe, Fergus R, R Shannon, R Derg.*

The bays and lochs were all marked in, as were many of the islands. The cities, county capitals, towns and villages were almost like afterthoughts, small pinpricks of red against all those rivers, mountains, battle sites, historical sites, which took up most of the space. Shannon, then a new town in the making, was not on the map at all.

Broken red lines led into Waterville and Valentia: *Trans-Atlantic Cables.* Sea routes were thin red lines. There were twenty-four of them then. *Cobh to New York 2800m, Waterford to London 215m, Dublin to Liverpool 120m, Greenore to Holyhead 70m, Belfast to Glasgow 113m, Moville to New York 2560m, Larne to Stranraer 35m.*

I still have that map of Ireland, along with several others I've acquired in the meantime. I like the fact that, like palimpsests, maps can contain anything: that one map of the same country can exist without showing you roads, and that another one is thick with roads. That one version can show you historical sites, and another only race-courses. I also like the simple but satisfying fact that, if you have been to a certain county, it means something different to you; you have a first-hand, three-dimensional experience of it. It becomes real in a way it didn't before.

Ireland is a country that is sentimentalised by virtually everyone except those who actually live in it. Here's the best example I can think of. Litter. The Irish, it has always seemed to me, are genetically programmed to litter. RTÉ journalist Valerie Cox did several reports about illegally dumped rubbish recently for the *Today with Pat Kenny Show*, going out on the road with litter wardens. In rural Sligo, they found a huge pile of half-burned rubbish in a scenic public amenity. The litter warden found an address in the mess and duly confronted the man who had dumped it there. When asked by Cox what this man's partner would say if she knew that he had burnt all this litter in a wooded picnic area, he said, "She'd kill me." When Cox asked him why he had done it, he simply replied several times, "I don't know." The thing is: he did sound genuinely baffled, as if he really had no clue at all what had prompted him to think that it would be an excellent idea to go to a local beauty spot and burn his unwanted rubbish.

So that's part of what Ireland is. It's there, the elephant in the corner, along with political corruption, drugs, racism, tribunals, a new culture of commuting, planning disasters, materialism, obsession with property, celebrity and the quite staggering fact (to me, anyway) that Brown Thomas now offers a bespoke Hermes bag made of crocodile skin and diamonds that sells for €120,000. All those things are now an integral part of the Ireland we live in. But they weren't what I wanted to focus on when writing this book.

I wanted to write a book that attempted to show that you can be surprised by your own place. Undoubtedly, many people who read this book will know the things I have written about inside-out. But prior to researching this book, I had never heard of the Seven Wonders of Fore at Westmeath. Or Dan Donnelly's arm in Kildare. Or explorer Thomas Heazle Parke, buried in Drumsna, Leitrim. Or Billy Dunbar's museum in Tyrone. Or the lost village at Ballyvaston in Down. Or the Fuldiew Stone in Antrim. Local people in those counties will probably know all those names and places intimately. I suppose my thinking was that you can't be a local in every county, so hopefully there are at least a few surprises for everyone.

Knowing a county well made little difference to what I chose to write about. Kerry, for instance, where my father is from, where my brother David now lives, where I once lived myself and which is a county I have known extremely well all my life, was almost the last place to yield up what seemed like the right idea. Similarly, I dithered for a long time about Clare, my home county. In the end, I chose subjects purely because they either meant something to me or intrigued me, thus I really wanted to research and write about them. Selection was as simple as that. Anyone could write a book like this one, and each one would be completely different because everyone would focus on different subjects, chart their own individual map.

The other criterion I set myself was that everything I wrote about was to be accessible in some way to the general public. Almost everything is. Anyone can go hunting for the route of the old West Clare Railway; or stay a night in Mount Melleray in Waterford; or visit the Chinese Room at Dalgan Park in Meath; or look at where *T'aint-a-Bird* landed in Cork; or visit the Folklore Library in Dublin; or ask for the key to Robert Percy ffrench's mausoleum. There are a few exceptions: I was invited to Inishlyre in Mayo by the islanders and invited to visit the Met Station at Malin Head in Donegal – invitations I accepted because I thought they would cast light on the bigger associated subjects I wanted to write about. But in the main, most things covered in this book are places anyone can go, should they want.

I put the chapters in the order that I visited the counties in, mainly because there are various references to weather through the year's research that give them a kind of natural unity as a whole. But the book can be read in any direction: probably the chapter everyone will read first will be of the county they are from. The idea is that the thirty-two chapters make a kind of jigsaw: that the various pieces all add up to make a picture of Ireland as I see it. My own customised treasure map, I guess.

When I started researching this book, in May 2004, I thought I already knew Ireland pretty well. I was completely wrong. Long before I had finished the research, I realised I didn't know it at all. That the more closely you look at something, the bigger and more complex and more densely textured it becomes. To me, the biggest and best surprise about writing this book was realising I will continually be surprised by Ireland.

Dublin, May 2005

~ GALWAY ~

A KEY

In Ireland, we grow up wonderfully used to taking castles for granted. Not just the posh ones that are now hotels, such as Ashford and Dromoland, or the pristinely restored ones you pay to visit, like Bunratty and Knappogue, but also the ruined ones. The bits and pieces that turn up all over the country; stone flotsam and jetsam from a tide long gone out forever. The huge slabs of walls at right angles to each other. The still-stark outlines of Norman towers. The fields with those roofless, floorless, soaring spaces; the walls thick as memory. The ruins we find familiar, and thus not remarkable. They are one of the more exotic things we take for granted about rural Ireland. The sheep and cows of Ireland really do graze in pretty astonishing surroundings.

I heard about a mausoleum in Monivea Woods twelve years before I discovered that it was in a building that looked like a miniature castle. My sister, Cáitríona, lives in north Galway, not very far from Monivea, to where she sometimes used to drive my niece Sarah to discos. I asked Cáitríona if she knew of a mausoleum somewhere in Monivea Woods. She had never heard of it. Monivea is very small. You would think that if there were something special there, someone who lived reasonably locally and was interested in these things anyway would have heard of it. I was not even sure what information I had originally picked up about the tomb, in the faintly remembered Chinese-whispers way that you hear things.

In the end, it was simple: I looked it up on the Internet. It took less than a minute to find out that there was indeed a mausoleum still standing in Monivea. It sounded both im-possibly extravagant and impossibly romantic.

The mausoleum at Monivea was built for Robert Percy ffrench, the last of the male line of his family. Their estate was the village's Big House, Monivea Castle, now ruined. ffrench was a diplomat and served as secretary to the British Embassy in St Petersburg and Vienna. On his travels, he met Sophia de Kindiakoff, the only child of fabulously wealthy Russian aristocratic landowners. They married in 1862.

They themselves had one child: a daughter, Kathleen. By the time her father died in Italy in 1896, she was one of the richest women in Russia, where she was then living. Not only had she inherited the estate at Monivea, she had also inherited all the Russian estates belonging to her mother's side of the family. Kathleen Emily Alexandra de Kindiakoff ffrench lived at Simbirsk on the Volga in what was described as "the largest of her palaces" until all her property was confiscated by the Soviet government after the Russian Revolution.

Meanwhile, after her father died in Naples in April 1896, his body lay embalmed there while Kathleen commissioned a tomb worthy of his memory. Designed by Francis Persse, the younger brother of Augusta Gregory, it took four years to complete. Kathleen's fortune explains the cost of the extraordinary commission – the equivalent of €2 million in today's money. The triple-lancet stained-glass windows, by Mayers of Munich (still in business today), were valued in the early 1990s at a million pounds alone.

One Saturday in May, I met my sister Cáitríona, niece Lucy, who had just turned nine, and five-year-old nephew Luke in Monivea. The wide-streeted village still has the irregular green patches that were once flax beds; the industry that supported Monivea in ffrench's time. Together, we went looking for the house near the entrance to the woods that holds the key to the mausoleum. It is not the first house or the one closest to the entrance of the domain, and there is nothing to indicate where the keyholders live. You find out by asking in the village – although, in the Irish way, you must first know what it is you are looking for.

The key we collected was a magnificent object. It was as long as Luke's forearm; a huge, heavy old iron key. The children took turns carrying it, thrilled by its size. I was pretty thrilled myself. At one point, Lucy dropped it. What we would do if you lost it, we teased her. But that can't be the only key, Cáitríona said. When we returned it later, we discovered that it was. There is only the one, original key to open Robert Percy ffrench's mausoleum, which you borrow from the keyholders for no fee and without even giving your name. I both loved and worried about the freedom of that trust.

We walked through Monivea's lovely woods for about half an hour, following an unmarked path through the dense forest. We were not quite sure which direction we should be walking in, and there was nobody around to ask. The children panted in the hot, still afternoon and asked how much further, but we didn't know.

The first sighting you get of the mausoleum is through a clearing in the trees. It is pure Hans Christian Andersen: a miniature castle hidden deep in the woods. It's the kind of castle you draw as a child: square and simple, with steps leading up to a gothic arched door and crenellations on the roof. There are no windows on the facing wall. We hurried towards it. Lucy clutched the key and ran ahead of us, her brother trying his best to keep up.

When we turned the key and pushed in the door, all four of us gave involuntary gasps. The children squawked with delicious fear. They seemed both freaked out and enthralled, in equal measure. They stood behind us while we went into a dense and beautiful silence.

The afternoon sun was at our backs. When we opened the door, the strong, bright light fell inwards and onto the effigy in the middle of the room. The life-sized effigy of Robert Percy ffrench is apparently a perfect likeness. His bearded, dignified face is inclined sideways on a marble pillow. He lies on his back, feet to the door and the forest beyond, draped in a richly carved cloth with a Maltese cross on it. He had converted to Catholicism and become a Knight of St John of Jerusalem; the order use this cross as their symbol. The entire effigy is carved from Carrara marble – the marble Michelangelo carved the *Pietà* from. Canova used it too. It is a pure white marble, from a famous old quarry in Tuscany, still quarried to this day. Its special quality is that it glows translucent when the light shines through it; almost in the way you can hold your hand in front of strong light and see the shadows of the bones within. Infused with sunlight, the effigy looked eerily alive. It was this quality that startled us all when we opened the door first.

This piece of carving by Terace is one of the loveliest I've ever seen, all the more startling for being in such an unexpected location. The genius is not just in the carving, but also in the positioning. On the wall opposite the door are the east-facing triple-lancet stained-glass windows; the morning light shines in through here. On a sunny afternoon, such as the one when we were there, the sun is in the west and ignites the marble with light when the door is opened. There is no electricity in the mausoleum, so the use of natural light remains as effective as it was a hundred years ago, when Kathleen de Kindiakoff ffrench commissioned it.

The building itself is perfect, in pristine condition; a place exactly in tune with what it contains; and a beautiful piece of architecture by any standards. It is in every way extraordinary. You could not call it a folly, because it is both beautiful in itself and serves the specific purpose of being a funerary chapel.

It also feels very peaceful, as ideally the final resting place of a person should. The mausoleum-cum-funeral-chapel is small and square, with a high vaulted ceiling of granite gothic arches. Four black marble columns mark each corner of the effigy. There is the distinctive smell of an enclosed place; a place that doesn't often have air – or people – circulating through it. On the side of Robert Percy ffrench's effigy is carved: *Il lui sera beaucoup pardonne car il a beaucoup aime.* He will be forgiven much because he has loved much.

We left the door wide open and explored further. Under the windows facing the door is an altar, with another Maltese cross carved into it. There were two candlesticks with half-burnt candles in them. I discovered later that Monivea Wood was acquired by the State in 1941. The forest is owned by Coillte, and the mausoleum itself is now owned by the Church of Ireland, who occasionally have services there. On the other two facing walls are more stained-glass windows, which depict twelve of the fourteen Tribes of Galway. There is also an exquisite, tiny holy-water font, composed of waves of the sea, stars and angels' wings.

There is a door on the left-hand side of the altar chancel. We pushed it cautiously. It opened. Beyond lay a spiral staircase, which led both up and down. We decided to go down first. The children pushed ahead of us, and then hung back some steps down, pressing themselves against the walls so we could pass by them to the basement, where it was very dim. We waited a few seconds for our eyes to adjust. "What," Cáitríona said, "is *that?*" pointing to the two shapes that lay facing east.

In the basement of mausoleum are the two lead coffins of Robert Percy ffrench and his daughter. Kathleen herself died in China in 1938; in Harbin, far north-east China, infamous for being one of the coldest places in China, where the temperature drops to forty degrees below every year. These days, the people of Harbin make ice-sculptures each winter to attract visitors. The biggest ones are several metres high and constructed around lampposts, which make them glow eerily from within – like Robert Percy ffrench's effigy in sunlight. It was strange thinking of such coldness on what turned out to be one of the hottest days of the summer.

Kathleen was the last of her line: she had no children. We walked around the coffins in the faint light. Kathleen's is on the left and her father's on the right. His stands on a carved stone, the letters of which are faintly visible: as if the coffin was intended for a vault that was never built. Between the two coffins is a small white marble cross, with a beautiful wreath of fragile jewelled flowers over it. The children were confused. They had thought the dead person was upstairs, and that there was only one person. "Is he dead?" they had kept asking, walking round the effigy. They recovered their nerve swiftly and scampered upstairs again. When we emerged from the basement, we found them sitting either side of the effigy, patting the head delicately and chattering away unselfconsciously to him.

The other part of the stone spiral stairs leads up to the roof. There is a fine view far out over the forest, all of which was once the ffrench estate. We could see nothing but the trees, hear nothing. The whole experience, I thought later, was like opening a series of Chinese boxes: the wood in the village; the miniature castle in the wood; the marble effigy in the castle, luminous and ethereal as a trapped star, should such a thing ever exist. The key that opened them all.

Months later, curious, I asked Lucy if she remembered the day we went to Monivea. "Oh, that was when we went to see Percy in the forest," she said brightly. "The dead man lying on the floor. He was nice. I think he gets lonely at night, though."

Monivea, Co. Galway, 29 May 2004

~KILKENNY~

THE RAGGEDY BUSH

On the right-hand side of the twisting road that runs between Kilkenny and Kells, contained in a scrap of a verge, is the Raggedy Bush. You register it from the corner of your eye; a confusion of branches and scraps of colour. *What* was that? And then it's gone; the thicket of branches and rags that bulges so unexpectedly out of the landscape.

I went past the Raggedy Bush for years, either coming or going from visiting friends in nearby Burnchurch, Helen Comerford and David Lambert. They acknowledged it as we passed; "Oh, there's the Raggedy Bush," they'd say, as we whizzed by. So I knew what it was called. But I never stopped to look at it properly. Partly because it is not very accessible. It's true the bush is on a roadside, but it is a very busy, fast, narrow road where, if you're on foot, you need sharp ears and quick reflexes to avoid being flattened. So I would glimpse the

7

Raggedy Bush at the last moment from the window of the car and then it would go by in a glorious, strange blur.

Sometimes I don't want to look at things too closely. The tantalising blur from the car or bus or train is enough. It's enough for something to be part of the texture of the landscape. For it to promise something; to offer arcane dimensions without needing to know exactly what those dimensions are; not to have everything around us constantly spelt out and demystified in the process. But finally, one hot June afternoon, I parked my car some distance up the road and walked back to look at the Raggedy Bush properly for the first time.

The Raggedy Bush, I realised that afternoon, looking at the tangle of branches and wall, is first of all a miracle of survival. It was difficult to know where the bush began or ended, and how much of its endurance depended on the stakes that held it up and the ropes that held it together. It was even difficult to see where exactly it was growing from; parts of it appeared to be growing out of a wall, and parts seemed to be mixed in with an alder bush. And yet it was thriving, green-leaved, with a nebula of whitethorn flowers on every branch.

And on every branch, also, items were carefully attached. The June day I was there, these were some of the items hanging from the Raggedy Bush:

> The white china lid of a teapot, decorated with red and blue flowers and tied to a branch by a piece of white lace.
> Several pairs of tights.
> Scores of single socks – grey, black, white, blue. Men's and women's. One pale-green sock with pictures of sheep. One child's sock with cartoon bears.
> A blue bead earring.
> A royal-blue tie.
> Several bras.
> A baby's bib, tied on the highest branch.
> Hair-ties and scrunchies.
> A woman's white cotton handkerchief with pink roses.
> An orange chiffon scarf.

A rosary beads, twined round a branch.
Hair ribbons.
Scores and scores of strips of cloth – silver lamé, pieces
of J-cloth, tea-towels, bathroom towels, clothes fabric,
sheets, blankets, bedspreads – and also a few strips of
plastic.
Red lace knickers.
Green silk camisole.
Several pairs of boxer shorts.
A crystal necklace.
A blue and white woollen scarf.
A white lace Secret Possessions bra, size 36B, tied very
carefully into the shape of a container, so that it looked
like a kind of secret Fabergé egg. Inside the shape it
had made was a man's black sock.

What did they all mean? I had no idea. The lid of the teapot,
in particular, mystified me, partly because it was the only piece
of china on the bush. Why, I wondered? Why would you hang
the lid of a teapot on a bush? I tapped it gingerly. The sound of
china rang back at me, but revealed nothing. Although why
would you hang boxer shorts and ties and knickers on a bush
either? I felt a little superstitious about touching any of the
items, but figured as long as I treated them with respect, it was
OK. I was also fascinated by the white bra tied around the man's
black sock. It was like a poem of intimacy; an anonymous love-
token of two people. Placed there for fertility? For love? For
luck? For the craic? I had no idea, but there was something both
touching and wonderfully light-humoured about the bra-and-
sock Fabergé-egg installation.

The baby's white bib had been deliberately placed on the
highest branch, some seven feet from the ground. It fluttered in
the small breeze and bizarrely made me think of Tibetan prayer
flags, tied to the highest trees so that the wind can carry the
prayers printed on the flags down-wind all the better.

And why so many socks? Perhaps because they were small
and more easily parted with than shirts or larger items of
clothing. But that was looking at it from a practical perspective

and, whatever they meant, I was sure the socks weren't there only because they were small and disposable.

Some of the items were so faded I couldn't make out the colours any more. They had become a uniform grey, stiff with wind and dust from passing cars. Some had rotted away almost entirely. I was struck by how secular the items on the bush were. I had seen many holy wells, where the items left are almost entirely religious: sacred pictures, rosary beads, prayers, memorial cards, candles and small statues. Although I looked very carefully for quite a long time into the branches, I could see only one rosary beads and one Lourdes picture, and the picture was in a plastic wallet lying underneath the bush, not attached to it.

I tried doing a rough tally of what items there were the most of, and concluded that it was the strips of fabric: the pieces of sheets, blankets, clothing, J-cloths, tea-towels, plastic and that marvellously flamboyant piece of silver lamé.

"What I heard about the strips of cloth," my friend Helen explained later that evening, "was that you tied something on the bush belonging to someone if they were ill, and when the cloth rotted, the person was well."

There had indeed been many strips of bedding: sheets and blankets and bedspreads. Perhaps they had come from that place located in the old-fashioned expression, the sickbed. But J-cloths? Tea-towels? Strips of plastic bags? The silver lamé? The whole bush was like a cypher; a code that everyone could attempt to crack in their own way.

Beside the bush was a recently carved stone, with the words, "St Patrick's Raggedy Bush. Age Old Tradition." I liked that. It told you everything, and nothing, all at once. There was a border of pansies beside the stone. I looked at the flowers, the carved stone and the careful way the bush had been propped up by stakes. Someone was taking care of the place. It was still registering as important in the local consciousness.

Later, I read the articles the librarians in the Kilkenny Archaeological Library had dug out for me. One was from a journal entitled *The Proceedings and Papers of the Kilkenny and South-East of Ireland Archaeological Society of March 1856*. A Mr E. Fitzgerald had recorded a piece about holy wells in the Ardmore district during the 1850s. Both the florid language of the period and the content interested me:

> At each of the wells, the visitor will find numerous coloured objects tied to the trees and briars in their neighbourhood. At my visit to St Bartholomew's well, the fine old venerable thorns which overshadowed it bore a most motley appearance, actually crowned with old red, blue, and green ribbons and rags, as if torn from the dresses of the pilgrims, and tied up as a finale to their "rounds" and prayers. An old crone engaged in giving her "rounds" told me they were tied up by each to leave all the sickness of the year behind them. Now, such matters as these are well worth our attention.

A couple of paragraphs later, Mr Fitzgerald went on to quote correspondence from a William Hackett of Midleton, "who has given much of his learned attention to our early mythology". Hackett writes:

> I stand at a holy well and see an old woman attaching a rag to the branch of a tree. I know that an Indian rajah who had presented the image of a cow, as large as life, all of solid gold, to a temple, completed his devotion by the same rite of tying a rag to a tree. I read of a Brazilian Indian, doing the same, 1,200 miles west of the Atlantic. The same is done at this day by the Arabs on Mount Hor, at the tomb of Aaron. Rich [no explanation of who he is] mentions a holy well at either Babylon or Nineveh; there was no tree, but nails were in the walls covered with these rags, not given as votive offerings, but in a sense identical with that of the old woman here in Ireland. In this lowly and inexplicable rite, I fancy I see a vestige of the early patriarchal religion – the first universal worship in the world. But although wells must have been in Oriental regions appendages of patriarchal worship, the veneration for them and the rituals

observed at them have come down to us through a
medium loaded with Paganism ...

The other piece which the Kilkenny Archaeological Library
found for me was a book entitled *Kilkenny City and County:
People, Places, Faces* by local journalist John Fitzgerald, which
reproduced a short article he'd written about the Raggedy Bush.
The people Fitzgerald talked to reckoned the bush to be about
a century old, reporting that it was marked on a map of 1903.

They also offered theories as to why people hung rags on the
bush. In the 1950s, colliers en route to Castlecomer would not
pass it without leaving a rag behind, to show respect. A theory
about the ribbons was that you tied one on when leaving to
emigrate and then another if you ever returned. Perhaps so. The
Americans, in particular, seem to have adopted the ribbon-tying
ritual in recent years to remember those in conflict far from
home. I couldn't, however, imagine the Irish being so overtly
sentimental. Superstitious, yes, but not sentimental. But
whatever about ribbons, there was no explanation offered as to
why or when underwear started to appear on the Raggedy Bush.
Or socks. Or the lids of teapots.

Before leaving that afternoon, I took one of my socks, made
a wish and tied it securely onto the bush. Not a lowly rite, as
Hackett would have had it some 150 years previously, but
certainly an inexplicable one.

Kilkenny–Kells Road, Co. Kilkenny, 5 June 2004

~ LEITRIM ~

THE MOUNTAINS OF THE MOON

Of all the things I've accumulated over the years, my favourite possessions by far are my passports, three to date. To me, they are impossibly romantic objects: their pages stiff with visas and stamps; each one dense with memories. They are especially dear to me since I've chosen never to own a camera, and thus don't have a single photograph of any of the countries I've travelled in, although I do keep diaries. So the passports are records: proof, tokens of adventures.

I can't be bothered with photographs. I prefer to let scenes and images of places surface later, unbidden and of their own accord. I literally never know when the darkroom in my head will suddenly develop an image and surprise me. Probably most frequently is while walking the daily beat to work: along the canal, down Leeson Street, through the Green, down Grafton Street and along College Green.

The images come at random. Telc's old town square, white on white in moonlight under January snow in the Czech Republic; the refracted fading light on broken mosaics of a ruined Mughal palace on an island in Bangladesh; the blue, blue tiles of Isfahan's surreally beautiful mosque in Iran; a horizonless horizon on the Nullabor Plain in Australia; an irrigated village like a chip-of-emerald shelf over a gorge in Pakistan, where its children play among the flowering apricot trees, mere feet from a sheer half-mile-long drop to the Indus river below.

Or any of innumerable images. Not all of them beautiful by any means, and some very disturbing. The haunted faces of the old on the streets of Phnom Penh; the bared-teeth snarl of the wild-eyed street dog that bolted towards me from nowhere, circled and then bit me viciously three times when I was alone on a back-street at night in Kathmandu; the small children in Calcutta, their limbs needlessly amputated, deposited thereafter outside tourist-traps each morning, human begging-parcels; the intimidating army signs all over Mandalay – *Oppose all foreign nations interfering in internal affairs of the State* and *Crush all internal and external destructive elements as the common enemy.*

Whether beautiful or disturbing, for a moment or two when these images arrive, I literally forget where I am, temporarily transported elsewhere by the magic carpet of memory. And then the lights change or someone jostles past or I start thinking about work and the image vanishes, as swiftly as it arrived.

When I discovered that Drumsna in Leitrim was the last resting place of the first Irishman to cross Africa *and* to see the Mountains of the Moon, my first reaction was amazement, the second awe and the third incredulity that his name is so little known. Then I realised I had been passing his statue in Dublin for years without knowing who he was. Surgeon Major Thomas Heazle Parke's statue stands in a prominent public position outside the Natural History Museum on Merrion Square, although it's a fair bet most people who glance at it en route up the path to the museum have no idea whom the statue represents.

Parke was born in 1857 in Clogher House, Kilmore, just

inside the Roscommon side of the Roscommon–Leitrim border. He trained at the Royal College of Surgeons in Dublin and soon after joined the British Army, working in the Royal Army Medical Corps. He was posted to Egypt in 1882 and quickly gained a reputation for cool-headedness and hard work. Almost single-handedly, in 1883, he dealt with a huge cholera outbreak near Cairo at a camp in Hiloun. The following year, he joined the Nile expedition for the unsuccessful relief of General Gordon at Khartoum, which took two years.

His most famous expedition was another relief operation: this one to relieve Prussian Edvard Schnitzer, who titled himself the Emin Pasha, who was stuck in what is now Zaire, then known as the Equatorial Province and a British territory. General Gordon had recommended Schnitzer's appointment as governor in 1878, although he was not a military man, but a rather eccentric linguist, botanist and medical doctor. By 1887, the Pasha's territory was surrounded. On three sides were foreign colonists and on the fourth were the Sudanese. His own garrison was made up of what he described as highly unreliable Egyptians. He sent a dispatch to England, requesting relief.

The resulting expedition was a classic example of British Victoriana. It was, first of all, strictly unnecessary: the Pasha could quite well have got himself out of Equatorial Province if he had been a little less lazy. It was also on a huge scale – there were six hundred Zanzibarian porters to carry the gear. They took with them two tons of gunpowder, six hundred rifles, thirty-five thousand cartridges and a twenty-eight-foot steel boat, which ended up being carried most of the way. Even the provisions were extravagant and impractical, with forty loads alone coming from Fortnum and Mason's, many of them perishable and wholly inadequate to the needs of so many over such a long period of time. The six-thousand-mile expedition took the longest and daftest possible route. Instead of cutting up north, expedition leader Henry Stanley, then internationally famous as the man who found Dr Livingstone in 1871, chose to follow the Congo from west to east, starting by sailing east to west, via Cape Town, a voyage of three thousand miles alone. Altogether, there were some 810 people in the expedition – but only eight Westerners, seven officers and Stanley – to rescue one, not terribly significant, governor of an obscure British territory. Only three hundred people survived the nightmare expedition, and many more would have died had Parke not tended to them. It was, perhaps, the Falklands of the nineteenth century.

But at the time, the expedition was seen as a magnificent thing for Britain; a morale boost overseas, after their failure at Khartoum. The money for the expedition – £21,500 – was raised by public subscription, and most of the tents, medical supplies and firearms were donated.

Expeditions, then and now, need doctors, and Stanley chose Parke for the job. I read about how it happened in Parke's diaries of the expedition, which are unpublished but held at Mercer's Library in Dublin, where they arrived in the 1990s. They were acquired from the legatees of the late Austin Byrne of Bray, Co. Wicklow. Byrne's father, George, had bought a bookcase, along with all its contents, from a sale of the effects of a Dublin solicitor. Parke's four diaries from the Pasha expedition were discovered among the books and were passed to Austin Byrne. He died intestate, and Mercer's were approached and asked if they wanted the diaries of one of their most famous ex-students.

If you make an appointment, you can request to see the diaries and are permitted to read them on the premises. There are four of them, all identical: tall, thin, fairly battered notebooks, with marbled endpapers in brown and blue. They all have a stamp inside them, which reads, "Issued from Army Forms Store, 30 October 1886." The lined pages are a pale blue, and Parke's slanted handwriting is still very clear. He has written the date of each entry in the margin.

For a morning, I lost myself in Africa of 120 years ago, turning the pages of the diaries with a heady excitement, while computers hissed around me and the librarian's phone rang. They are the diaries of a pragmatic, intelligent and resourceful man; one who also shows himself to be a very tough traveller. He gives virtually nothing away, though, about anything personal.

It's possible he wrote the first few entries after the events recorded there, since his obviously orderly mind would have liked the idea of a full record of the expedition, from beginning to end. Most likely, he only started writing the diaries day-by-day when he had been accepted on the expedition.

> *27 January 1887*
>
> Met Stanley at Abbato Hotel, Alexandria on his arrival by P&O boat. I applied for a post on his staff of the Expedition for the relief of Emin. His answer was that he could take no person except those he had already chosen. I gave him my card and he left for Cairo.

It didn't take Stanley long to reconsider. It took even less time for Parke to pack and board a train to Cairo – while also doing some housekeeping of his affairs in Alexandria.

> *28 January 1887*
>
> Received a telegram at [indecipherable] Club from Stanley, asking me to accompany him on the Expedition for the relief of Emin Pasha. I left Alexandria by 10.30 p.m. train and arrived at [indecipherable] about 6 a.m. having previously wired back "Yes. Coming to Cairo tonight." I also had some difficulty in getting a substitute to hunt the Alexandria Hunt Club Fox Hounds as I was Master and a meet was advertised for next day. However Major Wood of the Essex Regt after a little modest hesitation consented to relieve me out of the difficulty.

By June, they were well into their absurd journey along the Congo. The expedition itself may have been ridiculous, but the courage and endurance of those who undertook it is undeniable.

> *5 June 1887*
>
> We have not seen a village since Friday last. The islands in this part of the river [the Congo] are much longer and the bush extremely thick. It is impossible to get through them without bullhooks.

13 June 1887

I removed a large piece of the humerus of a Zanzabarian who had been accidentally wounded with a hatchet.

14 June 1887

Having stopped opposite a small village the men went on shore but could find no provisions except plantains. We stopped for the night and the natives fled into the bush. Tom Toms and horns were sounding high in all the villages around so as to prepare the inhabitants for the war path.

Food was a constant problem, especially for such a huge expedition

3 July 1887

Marched from daybreak until dark 7.20 p.m. so as to get out of the forest for we had nothing to eat. The forest here is a network of elephant tracks and we take advantage of them when they go in our direction.

9 August 1887

Stanley went on ahead and captured eight more goats which were given to the men as rations. The men are now beginning to steal food from us and also their comrades and crime is on the increase simply from hunger. One goat lasts six of us for two days.

As the months progress, the writing becomes quite a bit wilder and more untidy. Parke suffers from repeated bouts of malaria.

2 September 1887

Remained in camp all day and dried my clothes, medicines and dressings all of which have been wet for 10 days as there is not time to dry them for we march from morning until night and there is no drying in the bush, everything is damp.

28 September 1887

I shot two men who were in a canoe as I thought they

were escaping with a goat but the canoe went down-stream.

16 October 1887

Ate most of our donkey meat. Marched early. Not enough men to carry the boats as the men were dying along the road and we had to leave them but took their rifles.

5 November 1887

We cannot get anything to eat from these people. I fill in most of the men and ordered all able to walk to go on with Jephson as it was certain death for them to remain here where they would be starved or eaten by these savages.

Parke rarely makes any reference to his own feelings, which, for me, made this next entry poignant. It made him real, human.

16 December 1887

I shall be confined to bed for a long time as there is a very great inflammatory swelling about my left hip and thigh. I'm sure this is due to blood poisoning from hand-ling our ulcerated sick and living on the filth we eat. A most lonely sunset this eve.

Christmas Day 1887

Spent the day in bed lying on ammunition boxes [to protect them from theft]. My temperature was 106. I wish all at home a Happy Xmas.

3 January 1888

My boy won't confess what he has done with the valuable medicines although I forgive him the crime of theft if he returns the medicines. When I pointed my revolver at him he ran away. I intend hanging him up by one arm to a tree until he confesses. This is a simple but very effective method.

Stanley went ahead of them to the Imperial-held Fort Bodo.

8 February 1888

Arrived at 11 a.m. at Fort Bodo. Entered with our flag hoisted and fired a few rounds as is always the custom when a Caravan returns. Met Stanley. He gave me a warm welcome. Stanley was quite chummy for the first time. [It's clear from the diaries that Stanley was entirely wrapped up in himself and his sizeable ego.]

Towards the end of February, Stanley had been ill for several days. Though Welsh by birth, Stanley had adopted American citizenship and was extremely fond of his adopted country.

I sat up last night. At 9 p.m. Stanley had a severe fit of coughing. All draughts were avoided by stopping up holes in the wall and by his special request the American flag was placed as a shelter around his bed as he was rather low spirited.

Finally, the expedition party was noticed.

16 April 1888

After marching about six miles, a native brought a letter wrapped in American cloth and directed to Stanley and signed Dr Emin saying that he had heard of the apparition of a white man at the south of the lake and had come down with the steamers to see who we were. Letter dated 25 March 1888 and is wrapped in a piece of *The Times* containing a description of the Newmarket first spring meeting Tuesday 1887 including the two thousand guineas Irish Plate, won by Mr Manton's Primstead ridden by F. Barrett. We are all in great ecstasy as the trick is finished.

Four days later, Parke saw the Mountains of the Moon, the Ruwenzori Mountains, on the border between Zaire and Uganda. To this day, the cloud cover keeps the mountains elusive from sight. Sadly, all the record books report that Stanley was the first Westerner to sight them. He claimed them for himself later and, since Parke was conveniently dead by then, nobody objected.

20 April 1888

Jephson and myself were sent by Stanley this morning to bring the boat and launch it on the lake, where Jephson accompanied by the boat's crew was to go and search for the Pasha. We camped in a village and got three goats as a present. On the march, we distinctly saw snow on the top of an immense mountain to the south-west. As this was an unexpected sight, we halted the Caravan to have a good view. Some of the Zanzibaris said the white appearance of the mountain was salt but Jephson and myself were quite certain that it was snow.

29 April 1888

Stanley was the first to announce steamer as he had seen her through his binoculars on the top of an ant hill. As the steamer came closer and closer the Zanzabaris became wild with joy, now that they are certain of the existence of the white man whom they often disbelieved in during their terrible wanderings in the jungle.

Enter the Pasha at last, who appeared to be in fine fettle and not, after all, in need of urgent relief. In fact, he proved extremely reluctant to leave his little fiefdom. In this long entry, Parke goes on to describe the business of escorting the Pasha to their camp.

Jephson was busy keeping the Pasha from stumbling into swamps and holes as he is extremely short-sighted. The Pasha was very slight and short about 5 feet 7. He wore a clean white shirt and spotless coat and trousers. He looked cheerful and was exceedingly polite. Stanley gave him his armchair [Stanley had an armchair!] and he invited Casati, Jephson and myself to sit around on some boxes. Stanley disappeared for a moment and returned with a couple of bottles of Champagne which he had carefully concealed in the legs of a pair of long stockings buried in his box. [They were reduced to eating their donkeys, but they had Champagne!] We each drank the Pasha's health. The Pasha said he could scarcely express

his thanks to the English for sending relief but he did not know if he would come out after doing so much work in the Province and everything in perfect order. We all hope the Pasha will come out but curiously enough Stanley says that our object is to bring him relief and not to bring him out, as we shall have scarcely enough men left to drive through to Zanzibar and protect ourselves.

The farcical upshot of all this effort was that the Pasha got spectacularly drunk at a celebratory banquet in his honour shortly after and fell out of a window, fracturing his skull. Parke patched him up, and the Pasha did eventually depart with what remained of the expedition. However, he left them along the way and was later murdered by tribesmen.

Despite all this, the staggering loss of life and no Pasha to parade in London as a trophy, the three-year expedition was deemed a success. Stanley was hailed as a hero. Queen Victoria, Bismarck and US President James G. Blaine sent messages of congratulations. In May 1890, Parke went back to England and was given many tokens of recognition of his part in the expedition, including a medal from the Royal Geographical Society, which is also held now at Mercer's. He was promoted to the rank of Surgeon Major. In Ireland, banquets were held in his honour, both at the Royal College of Surgeons and at Carrick-on-Shannon's town hall. A subscription was taken up to honour him, resulting in the statue that now stands outside the Natural History Museum. But only three years after the expedition, he was dead, aged thirty-six, his health fatally undermined by the demands made on it in Africa. He never married and left no children.

In 1920, Florence Parke, Parke's sister, presented to the National Museum some items that her brother had had with him on his last, and most famous, expedition. They were: a water bottle, a gun holster, a leather belt, a cotton Nehru-type shirt and a pair of cotton breeches. They were held in the museum's Art and Industrial division, but nobody is now sure what was held in storage and what was on display. The clothes and holster were displayed in an obscure cabinet in the Natural History Museum from some unknown date until 2002. They are currently undergoing restoration at Collins Barracks, where they are due to be displayed in 2005 as part of a major exhibition of Ireland's military history. I looked at them by arrangement in the conservation department of Collins Barracks: the faded, patched clothes laid out like shadows, the battered water bottle, the cracked-leather holster. Proof, tokens of adventures.

In the village of Kilmore, just inside the Roscommon border with Leitrim, there is a small church, the key of which you must ask for locally. I called on Harry Nutley, who lives in the middle of Kilmore village and who is the keyholder. Harry invited me in, and while I petted his terrier, Spot, he went rummaging for the key. Few people ask for it these days and he spent some minutes searching. He found the key eventually on a hook over the range. Before he passed it to me, he warned that the church was in a bad state of disrepair and that I should be careful when in there. And what, exactly, was I interested in seeing, if I didn't mind him asking?

I wanted to see, I told him, the plaque that had been put up in memory of Thomas Heazle Parke. I had seen a photograph of it, but I wanted to see the actual thing myself. His face fell. "If it's the plaque you're wanting to see, you'll see nothing," he told me. "It has been boarded up."

Since I was there anyway, I took the key and walked up the road to the church. It didn't look too bad from the outside, but when I put the key in the door and went inside, I cried out, taken aback. Swallows, nesting in the church and startled by my sudden appearance, flew past my head, dipping and swooping. For a moment or two, until my eyes adjusted, I didn't know what they were. I closed the door behind me and stepped inside.

Kilmore Church is heartbreakingly beautiful in every sense of the words, as it is literally fading away to ruin. There is a large hole in the ceiling, where the birds and rain get in. It is small and richly decorated, with hand-made cassocks rotting on the pews. There is a wonderful antique organ, which was made by Cramer,

Wood and Company of Westmoreland Street, Dublin. Its lid is open and the organ is covered in bird droppings and what looks like woodworm. *Viola, Forte, Octave, Cello, Celeste, Melodia* read some of the little enamelled knobs. There is a fireplace beside the lectern and leaded glass in all the windows. There are extraordinary, exquisitely carved seventeenth- and eighteenth-century memorial plaques.

One, in white marble bas-relief, is adjacent to the altar and in near-perfect condition. It depicts a scene that could have come out of Kipling's *Kim*: an image of a man dying in his wife's arms, while three men in turbans stand in the doorway of what was clearly a Big House, one of them with a smoking musket in his hand. The inscription reads:

> Here be interred the remains of James Sawden of Kilmore Esq whose many virtues still live in the hearts of his surviving friends; for he was benevolent in his disposition, steady in his friendship, hospitable in his family, cheerfully amiable and equable in his tempers, fair in his person and blameless in his life.
>
> To the memory of such perfections, this monument was created by his forlorn and disconsolate widow, Mrs Jane Sawden, who still endures existence after having enjoyed uninterrupted felicity, in the society of such a husband for the space of 44 years and having beheld him breathe out his last in her lap.
>
> On the 7th day of January 1779, aged 70, he was barbarously murdered while unprotected, unarmed, and in his own house, at a dead hour of the night and by the hands of ruffians, some of whom his former bounty had fed.
>
> Reader, from this sad event, learn this useful lesson: that we must look beyond this world for that happiness and security, which extreme charity, unaffected piety and innocent manners cannot secure us in this.

As Harry Nutley had warned me, the plaque in memory of Parke is now boarded up. It is in the middle of the church, over the left-hand pews. I looked underneath it and could just see the sheen of the brass, sandwiched between the crumbling wall and the crude wooden board over it. I knew what the inscription said:

> In memory of Thomas Heazle Parke Surgeon Major AMS, 2nd son of William Parke Esq J.P. of Clogher House, Kilmore.
>
> Beloved and honoured by all who knew him. He entered the Army medical staff 1841. Served in Egypt with distinction accompanying the Bayuda Desert column of the Nile Expedition for the relief of General Gordon 1884–1885. From Jan 1887 to Dec 1889 he served on the Expedition for the relief of Emin Pasha as Surgeon.
>
> It is as a tribute to his constant gentleness and care for the sick and suffering and to the splendid services he rendered alike to Europeans and Africans during the three years march across Africa that this tablet is erected in grateful and affectionate remembrance by the two surviving officers of the Expedition.
>
> Henry Morton Stanley, Commander
> A.J. Mounteney Jephson, Lieutenant

When I had returned the key, I drove the couple of miles across the border to Drumsna in Leitrim. Thomas Heazle Parke is buried here, in this tiny village. There was once a railway station there, and Parke's body arrived from Dublin by train. The tracks are still there. He is buried in the lovely ruins of the tiny Presbyterian church that lies behind a gate down a laneway from the village's main road. The Parkes had burial rights here. It contains less than ten graves, none of them tended and some now badly damaged, with broken headstones. On the showery June day that I went there, I spent some time sheltering under the huge old ash tree that grows in the middle of the ruined church, its branches acting as a roof that suffuses the place with an ethereal pale-green light.

Parke's grave is beside the tree. The Celtic cross that marks his grave has the simplest of inscriptions, revealing nothing of his military rank, nor of his achievements. It reads: *In loving memory of Thomas Heazle Parke, second son of William and*

Henrietta Parke, Clogher, Drumsna. Born November 27 1857. Died September 10 1893. Blessed are the pure in heart for they shall see God. His parents lie buried behind him. The church receives very few visitors. His untended grave is thick with weeds. It seems an inglorious ending to an extraordinary life.

Drumsna, Co. Leitrim,
and Kilmore, Co. Roscommon, 26 June 2004
Mercer's Library and Collins Barracks, Dublin, 12 July 2004

~ANTRIM~

THE FULDIEW STONE

It had been raining on and off all day; sulky, relentless sheets of it, with yet more hanging grey and thick in the distance. The rain was keeping everyone indoors. I was in Knocknacarry, far up the Antrim coast, and I needed directions, but there was nobody around to ask. I was looking for a churchyard I had been shown two years previously, and I couldn't remember where it was. There were, of course, in the fine Irish tradition, no signposts.

In the end, I found St Patrick's Church again simply by driving around a lot and guessing. Just as I drew up alongside the boundary wall, the sky hissed open and torrential rain hammered down. I sat in the car and waited, not very patiently. Fifteen minutes later, it was worse. If I'd got out of the car with my notebook just then, it would have been reduced to pulp in seconds. I'd been driving for hours to visit this place and I wanted to record my impressions without being hurried. I just had to keep waiting.

There is something of the no man's land about the time spent unexpectedly waiting. It is an in-between time; a stepping-stone between action and inaction. A few months before I went to Antrim, my car had packed up one Sunday evening in Dublin, and I spent a good three hours at the side of Clanbrassil Street waiting for the tow-truck to arrive. Frankly, I hadn't bargained on spending my Sunday evening in the dark, staring into the window of Capital Glass, which is where I had cut out. ("It's Sunday and we're very short-staffed, but we'll have someone to you as soon as possible.")

I've never meditated, nor do I have any desire to do so, but I did a lot of thinking during those hours while waiting for the truck to arrive – though I guess the purpose of meditation is not to think at all, but to empty your mind of thoughts. That evening was like being in a cul-de-sac of time: on pause; shored up at the side of the street, waiting, when I was meant to be somewhere else and doing something else. I'm often on Clanbrassil Street, but I've never before spent three hours there at one time, just waiting in one place and thinking. It isn't the loveliest or most promising of locations in Dublin for a bit of enforced reflection on a cold and dark February night. Yet, months later, sitting in the car in Antrim waiting for the rain to stop, I remembered that night and realised that it had reminded me, literally, of time passing. It had been a sort of *memento mori*, and the fact that I was now waiting to visit a grave made it seem even more so. I found myself retrospectively being oddly grateful for that breakdown, for what agnostic does not want to be reminded occasionally to make the most of whatever time it is you have? And then the rain stopped.

Although I had been to this church once before, when my friends Bernard and Madeline MacLaverty had shown it to me, I still spent quite a while hunting round for the right grave. I remembered it being flush with the ground, not upright, which made it harder to spot. I walked past the gravestone twice before it finally registered with me. There was a sheen of water on its surface, glinting in the post-rain light.

What I was looking at was an oblong gravestone with carved letters top and bottom and, in-between the lettering, a crude but distinctive carving of a fully rigged ship with two anchors cast from it at opposite ends, each of them different. There was another object, a goat, carved on the top left-hand side. The letters, all in capitals, read, in this order:

CHARLES MC
ALASTER'S BURR
ING PLACE
HERE LIES THE
BODY OF JOHN
HIS SON DIED 11
MARCH 1803
AGED 18 YEARS

Underneath were the carvings of ship, anchors and goat, and then more letters:

YOUR SHIP
LOVE IS MOR
ED HEAD AND
STARN FOR A
FULDIEW

The story I had been told about this inscription by the friends who had first shown it to me was that John McAlaster was a seaman who had, at eighteen, recently become betrothed to a girl from Cushendun. While he was at sea on a voyage, his ship called at Liverpool, where he met a man from his homeplace who was en route back, to whom he gave a letter for his betrothed. It was to tell her that he would be paid off in a couple of weeks and that his ship would be coming back to Cushendun and to look out for it; that they would be married as soon as he returned and, mean-while, to start the preparations for the wedding.

When the sails of the ship were sighted on the horizon, the word spread. The ship dropped anchor in Cushendun Bay, and a small boat was lowered. The people on the shoreline thought it was being lowered to set ashore their neighbour and kinsman, John McAlaster. What they did not find out until the boat reached the shore was that the boat contained John McAlaster's body. He had died in a fall from the ship's rigging.

The story I heard originally was that his betrothed went quite mad with grief at his loss. When he was interred at the family plot in the churchyard, she stayed up all night carving with a flint the letters and drawings on the stone. In the morning, she was found dead: an Irish Juliet lying on a tombstone, dead of a broken heart.

I stood in the churchyard, trying to draw the anchors and then the goat (the ship itself and its complex rigging completely defeated me) and copying the lettering into my notebook, remembering the original story I had been told. The story intrigued me enormously, but the pragmatist in me could not believe all of it. Broken hearts, while undeniably painful, do not kill you of themselves. And there is no way a young girl could have done all this carving in a night. Even by moonlight. Even with proper tools, let alone with a flint. Yet the stone was undeniably there, in all its strange and lonely loveliness, carved in a way I had never seen a gravestone carved before.

The carving alone would mark this grave out as something very individual and special, even without the depictions of ship, anchors and goat. The letters, all in capitals, are carved deeply, but very unevenly. Wonky would be the right word to use. The letters are all different sizes, hence the words breaking randomly in peculiar ways. There is also a mistake, one a professional stonemason would never have made: the *E* of *DIED* is missed out and has been inserted as a smaller capital over *DID*.

But you can see the meaning of the words in the way they are carved: carved deeply, with more feeling than technique. The words are still distinctive and seem to have eroded hardly at all, despite two hundred years of weathering. You look at them and think, whoever carved that was grieving indeed. It is a little like looking at wild handwriting, where someone can't get the words down fast enough, so desperate are they to get the message across. And then there is the word "love". *Your ship love is mored head and starn for a fuldiew.*

Fuldiew means the money a sailor would receive at the end of a voyage for the work he had done: his full due. It is also a nautical expression, meaning something duly and thoroughly done, so that it does not need to be done again. So you could read the epitaph in a couple of different ways. That not only was John McAlaster's ship finally moored and his voyage in life over, but also it was moored for eternal love. But whose specific love? His betrothed's? His family's? Who knows? There is no record of his betrothed's name anywhere. She has become a shadowy, mythologised figure through the story of this gravestone, and is now more lost in the past than the young man who predeceased her.

Malachy McSparran lives in Knocknacarry and is one of the founder members of the Glens of Antrim Historical Society. I went to visit himself and his wife, Brigid, to ask them about the local perspective on what is referred to in the area as "the fuldiew stone".

"The McAlasters were without doubt a sea-faring family," Malachy said. "There was a story that one of the McAlasters had sailed with Nelson. When I was a boy, our schoolmaster told us he had visited the McAlaster house and been shown an old naval uniform and a sea-chest. The McAlasters have all died out now. The last of them, a granddaughter of the last McAlaster, died in about 1970. There was an auction in the house after her death, but the uniform and the sea-chest were not included in it. They had disappeared. We don't know what happened to them."

Malachy and Brigid are of the opinion that the essence of the story behind the gravestone is true, but has been embellished over time. Malachy showed me a book he had acquired some time ago: a Victorian travel book about Ireland, written by an American woman called Miss Mulock, entitled *An Unknown Country* and published in 1887 by Harper and Brothers of Franklin Square, New York. Miss Mulock (as the author chooses to coyly call herself) visited Antrim in 1885 and saw the fuldiew stone. It would then have been in the graveyard for eighty-two years. Miss Mulock writes of a girl on horseback by the church telling her about the stone:

> "There is one grave you must look at. A girl here who had second sight as they call it in Scotland, begged her sweetheart, a fisherlad, not to go to sea on a certain day as he would certainly be drowned. He was drowned, though they managed to rescue his body and it is buried in this place. The girl would sit for hours beside the grave, carving a ship on the stone, until at last she went melancholy mad and jumped from a rock into the sea at Cushendun."
>
> As she galloped off, we crossed the once carefully-kept graveyard to the stone she had indicated, and pulling the moss away, read the inscription. A few more half-obliterated marks that were supposed to represent an anchor and goat. I have since heard that these marks were scratched not by a love-lorn girl, but by the boy's father. My readers may choose either tradition.

Malachy waited until I had read the passages he had marked. I read them twice. "That could be the true version," he said. "When you think about it, she visited in 1885. So she was a lot nearer the event that we are now; eighty-two years. It's possible the story she heard had been passed on by relatives of people who still remembered the event. We are now two hundred years on from it all, and it's much further from us."

So what is the true story of the fuldiew stone? That John McAlaster fell from the rigging of a ship and died? That he drowned? That he was due to be married on his return from a voyage? That his anonymous betrothed carved the letters and drawings on his grave? That she died of a broken heart, stretched out over the tombstone? That she jumped into the sea and was drowned? That John McAlaster's father, Charles, carved the letters and images himself to commemorate his beloved son?

Like Miss Mulock over 120 years ago, my readers may choose either tradition.

Knocknacarry, Co. Antrim, 28 June 2004

~ARMAGH~

Mr Tayto

Probably our first introduction to economics is through the sweetshop. The first money you have of your own to spend is invariably a very small sum, and unless you are heroically self-disciplined and save it all, you will recall exactly what your favourite sweets and crisps cost throughout your childhood.

The first time I had any money of my own to spend was when a bag of Taytos cost 2½p. Even then, there was a dilemma when it came to parting with a portion of the 10p weekly pocket money, because a bag of Sam Spudz was 20 per cent cheaper, at 2p. Taytos invariably won out, though, because to me they tasted better. For a long time as a child, I thought that the brand-name of Taytos was actually the word for crisps themselves. Taytos *were* crisps, the two things mixed up together in the same way that the brand-name Hoover became a byword for the act of vacuuming and Xeroxing, for a time, meant photocopying.

For a while, I was very fond of Smokey Bacon. Or Smokey Bacoon, as I called them. For some reason, I thought the word "bacon" was pronounced "bacoon", like racoon, although how I might have become aware of such an animal in 1970s Clare is an unsolved mystery sadly lost to the past. Mrs Markham, the kindly shop-owner across the road from us, never corrected me when I asked week after week for the name of a crisp that didn't actually exist. She just smiled and handed the brown and orange bag over the counter. When I stopped eating the Smokey Bacon Taytos, at about ten, I never ate them again. Then there was a brief flirtation with Salt and Vinegar, which always tasted wonderful for the first few mouthfuls and then it was too much – too much salt, too much vinegar, too much dryness and too strong a smell. It was Cheese and Onion which was the constant choice; ever reliable and always the flavour that most of my friends wanted to dip their hands into when the bag was offered around at school.

As an adult, the only time I ever eat Taytos is occasionally in a pub with a pint of Guinness. I never, ever have this longing for Taytos anywhere else. But from time to time, nothing will do me but a pint and a bag of Cheese and Onion Taytos. I want the rattle of the bag, the taste of the salt and the familiar, friendly face of the charmingly absurd little Tayto Man, smiling out from the back and front of the bag.

Clichéd and all as it is, surely it's no coincidence that, over time, Taytos have been one of the most requested items from home by Irish people now living abroad. Asking for Taytos when you are far from home must have something to do with connecting with memory, identity and your past, since potato crisps themselves are so widely available. And not just any old crisps: often much more interestingly flavoured; posh, expensive crisps that are grand enough to be acceptable with aperitifs before a dinner party. My nephew Liam, who was eleven at the time, happened to be in the middle of writing a school essay when I was visiting my family in Galway a couple of years ago. The topic was "Irish heroes". Liam read out some of the essay to us after dinner. "My hero is Joe 'Spud' Murphy, because he invented Taytos, and to think of Ireland without Taytos is like thinking of a bog without turf," he read with feeling, as the entire family collapsed with laughter.

In the same way that I naturally assumed as a child that Taytos were crisps, I naturally assumed as an adult that there was only one Tayto company. About fifteen years ago, I was told that Taytos were made in Armagh, at a place called, improbably, Tayto Castle in Tandragee; told by an acquaintance from Armagh who had once been there on her school-tour visit.

Tandragee is a very small L-shaped town, five miles from Portadown. Driving into Tandragee at the end of June, I was left in no doubt as to where its allegiance lies. Red, white and blue bunting hung between every lamppost. A permanently fixed metal archway over the town's main street proclaims: *Fear God, Honour the King, and Love the Brotherhood*. There are various symbols incorporated into the arch. King Billy on his horse. A cannon. A cross. A coffin. Union Jacks fly at either end.

During weekdays, there are free tours of Tayto Castle, which you can book in advance. I was to tag along on that afternoon's 1.30 p.m. school tour. I spent the hour or so I was waiting by walking up and down underneath the bunting and browsing round the town's Spar (it was Tuesday, a day when most of the other shops were closed). I noticed that Walkers crisps were selling for half-price – a bag of twelve for the price of six – and was marvelling at the audacity of such blatant competition in the very home of Tayto itself, when I noticed the racks holding the bags of Taytos.

It was the first clue that something was different. There was a packet of Taytos called Ulster Fry, with a picture of rashers, sausages and tomatoes on the front of the bag – and a line on the back saying the product was suitable for vegetarians. I had never seen this flavour before. I stared at it, quite mesmerised. Then, when I started looking properly, I noticed lots of flavours I'd never seen before: Thai Chilli, Wuster Sauce, Barbecue Beef, Postman Pat Prawn Cocktail, Bob the Builder Pickled Onion, and things called Whisps, Bikers, Rollers, Ravos, Spirals and Fives, all of them with the Tayto name on them. I was confused. Why had I never seen any of these flavours before?

The Tayto Castle at the centre of Tandragee is indeed a castle, and a handsome one at that. You push open an imposing wooden door in a wall and go up the driveway that leads to the seventeenth-century castle, which was once the home of the O'Hanlons and later the Duke of Manchester. During the Second World War, Tandragee Castle, as it is officially called, was requisitioned by the War Department, and both British and American troops were stationed there. Then it lay empty and deteriorating until three local entrepreneurs bought it in 1955, one of whom was Thomas Hutchinson. A businessman with many interests, Hutchinson started manufacturing Taytos on the site in 1956. The Hutchinson family still own and run the company.

The current factory building dates from 1978 and is adjacent to the restored castle. Prior to the afternoon tour, I stood in a foyer with some thirty children from Killen Primary School in Castlederg, Co. Tyrone. We all left our bags and watches to one side and put on blue hairnets and white plastic aprons. Before our tour of the factory started, Mr Tayto came to meet us; a luckless employee dressed up in an outsized costume. The children screamed joyfully and begged their teachers to take pictures of them with Mr Tayto. I was very puzzled. This was not the Mr Tayto I knew – the rhombus-shaped, smiley, enigmatic man with the red coat, striped blue trousers, small natty shoes and trilby-type hat. This Mr Tayto had huge black clown-like boots, a red suit like a Butlins employee, a ridiculous red hat and, most unfamiliar of all, a potato-shaped head on a tiny little neck. The Mr Tayto I knew had no neck at all, just a head that continued into a magnificent kind of slope.

During the tour, we heard that the factory produces one million bags of crisps a day. It uses five different kinds of potatoes for production – Records, Premiers, Saturnas, Lady Rosettas and Clares. The potatoes are all sourced from twenty-five local farmers. Using artificial light, potatoes can be stored for up to eight months in the factory. Recycling is big: unused potatoes and peelings are sold as cattle feed; and the starch is extracted and sold to make paper, glue and animal foodstuff. And the most popular and best-selling flavour? Cheese and Onion.

Afterwards, when I had divested myself of hairnet and apron, I talked to Robert Brown, the promotions and PR manager for Tayto, in his office in the castle building. We had discussed statistics for a good fifteen minutes – products exported to forty-three countries over the Internet and so on – when I remembered Liam's essay and mentioned the name of Joe Murphy. I asked where did Joe Murphy fit into the story of Tayto, since the only name I'd heard since arriving was that of Thomas Hutchinson.

"But this is Tayto Northern Ireland," Robert said gently, in the way you might address a small and not very bright child. "Tayto Dublin are a completely separate company."

It was only at that point that I realised what should have been obvious to me all along: there were two Tayto companies. Tayto Northern Ireland, set up in 1956 and still owned by the Hutchinsons; and Tayto Dublin, set up by Joe Murphy two years earlier, in 1954, and owned by Cantrell & Cochrane since 1999. At the beginning, the two companies were connected but, although I tried hard to find out what exactly happened and when one became two, Robert Brown became a little coy.

"Everyone originally involved is dead now," he pointed out correctly. However, when I suggested that perhaps some current member of the Hutchinson family might be able to cast some light on the history of the company they owned, he wasn't biting. Robert did agree that it was "very unusual" to have two companies operating under the same brand-name on the same small island. He suggested that Thomas Hutchinson and Joe Murphy had come to "a gentleman's agreement" about the boundaries of their companies: that neither would sell their products on opposing sides of the border. "Maybe they met at a business meeting and came to that agreement," he offered. This policy of observing the borders when it comes to distribution is in place to this day. "We wouldn't think of selling in the south and they wouldn't think of going into the north," he explains. Then he added, apropros of nothing, "We employ people from both sides of the community in Tayto Northern Ireland."

Robert also told me that the flavourings and potatoes used by Tayto Northern Ireland are different from those used by Tayto Dublin. It explained why I had never seen flavours such as Ulster Fry for sale south of the border. But what I was truly astonished to hear was that the best-selling crisp of each company, Cheese and Onion, is made to different recipes. "They have a completely different taste, and depending on where you have grown up, you will have a liking for the flavour you have grown up eating," Robert explained.

When I got back to Dublin, I looked at the web sites of both Taytos: www.tayto.com, the site of Tayto Northern Ireland ("the taste of home"), and www.taytocrisps.ie, the site of Tayto Dublin ("the original Irish crisp"). The Tayto Dublin site told me no more than I already knew: "Tayto, a member of the Cantrell & Cochrane Group, was set up in 1954 by Mr Joe Murphy from Donabate in Co. Dublin." Neither company referred to the existence of the other.

I tried to find out more about Tayto Dublin. Their factory is in Coolock, but they do not offer tours. When I phoned looking for information about the history of the company, they directed me to their PR company, Slattery, who asked me to put my questions in writing.

I did this. Weeks passed. I left messages on the voicemail of Emily Cox, the PR person looking after the Tayto account, wondering how she was getting on. She periodically left apologetic messages on my voicemail, saying she had passed my queries on, but that Tayto were very busy with Christmas orders and she had heard nothing from them as a result.

After four weeks, I got on the phone and stayed on hold for a long time until I got Emily Cox in person. We went through the questions again. I heard that Tayto were busier than ever now, since it was so many more weeks closer to Christmas, and they had so many orders to look after …

Two days later, Emily sent me an e-mail that contained the official history of Tayto Dublin. There wasn't much new in it. Entrepreneur Joe Murphy started his crisp company in 1954, in a premises off Moore Street, with one van and eight employees. His wife Bernadette ("Bunny") spent hours peeling the potatoes. They had two deep-fat fryers. They called the company Tayto after their family nickname for potatoes. "His great marketing coup was to invent the world's first Cheese and Onion flavour."

Emily added a few extra bits of information about the Murphy family. Joe Murphy died in 2001. His wife Bunny is still alive and lives now in Marbella. As Tayto had been acquired by Cantrell & Cochrane in 1999, Emily explained, nobody working there now was familiar with the history of the company. She also confirmed that at some date in the past – exact year apparently unknown, but decades ago – Joe Murphy "sold the rights to use the trademark Tayto name in Northern Ireland and the UK".

Towards the end of the e-mail, she wrote: "Today, Tayto is Ireland's leading crisp brand and is one of the biggest purchasers of potatoes in Ireland. The company uses five varieties of Ireland's best quality potatoes to produce its market-leading crisps. The varieties used are Saturna, Lady Claire, Lady Rosetta, Homeguard and Premier and it is this combination that gives Tayto crisps the unique flavour and texture that has made them the market leader for half a century." Four of the five potato varieties are exactly the same as those used in Northern Ireland: instead of Homeguards, the Tandragee factory uses Records.

I had bought a bag of Tayto Northern Ireland Cheese and Onion and taken it back to Dublin with me. One Sunday, when I had my friends Oliver Comerford and Madeleine Moore around for brunch, I did a blind tasting of the crisps. The Northern version (which comes in a gold-coloured wrapper) were in one bowl and the Tayto Dublin Cheese and Onion (whose red, white and blue bag is as vivid as the bunting that hangs from the lampposts in Tandragee) were in another. Ollie and Maddy shuffled and mixed the bowls on the table with great ceremony, while I closed my eyes and we all laughed.

I always thought Tayto was a common language. That when you met someone Irish abroad, no matter where they were from in the thirty-two counties, you understood what they meant when they said they'd love a bag of Taytos.

They do taste different. Totally different. I recognised which was which straight away. I didn't even have to guess.

Tandragee, Co. Armagh, 29 June 2004

~ WICKLOW ~

MILLENNIUM TREE

The decision by the government in 1999 to give each household a candle and a native Irish tree to celebrate the millennium was received with decidedly mixed feelings by the population. There was an ongoing spate of letters in the papers and voices on the airwaves asserting that the money spent on the project could have been better used elsewhere – specifically, directed at the less well off in our society. However, controversial as they were, the candles and tree certificates were duly dispatched.

I was never quite clear as to how the ratio of candles and trees per household worked. In 1999, I was sharing a house in Dublin on Upper Leeson Street with three friends, Julie Cruickshank, Ger Hennessy and Mary Rose Crotty. Jools, Ger, M.R. and myself all eventually received tree certificates, but only one candle arrived. Our shared household had a pre-millennium dinner together some time in late December and rather cheesily burned the candle that evening, watching its gold letters melt away hour by hour. The candle was a nice enough gesture, but it also felt contrived somehow; portentous, really. I still have the millennium candle box. It's in one of my kitchen cupboards now, holding bandages, Solpadeine and flu-relief powders. From time to time, you see the boxes in charity shops or car-boot sales, although they're usually minus the candle.

The green-bordered certificate I received in November 2000 stated that, "To celebrate the new millennium, a native Irish tree has been planted for [my name]" and gave details of the location and a tree reference number. At the bottom was the facsimile signature of Seamus Brennan, then chairman of the National Millennium Committee. There were various logos on the cert, including one of eight figures standing together against a background of trees, which had a worryingly nuclear-looking sun behind it, radiating semicircles of yellow.

There are thirteen millennium forests in the Republic. They are at Muckross and the rather magnificently named Rossacroona-Loo in Kerry; at Tourmakeady in Mayo; Cullentra in Sligo; Derrygill and Rosturra in Galway; Derrygorry in Monaghan; Lacca in Laois; Portlick in Westmeath; Glengarra in Tipperary; Coill an Fhaltaigh in Kilkenny; Camolin Park in Wexford; and Shelton and Ballygannon in Wicklow. My millennium tree is at Ballygannon, in Co. Wicklow, numbered on the cert as BNDC013896.

The tree-planting project cost €5 million. A few years on, there has been ongoing controversy about the project, with protestors saying that too many trees have been planted per plot, and therefore only some of them can possibly survive in the long term, and that the whole thing was thus a cynical PR exercise by the government at the time. There were, in total, 1.2 million native Irish trees planted across the 1,500 designated acres: oak, hazel, birch, ash, alder, yew, cherry and the confusingly named Scots pine.

In July 2004, I dug out my millennium tree certificate and

decided to go looking for the tree. What I had liked about the project was that the cert made it feel personal, because the cert has your name on it and your own designated tree number. I got quite excited about it, especially since my own tiny, pebbled yard can hold only plants in containers. It's pretty, but a long way short of a real garden with grass – and trees. But, hey, I had my own tree! Out there somewhere in Ballygannon Wood! The species of tree planted for you is not specified on the cert. I was hoping it would be hazel, simply because I love the idea of divining. Failing that, ash, since that is the supple and resilient wood from which hurleys are hewn. Or oak, always a noble tree. After that, my affections were divided equally among the other species, apart from Scots pine, which is a tree I have a sizeable irrational dislike for.

Ballygannon is three kilometres north of Rathdrum. You park in a clearing on the right-hand side of the road (busy even early on a Sunday morning, buzzing constantly with motor-bikes) and cross the road to the Millennium Tree Site. There are signs, and also markers with oak leaves and arrows carved on them, to direct you. And I always need signs, since my sense of direction is abysmal.

Although the way was clearly marked, true to form I missed the sign. I realised this some half-hour later, when I had been walking in the sultry heat along an overgrown path by a boundary fence that was leading me deeper into the forest every step. I looked around me. There were a lot of trees pressing out the sky, and most of them seemed to be Scots pine. Now, I have an admission: forests freak me out a little. It's like Emperor Joseph II saying of Mozart's music that there are too many notes in it. For me, there are too many trees in a forest. I think it must have something to do with coming from Clare; a county where I grew up feeling at home among huge skies, the bare, stark landscape of the Burren and the vast horizons of the Atlantic. There are no horizons in a forest, which is quite possibly why I feel so uneasy when in one.

Whatever the reasons, I was definitely beginning to feel

claustrophobic. In addition, as far as I could see, Ballygannon Wood was totally deserted. As everyone knows, the Wicklow mountains and forests have not had a great press in the past, since from time to time bodies end up there. Only the previous week, a walker out with his dog in the Glen of the Downs had found the body of a Lithuanian man who had been lying there dead for some weeks. He was to be named ten days later as Arunas Gelzinis. I thought of his discovery and found myself looking round foolishly to check that nobody was following me. In fact, my mind was now rather more occupied with this than with finding my tree.

I fairly scampered back to where I had started, at the entrance to the wood. Of course, I then immediately spotted the marker that I had so unaccountably missed the first time. It was pointing in the opposite direction to the way I had just gone. There was a track beyond and some open space, which made me feel a lot better. Half-way up the track was a map of the wood under glass and a long column of figures alongside it.

I fished out my tree cert and looked down the column of figures for the corresponding number. The numbers are not listed individually, but in cohorts of several hundred at a time. My tree was located in the cohort BNDC013801–BNDC015180, in the Avonmore plot. There are four adjoining millennium tree plots in Ballygannon: the Avonmore, the Mass Path, the Copse and the Knoll. Under the map was written these directions:

> Locating where your tree is planted:
> Check to make sure the certificate states your tree is planted in this wood.
> Identify the tree number allocated on your certificate. Each square on this map represents a numbered plot where the trees are planted. A marker identifies each plot with a number attached.
> Locate the plot that corresponds to your tree number.
> Use the designated pathways to walk to the nearest plot where your tree is planted.
> The trees are very young and are extremely vulnerable. Please keep on the pathways and do not walk on the planted area or touch the young trees.

> We invite you to relax for a few moments beside your
> plot and to enjoy the birth of the People's
> Millennium Forest.

As I transcribed the instructions and invitation – *Check to make sure the certificate states your tree is planted in this wood*: well, *really*, did they think people were complete eejits? – the words of the Safe Cross Code, as immortalised by the *Wanderly Wagon* crew in the 1970s, kept resounding through my head: *1. Look for a safe place. 2. Don't hurry, stop and wait. 3. Look all around and listen, before you cross the road …*

I set off in search of the Avonmore plot. I walked past it, of course, not noticing the discreet wooden painted sign the first time. There are supposed to be cleared walkways within each of the four plots, where you can wander up and down before relaxing for your few moments and enjoying the birth of the People's Millennium Forest. I don't know what it's like in the other Millennium Forests, but in Ballygannon the walkways are so overgrown that, far from relaxing, you battle your way through briars and ferns, tripping over at intervals. It was July, and I soon regretted wearing sandals for my People's Millennium Forest visit.

I was not sure exactly what I had been expecting. I had at one point had a nice fantasy about visiting "my" tree every few years to see how it was getting on. I had thought vaguely of forests of saplings in neat rows, with plastic tags attached to them, each one listing a number – one of which would be mine. It's not like that. The Avonmore plot, where a tree in my name has apparently been planted, is so overgrown I could see virtually nothing, because almost everything there was very much taller than me. I couldn't see any saplings anywhere. I saw a lot of full grown trees, all of which seemed to be of the species I dislike most: Scots pine. I struggled my way up and down both walkways in the plot, peering through the tangled undergrowth, feeling more disappointed by the minute. I had liked that fantasy of my own designated tree, and I wasn't keen on letting it go, but go it went.

Later, in response to my questions as to why a) there was a

specific number on the tree certs when there didn't appear to be a tree to go with the number, and b) what trees had been planted in the Avonmore plot, Gerry Egan, Company Secretary of Coillte, sent me an e-mail.

> I was in Ballygannon yesterday and established that the Avonmore plot contains a mixture of oak, holly, and Scots pine trees, that regenerated naturally.
>
> To explain, in the Millennium Project, existing areas of native woodland were restored, some areas with exotic species were cleared and allowed to regenerate naturally with native species where it was considered that there was a good chance this would occur naturally, and some areas were planted. All three approaches were used in Ballygannon Wood. In the Avonmore plot the presence of a number of mature native trees suggested that this area would be a good candidate to regenerate naturally and that is what has occurred.

What I think this means is that nothing at all was planted in the Avonmore plot. The existing trees are just regenerating themselves. Tree BNDC013896 doesn't actually exist.

Ballygannon Wood, Co. Wicklow, 18 July 2004

∼WESTMEATH∼

THE SEVEN WONDERS

The Seven Wonders of Fore. I admit, when I first came across a reference to Westmeath's Wonders, I thought it was a joke. What I understood by the Seven Wonders was that they were not in Westmeath, or indeed Ireland. They were: the great pyramids at Giza in Egypt; the hanging gardens of Babylon; the statue of Zeus at Olympia; the temple of Artemis at Ephesus; the mausoleum at Halicarnassus; the colossus of Rhodes; the lighthouse of Alexandria. Or rather, they *had* been Wonders. Only the pyramids still endure.

But it's true. There *are* Seven Wonders in Fore. They are: the monastery on the quaking scraw; the mill without a race; the water that flows uphill; the tree that won't burn; the water that won't boil; the stone raised by St Fechin's prayers; and the anchorite in a stone.

I drove into Fore's pretty valley on the last Saturday in

August 2004. I had originally planned to come to Westmeath the previous Saturday. Instead, I found myself that day at my uncle's funeral in Monkstown in Dublin, attempting the impossible task of giving a tribute that would reflect something of what an extraordinary and special man he was. My uncle-in-law Gerald Bruen was ninety-six when he died, but he was a remarkable ninety-six: until a few days before he died, he was walking round, reading the papers and talking the talk. He even still had the trademark moustache he had had all his adult life. Along with my aunt Máine and my sister Cáitríona, I had been lucky enough to be with him when he died peacefully, and with dignity, at home in county Galway.

Uncle was a painter, and his studio in their Dublin house, with its easel in the middle of the room and canvases stacked against the wall, was one of my favourite places to be as a child. It was full of objects, some beautiful, like the blue glass vase with jasmine on it, some odd, like the Asian bronze representation of a man-cum-warrior with a second head sticking out of his body, and some puzzling, like the poppy-pin on the mantelpiece that appeared annually and that was neither an ornament nor a piece of jewellery, and which I was not allowed to keep for myself. Everything in the studio was interesting, but the most interesting thing of all by far was Uncle.

Uncle had been born in Poona, India, where he lived until he was ten. His father, Major William Bruen, served with the Connaught Rangers there and was later decorated with the Military Cross. It lay in a box on one of the studio shelves, but I didn't look at it often. I could not understand the significance of something so small and opaque as a medal. Uncle brought me places: the art galleries in Dublin, Dalkey Hill and Bullock Harbour, swimming at Seapoint, the Zoo, on his painting trips to Laragh and Annamoe in Wicklow, where he told me there was silver and gold in the streams. He tried to get me painting and drawing, which I enjoyed, but we both knew without ever saying so that I was no good at it. Uncle was a wonderful fisherman and cook, and loved good food and wine. He made me try olives, garlic, anchovies, soused herrings, chillies. He read the *Arabian Nights* to me, but I preferred the stories he invented himself. Every summer, he put up his old orange and navy tent in the back garden of the Dublin house and I disappeared into it for hours with my book, looking up periodically at the tiny pinpricks in the orange canvas to the sky beyond. Once, aged eight, when I was ill with measles in Dublin after a holiday there and could not return home to Clare, he phoned my teacher to tell her I wouldn't be back in school. I don't know what else he said to her, but two days later, when I was still feeling wretched in bed, the post arrived. There was one huge parcel for me, with forty-four letters and drawings inside – one from each of my classmates. It was the postal highlight of my childhood. He never had any children himself, but I and my three siblings all adored him, as did his great-nieces and great-nephews later on.

In December 2001 I was visiting Uncle and my aunt Máine at their home in north Galway. I took Máine out shopping to Roscommon. We asked Uncle before leaving if he wanted anything. He said he didn't. When we returned, we discovered Uncle had been and gone alone to Castlerea, a round trip of over thirty miles. He had gone to buy one thing: a bottle of champagne for me as my Christmas gift, something he knew I loved. He hadn't wanted to ask me to buy my own present, and it didn't occur to him to ask my aunt, a lifelong pioneer, to buy it. Instead, he drove all the way to Castlerea on icy roads to buy me the champagne himself, so that I would be surprised. He was then one month off ninety-three.

Driving into Fore that Saturday, the day's copy of *The Irish Times* lay in the back seat. It contained Uncle's obituary and a photograph of him, taken on his wedding day. I read it again before I got out of the car. Like all obituaries, it was very formal and factual, full of Uncle's achievements – including some I had never known about before – but not what he was like to those who loved him. Which is how obituaries are: they must record the facts, not the sentiments. As a journalist, I knew the obituary was faultless, but to me, his niece, it was like reading about a stranger. You shouldn't be sad when someone dies who has been so loved and had such a long and full life, but I still was sad.

Fore's only pub has a magnificent name: the Seven Wonders Lounge Bar. There is a petrol pump outside, as well as barrels of Calor Kosangas and a sign for HB ice-cream. Small wheelbarrows filled with flowers flank the entrance. The Westmeath colours hang on the façade. You go in here to collect the key that will open the door to one of the Seven Wonders: the anchorite in a stone. The yellow plastic key-fob is quite magnificent also. On one side is written "Key to hermit's cell." On the other is "Return to Seven Wonders pub, Fore, Castlepollard, Westmeath."

Fore was once home to three hundred monks and two thousand novices: a site of considerable religious significance and one that still receives many visitors and pilgrims throughout the year. The monastery was founded by St Fechin in the seventh century. Prior to his arrival in Fore, he had founded a monastery in Galway, the famous one on High Island, off the Connemara coast. Like on Skelligs, the monks at Fore lived in beehive huts, although no trace of these now remains.

I walked across the fields to the first Wonder, the monastery in the quaking scraw, or bog. This is the site of St Fechin's original monastery. It's where the ruins of an extensive Benedictine priory now stand. The priory was suppressed by Henry VIII. It's a Wonder, not just because of the significance of the site, but also that such a large and heavy building survived being built on a bog and did not sink. I crossed a few streams on the way to the ruins. One of them glinted with coins.

The ruins are quite beautiful, as is the whole setting of Fore, which is located in a lovely green valley. There were several tourists around, most of them foreign. I listened to their accents: German, Italian, English and American. I wondered where they had heard about Fore and what had brought them so far off the usual beaten tourist path, but by the time I got round to thinking of asking them, they had gone back to their cars, scattered by a sudden downpour.

The next two Wonders are beside each other: the water that

will not boil and the tree that will not burn. Or rather, they are there in theory. The old ash tree that used to stand near the car-park, and which was reputed to only have three branches, in honour of the Holy Trinity, is now dead. There is only a stump left. It was reputed that the wood could not be burnt, but it was not fire which did for it in the end. The tree died of copper poisoning from the coins that were tapped into it for luck over the years. A new one has been planted, close to the original, but it still looks very new and somehow raw.

The water that will not boil was in a holy well, out of which the original tree grew. The water from the well was taken as a famous cure for headache and toothache. Small children were brought there when ill. It was said that the water could not be boiled, and that if one attempted to do so, tragedy would strike. This may have perhaps originated from a desire to respect the well-water. Maybe people would have been tempted to make tea with the boiled water. Who knows? But the day I was there, the well was totally dry and looked as if it had been dry for some time.

The fourth Wonder is the stone raised by St Fechin's prayers. This is a two and a half ton stone, which is the lintel for St Fechin's church, across the road from the priory. It looks as huge as it sounds and has a carving of a Greek cross enclosed in a circle. There is uncertainty about how old the church is, but the general consensus seems to be that it dates from around the tenth century. The facts are blurred, since it seems that if the church does date from the tenth century, St Fechin would have been long dead and could not have raised the stone – unless, of course, he posthumously performed a miracle.

The story goes that, when the church was being built, the workmen could not lift the huge stone into place. They tried and tried and nothing worked. They went off to eat, and when they had returned, the stone was in place. Put there by St Fechin.

I walked up the hill to the fifth Wonder, the anchorite in a stone. The sky was a huge bright confusion of dark-grey cloud and shifting light. The fields glowed. I fished in my bag for the key to the locked building.

There are two parts to the building called the anchorite's cell. The oldest part is a small square tower, which apparently dates from the fifteenth century, although it was altered over time. It was built for anchorites, or hermits. Hermits occupied the cell in Fore for hundreds of years. There was only ever one there at a time. When one died, another one took over, to meditate and pray. They stayed there until they died and never left the cell once they entered. They were held in high regard and food was brought to them daily by local people. The last recorded hermit to live here was Patrick Beglan, in the seventeenth century, who is thought to be the last anchorite in Ireland.

The tower-cell was built onto later by the Greville-Nugent family. They built a small adjoining oratory and mausoleum, and several generations of the family are interred there.

I unlocked the door. It opened reluctantly, swollen with rain. I had to shove it hard and thus stumbled in after it when it finally yielded, feeling like an intruder. The place smelled of damp and was very dim. I left the door wide open and wished I'd brought a torch. I climbed the winding stone stairs at the back of the building to the anchorite's cell. It was eerie up there, dark, claustrophobic, dank. There was a very strange atmosphere trapped in there: something solid and unknowable and disturbing. I loathed the place. I couldn't find anything admirable in the fact that men had withdrawn from the world to meditate and live here alone all their lives: alive, but virtually entombed. To me, it just seemed horrible: a horrible waste of a life, especially when I thought of what my uncle had done with his own long life. It was a struggle to stay there long enough to look at the place properly. I paced the earth floor to find out what size the room was. Three and a half paces in each direction. Those were the dimensions of the world for the anchorites who lived here. I almost fell down the steps, I was so anxious to get away.

Patrick Beglan is interred downstairs in the adjacent mausoleum. The memorial inscription on his tomb is very elaborate and written in Latin. Later, I found a translation. It reads:

> Behold me, Patrick Beglan, dweller in the sacred hermitage. I am hidden and buried in this hollow heap of stones; beneath the towering rock for a monument and a sanctified abode. An undefiled sanctuary, a house hitherto without stain. The wayfarer, therefore, whoever he his, will perceive this tomb. Let them say may the soul of the hermit who dwells here reach heaven. AD 1616.

I locked up and stood for a while outside, looking over the valley. The sky had cleared. I still had two more Wonders to look for: the mill without a race and the water that flows uphill. But I didn't have the heart or the energy to look at anything else. The afternoon spent looking at ruined churches and tombs had made me sad. I went back to the car and drove away, two Wonders short, thinking of Uncle and the many wonders he had introduced me to all his life.

Fore, Co. Westmeath, 28 August 2004

~OFFALY~

Bog Train

I can't remember the first time I saw bog or heard the word turf.
They were always realities: always known things, always part of
the texture of my life. I loved throwing sods of turf into the fire
as a child. You had to shovel coal because it was so dirty, and the
briquettes were so dull, each little compressed peat parcel exactly
like the other. But sods of turf had individuality. I loved the
matted feel of them in my hand, often surprisingly light for their
size. I loved their irregular shapes and the way they looked so
untidy and wild in the fireplace. And I loved also the smell of a
turf fire, the way it hung in the air and lingered there.

You can't buy turf in Dublin, or, at least, I've never found
anywhere you can get it. Perhaps that's because you are not
meant to burn it in the city, although I do burn it sometimes,
whenever I've been back west and have been given some by my

sister Cáitríona or my aunt Máine, who both have turbary rights. Storage space is almost nonexistent in my cottage, so I can never take much turf. Rather than burning it all in one night, I tend to save it, burning a couple of sods a night to take the bare look off those too-neat urban-looking briquettes. The smell makes me feel happy. And it also makes me miss the west of Ireland terribly. It's not very scientific, but it's true.

I don't understand people who take out their fireplaces and replace them with gas-effect fires. It baffles me. When I finally went looking for a house to buy, apart from the obvious constraints, my two chief priorities were that it had to have lots of light – and an open fire. I love everything about a fire: the ritual of clearing it out, setting it, lighting it, sitting by it, watching it. To me, it is the homeliest thing about a home. I understand perfectly why extinguishing the fire was always the first thing landlords did in the nineteenth century when arriving to evict tenants. My idea of house-heaven would be having a fireplace in my bedroom too, so that I could fall asleep watching a fire at night in winter.

The midlands contains most of our bogs, which cover 14 per cent of the country. The midlands, with the Bog of Allen at its centre, is like a dark well, out of which many things have been windlassed over time. Our bogs have given up eighty-six bodies in the last two hundred years. They have also yielded butter, thousands of years old, and many treasures now held in our museums. But mostly, bogs are about the business of producing turf.

Near Shannonbridge in Offaly you can take a tour on a bog train. The train is called, very grandly, the Clonmacnoise and West Offaly Railway, which makes it sound as if it is an extensive line. Through April to early October, the train goes daily on the hour on a circular nine-kilometre journey through the Blackwater Bog, which is worked by Bord na Móna. One Sunday in August, I paid my €6 and hopped on the train.

The best way of describing the train is to say that it looks a lot like a bus. Honestly. It's like a 1980s-issue Bus Éireann bus, complete with brown and orange seat-covers inside. The cab it's pulled by is a lot like a tractor. So the bog train is like being on a bus in the bog, which is pulled by a tractor. It's wonderfully low-tech, and it's fun. It also doesn't go faster than five miles an hour, and since the tracks are laid on bog, they tend to be very wonky. Or, as the tour-guide told us rather magnificently, "The rail-track is floating on the bog." So it's a pretty bumpy ride, which adds to the authentic feeling of actually being on a bus. There are also intriguing signs at intervals along the route, which read: *How fast are you going?* You'd expect them on a motorway, but in Blackwater Bog, where it's not possible to do more than five miles an hour in a bus-train, they do seem a bit hopeful.

There were eleven of us on board the bog train the day I was there, mostly Americans. I was the only Irish person. Irish people do go on the train, though. I looked in the Visitors' Book at the centre where you buy your ticket, and, while there were addresses from Latvia, Denmark, America, England, Germany and Spain, there were also ones from Galway and Kilkenny and Cork. Schools sometimes use the train for educational tours. You can also rent the train for a birthday trip, where €9 gets you the train ride and a party bag with a soft drink and a surprise. Coming up to Christmas, they do trips out to see Santy in his bog kingdom. It's pure cheese, of course, but I'd still prefer to take a child to see Santy in a bog rather than in some tricked-up tinsel grotto in a city department store.

Blackwater Bog is a blanket bog, three metres deep. The train first trundles through bald-looking brown bog, where the surface layers have been taken off to be processed at the local Bord na Móna factory. Then it goes through the bog landscape I love most: the flat, matted horizon looking like the hide of some primeval animal, interspersed with flowers, bog-cotton, bog-pools, ditches. Every bog looks different in the same way. I can't describe what I find so satisfying about looking at bogland, other than to offer that it's a bit like an inland sea, where the waves endlessly remake themselves into something new. I can watch the ocean for hours. I'm not certain, but I think I could do the same with the bog.

At one point, the train stopped and we all got out to look at a stump of bog oak. "A fossilised tree. Thousands of years old," the guide told us. Some people took pictures, taking turns to pose beside it. An image came into my head. My mother, somewhere in Connemara when I was a child, tugging and tugging at a big piece of bog oak. She had spied it from the car window and made my father pull over while she went to try and extract it from the bog, because she loved the shape of it. My father, always attempting to reduce the flow of such found items into the boot – rocks, wildflowers, felled branches, fallen nests, slate, stones – did not offer to help, but told her if she could get it out by herself, he would allow it into the boot. I don't think he believed she would manage to pull it out. I didn't believe it either, since I had a few gos at it myself and it would not budge. But my mother managed to get it out somehow. She held it aloft momentarily, out there on the bog, solemn and triumphant: an Irish Statue of Liberty. For years, it stood on our landing. Sometimes, I touched it when I passed, loving the feel of the tiny smooth ridges under my hand and the fact that it was so old, possibly the oldest thing in our house.

At the place where we stopped to look at the bog oak, there was a small cart, piled with sods of turf. The guide handed one out to everyone. The Americans went wild, photographing each other holding sods of turf in the Old Sod itself. I couldn't bring myself to take the token sod that was offered to me as a novelty: it would have felt somehow fraudulent. I was saving turf when I was ten. I watched my uncle Larry Rogerson bring back his hand-cut turf from Cloonminda Bog in north Galway back to the barn with a donkey and cart; a memory I treasure and one that now seems to belong to an era far longer ago than it actually was. I don't know what was weirder on Blackwater Bog that day, seeing something so utterly familiar being presented to me as if it were an alien object, or watching the other people on the tour finding the turf so unfamiliar and strange. "This is real turf?" one man from South Carolina asked in marvel, examining his sod closely. As opposed to what, I wondered. Fake turf?

The guide told us that in fifteen years the nearby Shannonbridge generating station would stop burning turf and switch to oil or coal. Eight per cent of Ireland's electricity is generated by burning turf. Commercially, Blackwater Bog has only fifteen years left in it. I just hope there will be enough left for me, and all the other domestic turf-burners, to keep our home fires burning.

Blackwater Bog, Co. Offaly, 29 August 2004

~CORK~

T'ain't-a-Bird and Tojo

In 1943, when Ireland was officially in Emergency mode, an American B-17 Flying Fortress en route from Marrakesh to England got lost and went off course. Almost out of fuel, the crew of *T'ain't-a-Bird* made a forced, unscheduled landing in White's Marsh, outside Clonakilty. Looking out, the crew of ten thought they were in Norway, until curious locals started arriving on bicycles and enlightened them. By all accounts, they were given a sustained and rousing welcome. Interned in O'Donovan's Hotel in Clonakilty, the crew made merry while efforts were made to build a makeshift runway.

Those were definitely less PC days. The crew had with them a mascot: a monkey called Tojo, which they had picked up in Brazil before flying to Africa. The monkey, named for the then Prime Minister of Japan, had been swapped for three bottles of rum in Brazil. Tojo, unfortunately, couldn't adapt to the Irish weather and died two days after arriving in Cork. He was given a funeral with full military honours and buried in the hotel garden. Meanwhile, the attempts to lay a temporary runway didn't work. The men were brought out to the Curragh by truck after three days, and *T'ain't-a-Bird* was flown out later by persons unnamed, when special steel mesh had been laid as a runway on White's Marsh.

I found a passing reference to this story in an Irish guidebook a long time ago and never forgot it, mostly because of the marvellously surreal detail of the hapless monkey. But I didn't know how much of the story was true and so e-mailed the current owner of O'Donovan's Hotel in Clonakilty, asking for confirmation of the facts and contact details of anyone they knew in Cork who might still remember the event, sixty-one years on. I also inquired if Tojo was still buried in the hotel garden.

O'Donovan's Hotel has been in the same family for five generations and the current proprietor is Dena O'Donovan. She replied, confirming the story and giving me the names of some people whom she thought would be happy to talk to me. Of Tojo, she wrote: "Yes, the monkey's body was, and is buried in the hotel, but is now [due to extensions] under the function room floor."

White's Marsh is a couple of miles from Clonakilty and on the way to Inchdoney Lodge and Spa (where the government happened to be holed up for their annual pow-wow the day I was visiting the area). Dena drove me to the site where the plane had come down: a green boggy field, now partially drained by digging ditches. There is no marker of any kind, but all the local people know exactly where the plane landed: the location handed down aurally from generation to generation.

There is a plaque by the main entrance outside the hotel itself, erected by the Warplane Research Group of Ireland, which went up in 1988 and which records the crew's stay in the hotel. Inside the hotel, there are a number of display cabinets, with family bric-à-brac and assorted other things on show. In one of them, there are a few items belonging to the crew-members; found during renovations, where they had slipped through cracks in the wooden floorboards. Among them are uniform buttons and a small, still-unopened, tin US Army-issue first aid kit; its tab unpulled after all those years.

Part of the large, busy function room at the rear of the hotel used to be a billiards room. Tojo was buried in the adjacent garden. Then the room was doubled in size and turned into a dance hall. It is now a restaurant by day, in the season, and a disco and bar by night. There is only a scrap of garden left, which is used as a beer garden and is newly popular as a refuge for smokers. The floor is wooden and well worn. Dena showed me the piece of floor (close to the blue and yellow mezzanine) under which Tojo lies. Her father showed her the place when she was a little girl. "My father tells me he was never dug up," Dena explained briskly, while I looked down at the piece of floor she indicated. There is nothing to mark the spot, which is probably wise, as it might excite the late-night revellers a little too much.

O'Donovan's gets a steady flow of American tourists looking for Tojo's last resting place. This can prove complicated, as they tend to arrive in summer, when the restaurant is at its busiest. You can understand why it might not be so great for business if the unwitting dining punters discover that there is a monkey buried quite close to the table where they are tucking into lunch. Thus Dena has come up with a classic Irish solution to an Irish problem.

In the beer garden at the back of the hotel, there is a large rusty metal cross that has been stuck into the earth and acts as a decoy grave-marker for Tojo. "What we've been doing is taking people out here," Dena explained. "We've actually told people we've moved the body out here – which is totally incorrect. But what do you do with five or six Americans in the middle of lunch when there's a function on and they insist on seeing the grave? So this cross is just for show." The tourists take photographs of the cross, and everyone is happy.

Hannah Coakley keeps a small, brightly painted shop in

Clonakilty, of the kind that is disappearing and sadly not being replaced. She sells homemade jam and tins of peas, bottles of Lucozade, packets of soup and boxes of Major and Carroll's cigarettes. A Child of Prague stands between Bran Flakes and boxes of Barry's Tea on the top shelf. On the blue formica counter are an old Avery weighing scales and six mission boxes.

Hannah, now approaching eighty, was seventeen when *T'ain't-a-Bird* landed in White's Marsh. She was working in O'Donovan's Hotel at the time as a waitress. "I'm the only one left now who was working there then. All the rest are dead and gone," she told me over tea and cake in her back-room, where her little dog laid his head on the bottom tray of the trolley she wheeled out and tried hard not to look too hopefully at the cake. She had worked in O'Donovan's since she was a child of ten: when both her parents died, the hotel took her in. "Different times now, says you," she said brightly.

They heard the plane flying over in the hotel. "It was so loud we knew it was going to land nearby." The subsequent arrival of the crew to stay in the hotel was an event in the 1940s in a way it could never be today. We pride ourselves these days on being sophisticated. It takes a lot more to get us excited about things. But Hannah loved the fuss and excitement generated in the hotel and in the town by the presence of the unexpected American visitors. Technically, they were supposed to be interned indoors at O'Donovan's, but the reality is that they were given the run of the town. "For the town and for the children, it was so exciting," she recalls. "And the monkey! I'd only ever seen one in the pictures, not in real life." She was there when they had the funeral for Tojo. "The poor lad whose monkey it was was fierce upset, so they gave him a funeral to take his mind off it."

When the crew left, they tipped the waitresses generously, a fact Hannah still remembers with gratitude. "We weren't very well paid in those days," she confessed. When the plane eventually took off, she says she couldn't bear to look at it.

In later years, some of the crewmen returned to Clonakilty to thank people for the hospitality that had been shown them there. They all looked up Hannah, and some of them exchanged letters with her, right up until their death. Some who never returned also wrote. She showed me the last letter she received from crew-member Jim Stapleton, dated 9 July 1994, with an address in California.

> Dear Hannah,
>
> My memory isn't quite as good as it was fifty years ago, so I don't remember many names or faces, but Clonakilty and the people of the town have always remained a fond memory throughout the years. In your letter, you said if I ever returned to Clonakilty, I should bring with me the medal. I am not sure if that was the word but it looked like it.
>
> The only thing that I recall is that some young lady gave me a small gold heart for good luck and I did keep it all these years. I gave the heart to my youngest son who was also a pilot in the Air Force and he still has it. If this is what you meant and if I ever return to Clonakilty, I shall bring it with me. Again, thank you for the kind letter.

Jim Stapleton never did return to Clonakilty and has since died, but Hannah keeps the letter safe and intends to keep it always.

Paddy Hart was eighteen when *T'ain't-a-Bird* landed in White's Marsh. He was working as an apprentice joiner at the time and was in his workshop when he heard the plane overhead. He came out and saw it circling very low. "I got on my bike and went looking for where it had landed," he recalls, sitting in his daughter Aileen's coffee shop, Hart's, on Clonakilty's main street.

He was one of the first to arrive on the scene. "People kept arriving. And when they brought them back to the hotel, there was a carnival atmosphere in the town. You could say there was a fair bit of partying done. The crew were the centre of attention – although more from the ladies than from the men." One of the crew gave him a bullet as a souvenir, which he still has. When the crew were leaving Clonakilty in the back of an army lorry, one of them dropped and smashed a bottle of whiskey he had been given as a gift. "One of the locals went straight into a bar, bought another and handed it up to him."

It was some weeks before a suitable runway could be built to take the plane out. "It was like a pilgrimage site," Hart explains. Even when the crew were gone, people came for miles to look at the plane. Some brought picnics with them and made the journey into a day out. The laying of the runway on the marsh was also considered a spectacle. "They laid some kind of mesh down and reinforced it with iron bars. Iron was very valuable at the time, and when they took the runway up again, a lot less iron bars went back than had arrived."

In the end, they were all caught by surprise when the plane took off. "It was rumoured it was going on a different day," he explains. "We were at a football match, and the plane flew over the pitch and dipped its wings at us, and then off she went."

Matty Teehan, who is now eighty-one and still a respected practising traditional musician, was in the Irish Army from 1940 to 1945. In 1943, he was stationed at Bandon. An SOS message came from the Garda barracks to the Army camp that "a Yankee bomber had landed in Clonakilty. We were ordered to get into battle order and to get down there as quick as possible. There was high excitement."

Matty lives in Cork city now, in Ballyphehane, where he talked to me at his home. Matty and ten of his comrades were scrambled and they tore off to Clonakilty. The bewildered crew were still in the plane when they arrived, but it's fair to say that their Irish Army counterparts were equally bewildered when they boarded the plane and discovered Tojo. Matty was particularly impressed by their gun. "It had a revolving seat, like one you'd sit in at a barbers. You could swing the gun any direction."

The Irish Army escorted the crew of *T'ain't-a-Bird* to O'Donovan's. Matty was posted on White's Marsh for two days to guard the plane from the curious public: the plane had a guard on it the entire time it was there. "There were fierce crowds came out to see it. And the crew were treated like celebrities. Did I socialise with them? Oh, I did." He grins hugely at the memory. "God," he says, "you'd never have known we were a neutral country."

Clonakilty, Co. Cork, 7 September 2004
Cork city, 8 September 2004

~FERMANAGH~

BORDERS

In 1993–4, I spent a year travelling overland back to Ireland from Kathmandu: via Nepal, India, a side-trip to Sri Lanka, Pakistan, Iran, Turkey and up through Eastern Europe, where I had spent several months two years previously. I found myself thinking a lot about borders during that time. Apart from Sri Lanka, I crossed all borders over land, by bus and train and taxi, and as I waited with my rucksack and passport at check-points, I always wondered what made one bit of land different from another; where did one place end and another one begin? Why exactly there, at that point? And how did one place feel different from another once you had crossed over: how long did it take for you to know that you were somewhere else? Sometimes, not long at all. I walked out of the passport-control office at the flyblown border crossing at Taftan in Pakistan, and into Iran.

On the wall adjacent to the exit were the words *Down with USA* painted in huge capital letters.

Other borders were more subtle. I spent a month in northern Pakistan, some of it in Baltistan, at Skardu and Sighar. The people of Baltistan speak Balti, an ancient form of Tibetan. It is an unwritten language, thus their history is one which is not recorded. It is a place that eludes certainty, dependent on memory and recollection, where many people do not even know their date of birth. The past is a fluid place in Baltistan. Unsurprisingly beloved by anthropologists, nobody really knows what it contains. It remains by far the strangest, and most memorable, place I have ever been to.

Then as now, adjoining Kashmir was disputed territory between Pakistan and India. A 1987 *National Geographic* article on Baltistan described the place as a "cultural fossil". Until the vertiginous, nausea-inducing Indus Highway, which links Gilgit and Skardu – unquestionably the most terrifying bus journey of my life – was completed in 1981, the only other way out of Baltistan was the track over mountain passes to Srinigar in Kashmir. When I was there, no civilians had used the route to Kashmir since Partition in 1947, even though it is only a two-day walk. The "Highway" bit of Indus Highway, by the way, is an oxymoron, standing as it does for a mere unsealed track the width of an overloaded, clapped-out bus with failing brakes (ours), carved out of the side of a sheer mountain half a mile up, composed of hairpin bends, with no barrier of any kind between the wheels of the bus and the edge of the track. Buses and jeeps regularly fall off when taking the hairpin bends too fast. Or else they are flattened by rockfalls: at intervals along the way, there are permanent teams of men living on little shelves of rocks, their sole, unenviable task to clear the track of landslides and rockfalls. A bus fell off en route from Gilgit before I arrived in Baltistan: not only were no traces of any bodies ever found in the Indus river far below, they could not even find the *bus*, so deep and dark is the Indus. It took ten hours to make a journey of less than eighty miles from Gilgit to Skardu. I spent the entire journey suffering from the ever-growing conviction that I was going to die, and I didn't scare that easily back then.

In Baltistan, I thought a lot about borders. On the Siachen Glacier above me in Skardu, six thousand metres up in the thin air, the Indian and Pakistani armies were fighting for control of an expanse of ice. I had seen the High Altititude Combat School on the outskirts of Skardu. *Shoot to Kill*, an expression familiar to me from Ireland, was painted on its gable wall. It was, in fact, the elements and not bullets that claimed most lives on the glacier. Avalanches, crevasses, altitude sickness, the bitter cold. The camps were two miles apart on the ice and the soldiers lived under conditions most mountaineers – this is K2 territory, where most of the world's highest mountains are located – would baulk at. On my way back from walking to Satpara lake one afternoon, I saw an army helicopter land close to me and watched the body of a soldier being taken out. He had died of altitude sickness.

Pakistan was named in anticipation of Partition. The name is an acronym, intended as a definition of its future territory: P for Punjab, A for the Afghan Borders, K for Kashmir, I for Indus, S for Sind and TAN for Baluchistan. The K that gives the name Pakistan its hard-sounding backbone is a missing land; a ghostly absence in every mention of the country; a still-contested border.

There are two villages in Fermanagh that are bisected by borders. One is Tullyhommon/Pettigo. If you think of the village of Pettigo, it's most likely you think of Donegal. But there is a shadow-side to Pettigo, its lesser-known twin double, named Tullyhommon. Tullyhommon is in Fermanagh, and the county border that divides Pettigo/Tullyhommon in two is the tiny Termon river, which winds usefully between the two.

Further south along the Fermanagh border lie the villages of Belcoo and Blacklion. Belcoo is in Fermanagh. Facing it, on the other side of the stream that connects Upper and Lower Lough Macnean, is Blacklion in Cavan. At Belcoo/Blacklion, a long stone bridge lies between the two settlements. Facing each other on the bridge, 117 of my paces apart, are contrasting road-speed signs. On the Fermanagh bit of the bridge, they are thirty miles per hour. On the Cavan bit of the bridge, they are fifty kilometres per hour.

Although the combined population of Pettigo/Tullyhommon is only 275, according to the 2002 census, there are two post-offices there, one An Post and one Royal Mail. There are very many bigger settlements in Ireland that have no post-office at all. But borders are political, and thus the presence of both governments in the form of separate post-offices at Pettigo/Tullyhommon.

The Donegal side of the tiny village has the few shops – several of them now derelict – and two of its four churches, Catholic and Church of Ireland. The Fermanagh side, even smaller, has Presbyterian and Methodist churches. On the Donegal side are both the village's war memorials. One, an elaborate stone plaque high up on a wall, is in "proud and grateful commemoration" of the local men who died in the Great War of 1914–18. The other, a statue of a man holding a rifle on a plinth, is mere paces away at the Diamond and commemorates those local men who died "fighting against British forces in Pettigo" in June 1922. Each side has a public phone-box: the BT box has a yellow sign around the top of it saying, "Euro also accepted here."

At Belcoo/Blacklion, in the restaurants and shops on both sides of the border, there is a little free pamphlet on display that you are welcome to take away with you. Distributed by Belcoo and District Historical Society, it covers the area's flora and fauna and its cultural landmarks. The last page is called "Belcoo, Today and Tomorrow".

> After the Great Famine life slowly got back to normal in West Fermanagh and as farming recovered from its tragic years, industry and commerce gradually re-established themselves … Another upheaval followed in 1922 when Ireland was partitioned into two states. Overnight, sleepy Belcoo, in Fermanagh, and its close neighbour Blacklion, in Cavan, found themselves on opposite sides of the new border between Northern Ireland and the Irish Free State (later to become the Republic).

James Gallagher is the softly spoken postmaster at the An Post office in the Pettigo part of the Pettigo/Tullyhommon village. His father, Patsy, was postmaster for forty years, and his grandfather, James, was the sub-postmaster, so he is the third generation of Gallaghers to serve in the post-office. He has been working in the post-office for twenty years himself. Now on Main Street, the office moved in the 1970s from its earlier location in Mill Street. Today, the post-office counter is in a large general grocery-store, where containers of Calor Kosangas are lined up on trolleys outside the shop and a sign in the window proclaims a €1,642,445 Lotto winner.

James knows all his customers and reckons he does better business than the competition over the river. He opens Monday to Saturday, nine to one and two to five-thirty. Wednesdays are a half day. Friday is the busiest day, when pensions and other social-welfare benefits are paid out. The post goes out once a day, at 3.10 p.m. The two post-offices do not share their collection service. He himself very seldom uses the Royal Mail office, but has done so once or twice when sending parcels to sterling counties. He accepts sterling, both coins and notes. Tourists, he says, don't comment on the oddness of one village having two post-offices, since they don't get many tourists. James lives over the shop, and despite the fact that he can see Fermanagh by looking out of his windows, he has never considered himself anything but a Donegal man. "I support Donegal," he says firmly.

Belcoo/Blacklion is considerably bigger than Pettigo/ Tullyhommon. Both Belcoo and Blacklion have a post-office, several pubs, restaurants, garages, supermarkets, bed and breakfasts and police stations. The Belcoo Police Service of Northern Ireland station is on the corner near the bridge, by far the biggest building in either village and still heavily fortified. There is a small Garda station in Blacklion.

It was polling day for the British and Northern Ireland elections the day I was in Belcoo/Blacklion, and the posters were visible right to the nearest lamppost on the Belcoo side of the bridge. I watched a campaign van with a loudspeaker on the roof travel up and down Belcoo, urging people to come out and vote for their particular candidate. At the bridge, the campaign van made a sharp, awkward turn in a scrap of someone's private driveway and went back up through Belcoo village again. It didn't seem an option to drive across the bridge and turn more easily in Blacklion, a journey of a minute or less: some invisible wall, a border, kept the van firmly on the Belcoo side, even though you could hear the loudspeaker perfectly well in Blacklion, as I did, some minutes later.

I walked backwards and forwards across the bridge and between the two villages of Belcoo/Blacklion several times that day, glancing down each time at the river that passes for the border. The two opposing villages *do* feel different, much more so than Pettigo/Tullyhommon. It's not just the fact that smoking in pubs and restaurants is legal on one side of the bridge and illegal on the other. Or that I paid in sterling for my newspaper in Belcoo and, a couple of minutes later, in euro for a bottle of water in Blacklion. Or that to spend the night in the Custom House Bed and Breakfast in Belcoo would have cost me £40 (€59) in Belcoo, and €45 in MacNean's Blacklion. Or that the speed limits change from kilometres to miles on the bridge. It was something far more subtle, yet also far more obvious: something I couldn't quite locate, but recognised nonetheless.

It takes less than a minute to leave James Gallagher's post-office in Donegal and cross over the Termon river to Fermanagh. There are no street or road signs that advertise the fact you are now in both another county and another currency zone. There are, though, the BT phone-box and the red post-box on a post, with its ER insignia.

The Tullyhommon Royal Mail post-office has been even more mendicant than its counterpart across the border in Pettigo, moving location several times over the last two decades. In the 1970s, a soldier was blown up defusing a bomb that had been left in the post-office. Over the years, the office moved from the top of High Street to the bottom and for the last three years has been at its current location close to the bridge. There used to be a large

Royal Mail sign outside the office when it was on High Street, but there is no sign of any kind at its new location.

"We were to get a sign but we never got round to it," explains postmistress Lorraine McGrath. Lorraine works in Fermanagh and lives in Donegal. Although she works in a sterling zone, she is paid in euros. The post-office accepts euros in notes only, no coins. She is busiest on pension days, which are Monday and Tuesday. The office is open Monday to Friday, nine to one and again from two to five. Their daily collection goes out at noon.

We were talking in the room adjacent to the post-office, which is the information office for the Catholic pilgrimage centre of Lough Derg, some four miles distant. It turns out that in addition to being the postmistress, Lorraine is also the information officer for Lough Derg. There is a connecting door between the two offices, and McGrath divides her time as necessary between the two jobs. Lough Derg currently holds Tullyhommon's Royal Mail licence: a fact that seems to me quite wonderfully surreal. Two more different institutions one could not imagine sharing the same metaphorical umbrella. Lorraine says she finds nothing unusual about the arrangement, but to me, it seems marvellously and profoundly ironic that a Royal Mail post-office is being run by one of the most prominent Catholic organisations in the country.

Whatever about the two postal services, my mobile phone remained firmly on BT/O2 network coverage as I crossed and recrossed the border that afternoon from Donegal to Fermanagh and back again.

In Belcoo/Blacklion, it was just the opposite. My phone stayed on O2 all the time, without the usual little message welcoming me to another network and another country. Even technology couldn't work out the complexities of a border dividing two such geographically close yet different places.

Pettigo/Tullyhommon, Co. Donegal and Co. Fermanagh,
14 September 2004
Belcoo/Blacklion, Co. Cavan and Co. Fermanagh, 5 May 2005

~DONEGAL~

IN HOOKS INVADING THE SKY

We have a few collective national obsessions, and one of them is the weather. It's a national standing joke: when you've nothing else to talk about, you talk about the weather. Even when you do have something to talk about, you still get the weather in there somewhere. It's partly a necessary obsession. In an island country, fishermen need to know what the weather forecast is going to be: their lives, quite literally, depend on weather conditions at sea. And throughout the cycle of the agricultural season, farmers require certain weather conditions for the success of their crops.

The rest of us just talk about the weather all the time anyway, even though our lives or livelihoods don't correlate to it in the same essential way as fishermen's and farmers'. It's not even as if we get out that much in the weather: the 2002 census statistics revealed that only a miserable 11 per cent of us walk to work. *Terrible day, grand day, soft day, it's brightening, it's raining, it's clearing, it's freezing, it's windy, it's mild, it's warm, it's boiling, it's clear, it's miserable, it's misting, it's drizzling, it's pouring, it's pissing, it's down for the day.* We are all walking weather thesauruses. We speak like characters in a Beckett play, endlessly repeating ourselves. The weather is our Godot. We're always waiting for something to happen with it.

We each have a personal weather obsession. Mine is light. What really makes the difference between a good-weather day and a bad-weather day for me is the amount of light that gets through whatever clouds are currently up there. I do like warmth, but I'd prefer a cold, clear bright day in winter to a dull warmish one in summer. My cottage is south facing, and one of the things that made me buy it was the light, which reaches into every corner. I put in a Velux window over my bed and now lie there at night looking at the stars, the moon, the occasional lights from a plane. It's my periscope to beyond. I didn't think I'd see anything through the city's sodium, but I do. I don't pull blinds or curtains in the bedroom, so the first thing I see each morning is light, or the lack of it, depending on the time of year. And the first thing I do virtually every morning is switch on the radio and listen to the news – and weather forecast.

After the foundation of the State, responsibility for monitoring the weather was taken over from Britain in 1936 by the newly established Irish Meteorological Service. In 1948, they began providing the forecasts for broadcast (until then, they had come through London). In 1951, the Met started sending forecasts to national newspapers. In 1962, Met forecasters started presenting the weather live on Telifís Éireann. Met Éireann use ten weather stations to provide us with the forecasts we have come to take for granted and that punctuate each day with reassuring regularity: Belmullet, Birr, Claremorris, Clones, Finner, Kilkenny, Malin Head, Mullingar, Roches Point and Rosslare.

Malin Head Weather Observing Station is located 55 22'20" degrees north, 7 20'20" degrees west and 22 metres above mean sea level. Malin Head is distinguished by being not just the most northerly station, but also the one which records most wind speed. The highest measured wind there to date was in 1961, when the tail end of a hurricane pushed the wind speed up to 98 knots. That's about 113 miles an hour. Despite the station being located more or less in precisely the most northerly point in Ireland, I couldn't find it at first and pulled up at the side of the road some distance out of Malin village to call on my phone for directions, feeling very dim indeed.

Malin Head weather station (coded 980) is a small complex of low, flat-roofed 1950s buildings overlooking the sea, with a collection of arcane-looking objects scattered round the lawn to the north. I was lucky to be there on a gorgeous September day, clear and blue, so I could see literally for miles. The station has a wonderful, wild, expansive aspect. You're right *in* the weather here: looking out to sea, watching those huge horizons. You can smell the brine on the air. The place feels fresh, elemental, alive. It's a place where the weather pulses.

Paddy Delaney (fifty-seven), originally from Tipperary, has been the station manager at Malin head for thirty-five years. This was his first station after his period of training. He has been here ever since. "I actually applied for a transfer after the first few days when I came here," he says, straight up, sitting in the main room of the station, "but I fell in love and got married and that kind of stuff and that sort of made it permanent here."

There are six meteorological officers stationed at Malin Head. Between them, they maintain a 24-hour weather watch, 365 days of the year. Every hour, they check a number of instruments, both inside and outside the building, and make their own skilled visual observations, e-mailing the information in the form of codes to the Forecast Office on O'Connell Street in Dublin. If the electricity goes, which it sometimes does, the reports are filed over the phone. Occasionally, their phone-lines have gone too, and Paddy recalls times during winter when his officers drove to the local radio station hourly in the middle of the night to use the phones there to file reports. The collective information from the ten stations is used to produce the weather forecast given to the media: a jigsaw of wind-speed and Hector Pascals, of visibility and rainfall and cloud cover.

Why does he think we are so obsessed with the weather? "Because it's so variable," Paddy says without hesitation. He gives an example. "A few days ago, some of the locals were complaining about the heat. We had temperatures in excess of twenty here and within two days, the temperature was down to ten and it was blowing a Force Eight. You can't get more variable than that."

Among the things checked every hour is visibility; both over land and sea. It might sound obvious, but checking visibility is something done with the unaided eye. It means Paddy or one of the other five officers standing on the roof of the weather station and looking around them 360 degrees to see how far distant or not they can see. Literally, as far as the eye can see. There is a photomontage on the wall of the station: pictures taken by Paddy on a clear day from the roof of the station, which form a panorama. It is a montage of a neighbourhood: houses, the local radio-station building, hills, fields, the local hotel. These are the visual reference points that all the Met officers look for when doing their visibility reports; distance points. If you can see Inishtrahull Island, that's 9 kilometres. Islay, 73 kilometres distance, had been seen earlier in the day when I was there, but had vanished from sight by the time I arrived. The Crossroads Hotel is 965 metres away. And so on, with the hills and the scattered houses. They all have their precise distances from the station marked in. Less than a thousand metres' visibility is considered fog, thus there are several houses marked in the photos that are in or around the nine-hundred-metre distance from the station. I loved the idea of a neighbour's house down the road from the station being the visibility yardstick by which a weather report is partly composed. It makes the process of collecting the weather-forecast data wonderfully personal.

Every job carries with it its own language. There are ninety-nine codes for describing the weather, which are divided into various categories: smoke, haze, mist, sandstorm or blowing snow, fog, drizzle, rain, snow, shower, thunderstorm. This is the official international coding system used for recording present weather – which accounts for the presence of sandstorms on the list; not a regular feature of Irish weather. There are, surprisingly, no codes for sun, only for those that record the absence of it. Within those categories, each weather type is given specific descriptions. Rain, for instance, comes in six classifications: intermittent slight rain, continuous slight rain, intermittent moderate rain, continuous moderate rain, intermittent heavy rain, continuous heavy rain. That's not all. There is a separate classification for showers.

"Which codes do you use most often?"

"The rain and the showers. Unfortunately, they're the most common."

The present weather chart is a fascinating document to look at. Every weather description has both a code and a symbol. Our old friend rain is a dot – a Black Hole. Fog is three horizontal lines stacked over each other, like window blinds. Snow is a six-pointed star. Drizzle is an apostrophe, as if to suggest something more to come. Haze, an eight on its side, looks like a pair of binoculars.

Among the things also measured and recorded are wind direction and speed, for which an anemometer is used. The sensor itself is outside, poking through the roof, atop something like a fireman's pole. At the bottom of it, in a little room adjacent to the main office, is a revolving paper barrel. Some gadget translates the wind speed by inking on lines each hour. It looks a bit like a heart monitor.

"After a month of gales, it's the silence you hear," Paddy says.

You find Hector Pascals in atmospheric pressure: their cartoon-like name familiar to us all. I saw the Hector Pascals being recorded. The instrument for measuring atmospheric pressure is in a small glass box with another paper barrel on the left and various baffling-looking brass pieces to the right.

There are several other instruments on the lawn outside, all of which need to be checked hourly. Rainfall is measured by a small hollow copper object set into the grass, with an open top. The rain falls into this and is collected inside by what looks like a glass milk-bottle. Each hour, the bottle is lifted out and the water-level checked.

Most of the instruments are not high-tech. "The instruments we have here are really antique," Paddy says, but he doesn't mean it in a disparaging way. "Most of them don't depend on electricity, including the anemometer. It's old hat, but very reliable."

Every hour, the cloud cover has to be measured. "We break up the sky into eighths. It's the amount of cloud in the sky – in eighths," Paddy explained. He gestured out the window. "For the moment now, there's seven-eighths of the cloud in the sky." I looked out also. I had thought I was looking at a virtually clear blue sky.

"How do you measure it?" I asked, bewildered. They do it at night too. Every hour on the hour.

"It's just practice," Paddy assured me. "You get used to it. But it is one of the most difficult things for new weather observers to get right, especially at night."

The cloud formations in the sky are also recorded. *Cirrus, Cirrocumulus, Cirrostratus, Altocumulus, Altostratus, Nimbostratus, Stratocumulus, Stratus, Cumulus, Cumulonimbus*. It's not only the certain cloud formations that are recorded, but also where they are in the sky – low, medium or high – and how dense they are. The clouds themselves come in many different types, which, described on the weather chart, sound like something out of Tolkien: *in hooks invading the sky; continuous veil above; in chaotic layers; with anvil; in bands growing denser*. Recognising all these is "second nature" to Paddy and his fellow officers.

It must get lonely and sometimes tedious at night in a weather observing station. "It can be very repetitive," Paddy admits. "You're a slave to time. Hourly weather reports have to go out on time. If you're not looking at the sky, you're looking at your watch." They are all avid readers. Paddy stargazes. Astronomy is his hobby. "I have a fine telescope at home. If I say so myself." He loves the Malin Head sky because there is so little light pollution. He has often seen the Aurora Borealis at night, when he's out with a flashlight, collecting data and checking the instruments. "They cover the whole sky." He hesitates, then adds, in something like embarrassed delight, "like curtainy ripples of light."

Malin Head, Co. Donegal, 15 September 2004

~TYRONE~

A CABINET OF CURIOSITIES

Cabinets of Curiosities have always fascinated me. Collections of disparate objects, not usually very valuable, linked by little more than the owner's personal interests and an eye for the esoteric. The Victorians, collectors supreme, particularly loved them.

I have my own modest Cabinet of Curiosities, to which every visiting child is unashamedly drawn and in which every visiting adult shows a lot more sneaking interest than they pretend. Among the contents are: a piece of the Berlin Wall; a mother-of-pearl pen owned by my grandmother; a fossil I picked up in White Park Bay; gold-leaf from Burma; a miniature painting of a hunt on half a cuff-link from Iran; a model of a Tuk-Tuk from Thailand; a whistle for calling hens from Laos; a waterproof diver's notebook; an old John Hinde tray; a match-box from the Orient Express; a musical thatched cottage in a snow dome which plays "When Irish Eyes Are Smiling"; a sachet of sugar from Turkey which says *Pamukkle Buses Take You to Your Lovers*; a fiendish, tiny hand-made jigsaw puzzle, found in a charity shop in Leeds, which reveals the initials of the creator when completed; a wind-up duck on a bicycle; my first mobile phone; an old lock from China; an inch-high leather-bound edition of Tennyson's *Collected Poems*; a Russian doll from Prague of Bill Clinton holding a copy of *Monica's Story*, with Monica within, in her blue dress, followed by ever-smaller versions of Gennifer Flowers, Paula Jones, Hillary Clinton and, er, a cigar.

More than anything, my Cabinet of Curiosities makes people laugh. It is kitsch and treasures all mixed in together. While doing research for this book, I read a lot of guidebooks. In the sixth edition of *The Rough Guide to Ireland* (2001), much to my delight, I came across the following in the chapter on Tyrone.

> Newtownstewart's real draw is the gem of a museum that's housed in the tiny tourist office. Local historian Billy Dunbar, a walking encyclopedia, donated his collection of vintage packaging, man traps, stereoscopes and war memorabilia to the museum when he could no longer navigate from one end of the house to the other. Highlights include a Bordalous (a mini-chamberpot named after a French priest renowned for his over-long sermons), and threepenny bit engraved with the Lord's Prayer.

However – this is both the advantage and disadvantage of consulting out-of-date guidebooks – once I began to make inquiries, it turned out that the exhibition and museum were no longer at Newtownstewart. Displayed in its entirety, it had been leased by Strabane District Council for three years there, before being dismantled in 2000. Further inquiries revealed that the collection had been acquired from Billy Dunbar by Strabane District Council and is now held at Gray's Printing Museum in Strabane. The collection is intended to be displayed now in rotation, by themes, and thus the majority of it is in storage.

Adrian Beattie is the curator of Gray's Printing Museum, an attractive old building in the centre of Strabane. He is hugely enthusiastic about the Dunbar collection, which he describes as "eclectic". Its value to the museum is partly in its representation of children's antique toys, but chiefly in the social-documentary element of many of the pieces. They put on many exhibitions for schools.

"A lot of the material refers to ordinary soldiering," explained Adrian. There are: ration cards; gas-masks; medals; a tin of Bourneville chocolate (with chocolate still in it) which Victoria sent to every soldier in the Boer War as a Christmas gift in 1900; black-out screens for cars; a Nazi-issue dagger; a Mother's Medal given by Hitler in 1938, one of the countless such presented to German women who had multiple births; an air-raid warning siren; an oil painting done by a German POW; a packet of "liquid silk stockings", which enterprising women painted on their bare legs in the days of rationing – one packet was apparently "sufficient for 24 applications, and cannot harm the skin". It's not difficult to see how useful Dunbar's magpie collection is to a museum. These kinds of things are the ephemera and details from wartime that do help history come alive for children – and adults.

Due to lack of space, only a hundred items or so are on display at Gray's at any one time. Adrian showed me the full inventory of the fifteen hundred items: a lovely litany of the strange, wonderful and unsettling, some of which I transcribed.

> 1906 Edison light bulb
> Kid gloves
> Pair of spats
> Smelling salts
> Man trap
> Bill from a swordfish
> Hand-held monocle
> Great Northern Railways cream jug
> Victorian mourning bracelets made of human hair
> Jar of nineteenth-century counterfeit pennies
> Paperweight containing piece of the *Mary Rose* ship
> Walking stick containing a telescope
> Walking stick containing a gun

Walking stick containing a glass phial for spirits
Whale oil
Magic-lantern oil lamp
Gurkha knife
Rubber and plastic bullets
Hand grenade
Persian shield
Thistle puller
Long Way to Tipperary bowl
Victorian child's exercise book from 1867
Clockwork dancing lady
Glove stretcher
Sword used by an executioner
Painted ostrich egg
Snowshoes
Thatcher's needle
Framed death warrant
Estate bell from country house
Edwardian push-chair
Anamorphic painting in glass dome
Victorian glass kaleidoscope from Annaghmakerrig,
    owned by Tyrone Guthrie

Apart from the items that refer to wartime, Adrian considers
the medical ephemera to be of most value, again from a social-
history perspective. Some of these are displayed in cases on the
first floor of the museum, and they would almost be comic were
they not so disconcerting. There is one item in particular: a
wooden box with a horrific-looking set of metal wires and
sockets, and a crank of the type found in the old manual public
phone-boxes. This is called The Improved [improved from
what?] Patent Magneto Electric Machine for Nervous Disease.
It won a First Prize Medal – for whatever horrible things it did
– in London in 1862 and a Silver Medal in Paris in 1878.
    Inside the lid are these instructions:

> Connect two metallic cords or wires with the sockets in
> the end of the box and apply the handles connected with
> the other ends of the metallic cords to any part of the

person through which it is desirable to pass the current of electricity. Then, turn the crank, regulating the strength of the current by the speed and by the knob at the end of the box, it being desirable to increase the strength only to that degree which is agreeable to the patient. It is less unpleasant to the patient if wet sponges are placed in the ends of the handles and then applied to the skin, as they prevent prickling sensations.

TB spawned many hokum cures. One of them is also on display. It's an unopened cardboard box containing a Gamgee Tissue Pneumonia Jacket, "which completely covers the chest and lungs. Sold in six sizes for old and young, it's an excellent protector for the chest and lungs, invaluable in cases of pneumonia, bronchitis etc." (They didn't dare mention TB by name, the social stigma of having the illness was so great.) The picture on the front of the box is that of a Florence Nightingale-type nurse seated on a bed, looking sweetly at the man lying in it wearing what looks like a large inflatable white bib: the Gamgee jacket itself.

In the same case as the Gamgee is the "Babies murder bottle", a melodramatic and overly sensational name for a sad example of needless infant mortality due to ignorance. It's an early feeding bottle, made of glass, with teats that couldn't be sterilised. There was a high mortality of babies who were fed using this model, until someone realised what was wrong.

The items in storage are kept in the attics, in boxes on open shelving, wrapped in white acid-free paper. Adrian took out some things to show me. I held the Nazi-issue dagger for a moment or two, until revulsion made me drop it. But there were also many beautiful objects, such as the work-of-art, tiny inch-high Bible in its jewelled red and gold case; the Victorian glass kaleidoscope that came from Annaghmakerrig, and which I twisted and looked into, the changing colourful images revolving like miniature rose windows, delicate as lace; the Chinese silk parasol; the Chatelaine's belt, with scissors, thimble, key-ring, propelling pencil and wee notebook; the pearl-handled pistol, which a lady would keep in her wrap; and

Beattie's own favourite piece from the collection, a lovely Japanese Netsuke carving.

Billy Dunbar (sixty-nine), the man who assembled this remarkable collection over a lifetime, lives in Omagh. He was in the Air Force for five years and then practised as an electrician in various State bodies, including hospitals. When he was a child, his father, returning from Dunkirk, brought back a toy tin money-box in the form of a Buckingham Palace soldier in a sentry box as a gift for him. This was to be the first item in his collection, and tin-plate toys continued to be of special interest to him – objects now highly sought after by specialist collectors.

He started seriously collecting with antique guns. "But when the Troubles started, I disposed of them, because I thought they might be seized," he explains. We're sitting in his living-room in Omagh, where the sentry-box money-box stands on a whatnot. When he sold the collection in 2000 to Strabane District Council, he kept back a few items, including his father's gift and the threepennny piece with the Lord's Prayer etched onto it, which he gave his sister. "And a pair of spectacles reputed to have belonged to Nelson's surgeon."

Twice a week, for years, he went all over Northern Ireland, to antique shops, fairs and dealers, although never to charity shops. "I tried to look for things in different directions, every time I went out. I usually went for something unusual," he says. "And then when I got something, I'd keep my eye for something that would complement and expand the collection." He taught himself by consulting reference books, thus cultivating an awareness of what things were worth and then keeping an eye out for bargains. Billy could usually get dealers to reduce their prices, especially as he became known. He can still remember what he paid for most of his objects, even those collected three decades ago.

Until the collection was leased to Newtownstewart in 1997, he displayed it all in his own museum, called Bygones, located in a shed at the back of his Omagh home. He put a sign out on the pavement at weekends to attract visitors, although not many ever came. Anyone who paid their pound and did come down the garden path must surely have been astonished at Billy's amazing private Cabinet of Curiosities.

The shed is still there, at the bottom of the garden, the Bygones sign on its side against one wall. There are still a few bits and pieces stacked on shelves around the place, enough to get a sense of what it must have been like when the fifteen hundred items were all here. Although some of the pieces in his collection were clearly valuable, Billy says he never worried about security, although there is a sense of relief that he no longer has the responsibility of having them on his premises. Once he decided to sell, he knew what he wanted most was for the collection to be kept together. He had created a distinctive shape and meaning to it by what he chose to put into it. Quite possibly, had he auctioned the items – Christie's valued one of his tin-plate toys alone at £600 – he would have made more money, but, refreshingly, money in itself wasn't what it was about for him. It would have been inappropriate of me to ask how much Strabane District Council had paid him for the collection (and I wouldn't have got an answer), but he says he was happy with what he got.

"For me, it's an added bonus to know the collection will be kept together now in Northern Ireland and not auctioned off," he confessed openly. He is also chuffed that the collection carries his name: it is known officially as the Dunbar Collection.

Wandering round his old, now near-empty Bygones museum, Billy showed me a box of Victorian magic-lantern slides he was currently sorting through. I'd never seen these old glass slides before and held them to the light, marvelling at the detail. He made me choose whichever I wanted. Eventually, I selected two. They're in my own Cabinet of Curiosities now.

Strabane and Omagh, Co. Tyrone, 16 September 2004

~ DERRY ~

CROKE PARK SAND

It was easy to remember Lough Neagh's name at school. No
other lake on the map came anywhere near that immense size;
at twenty-five kilometres by fifteen, it almost qualifies as
Ireland's thirty-third county, a big blank eye dominating the top
right-hand corner of the map. Flicking through my Ordnance
Survey mapbook of Ireland one day, my attention was caught by
the page with Lough Neagh on it. Broken lines divided the
lough into five unequal parts: the county boundaries of Antrim,
Derry, Tyrone, Armagh and a tiny bit of Down go through it. It
had never occurred to me that a lough would have county
borders, although I guess I'd always taken for granted the fact
that the Shannon flows through several different counties. But
what really astonished me when I started doing some research
into the lough is that it is privately owned. Lough Neagh is

owned by Lord Shaftesbury, an absentee landlord and a member of an established old English family who lives somewhere in the south of England. (Nobody could tell me exactly where.) I didn't think you could own lakes in Ireland, or at least not ones the size of Lough Neagh.

It is not really possible to drive along by the lakeside. The roads run off it at right angles, like tributaries. I was driving roughly along the north-western side of the lake, into the part that bordered Derry, and I couldn't see it at all. Finally, I drove down one of the tributaries. Extensive as it is, I had never seen the lough before, from any one of its five border counties. At the part where I was, I couldn't see the shoreline on the far side. A boat rocked beside a little pontoon and big steel-coloured clouds rushed over the almost-black lake. There was nobody around; no houses, no buildings of any kind, no people. It felt forbidding, somehow, and yet it was also strangely mesmeric. I got out of the car and walked around for a while, watching sky and water grow darker and darker. It started raining, and I still stood there, looking out for a responding shoreline that I couldn't see.

There used to be a freshwater laboratory on the shores of Lough Neagh, at Traad Point, which was run by the University of Coleraine from the 1960s and was open to the public by appointment. It closed in 2000. For most of the time the laboratory was in existence, it was run by Brian Wood. Now retired, he was the university's Professor of Environmental Science.

In his home near Magherafelt, Brian filled me in on some eye-opening facts. The lough is famous for its eel population, which I already knew: I just didn't know quite how big the population was. For weeks after I had been to Derry, I kept asking my friends: "Guess how many eels there are in Lough Neagh?" so I could see the inevitable expression of horror and amazement that crossed their faces when they discovered the answer. Two hundred million. No, that figure is not a mistake, nor is it a misprint: it is true. Lough Neagh is 375 square kilometres and it contains two hundred million eels. When I heard that, I made an instant, automatic vow never to go swimming in it.

Eels have mysterious lives. Nobody has yet discovered quite how they breed. What is known is that eels go to the unique eco-system of the Sargasso Sea to mate. The Sargasso Sea, which is thousands of square miles, is as mysterious as the eels it contains. It is unique among seas in that it has no coastline: it's a free-floating sea, the surface covered with seaweed. It rotates slowly in its North Atlantic location, bordered by the Gulfstream, the Greater Antilles and Bermuda. It's also known as the Horse Latitudes: when becalmed there in centuries past, sailors were forced to throw their horses overboard to conserve water. The Bermuda Triangle lies within the Sargasso Sea: the infamous area where many planes and ships have vanished.

When hatched, the eel larvae rise to the surface of the sea and start their onwards journey. Brian told me that eels migrate by night, but not when the moon is shining. "They travel in the dark side of the moon." It takes three years for them to reach North Europe. By then, they have grown to elver size. They're transparent at this stage of their lives and so are called glass eels. After crossing the Atlantic, the eels swim thirty-eight miles down the Lower Bann river to reach the lough. All two hundred million of them. It takes a further eight years for them to reach maturity. When you consider that even quite large animals usually reach maturity in a year or two, it makes the eel a very complex piece of marine life.

I asked Brian how the lough had acquired its arbitrary-looking boundaries: how had somebody decided that the lough would be divided up so unequally between Derry, Antrim, Down, Tyrone and Armagh? He didn't know, but suggested that the lough had been divided up so, if someone drowned in a certain part of it, one particular jurisdiction would have responsibility for dealing with the tragedy.

Brian was puzzled by my interest in county boundaries. He told me that they have little significance in Northern Ireland. "Everything goes by District Councils here. The people who play GAA would be the only ones to observe county boundaries."

We drove north towards Toomebridge, where the Fishermen's Co-Op is based. The lough was silver and grey and horizonless. I couldn't work out what was odd about it, and then I realised that there were no waves. It looks like the sea and yet it doesn't. It foxes the eye.

All those eels are big business. In 1971, the Lough Neagh Fishermen's Co-op was set up to control all the eel fishing. There are some two hundred fishermen on the lough at present, and seven hundred tons of eels are fished each year. The majority of the eels are exported live, packed in ice. They go to central Europe, where the Dutch distribute them onwards to other markets. We don't seem to be too keen on eating them ourselves: I don't recall ever seeing eel on a menu anywhere in Ireland. Brian explained what they taste like: "Light and floury. You chop it into steaks and it fries in its own juice."

The arrangement is that the Lough Neagh Fishermen's Co-op now owns the contents of the lake and the Shaftesbury Estate owns the bed. It didn't seem like a great deal to me at first. When driving up to Toomebridge, we passed a lakeside factory. "Sand extraction," Brian explained. There were dredgers out in the lake and large hills of bright sand heaped on the foreshore. Then I discovered that sand extraction on Lough Neagh is a bigger commercial business even than those millions of eels. It is used in the construction business throughout Ireland to produce everything from roof tiles to bricks to sections of motorway bridges. The dredging companies located around the lough pay the Shaftesbury estate a fee to extract the sand, which must add up to a very hefty sum. Many of the Guinness barges that used to transport barrels of the black stuff from St James's Gate down the Liffey to the docks ended up in Lough Neagh, where they were converted into dredgers. They were sold off in the fifties by Guinness when they started increasing their use of road transport. Some of them now lie wrecked under the water in Lough Neagh or form parts of breakwaters.

The sand from Lough Neagh has ended up in some more unusual places than in bricks and tiles and pieces of motorway bridges. When Croke Park was last renovated, seven thousand tons of Lough Neagh sand was used to form the base of its new playing surface.

Near Toomebridge, we met up with Michael Savage, an auxiliary coastguard who has written a comprehensive pilot's guide to the Bann and Lough Neagh. Before the wind got up, he had offered to take us out on the water. I had wanted to go out in a boat, to get a better sense of the place, but it was too windy and the plans we had made had to be abandoned. You don't argue with the man who's written a pilot's guide to the lough.

Instead, we walked along a series of paths and through gates which Michael's impressive collection of keys opened. We went to the weir that crosses a neck of the lough. The weir is a long bridge-like structure that we clambered up metal steps to, buffeted by the wind. Through the holes in the steel mesh, we could see the water rushing past, under our feet. Up to eighty thousand eels a night are caught at this weir. To ensure that some of them can escape to travel back to the Sargasso Sea to breed, there is a wide gap, known for some reason as the Queen's Gap, through which the water rushes furiously, pushing the eels onwards, to travel back up the river Bann and out to sea again. It makes a huge noise, the roaring of the water. I looked down and tried to imagine the eels under the water. Two hundred million of them in there. I didn't see even one, but it was very peculiar knowing that they were definitely there, in such staggering numbers.

Michael loaned me his binoculars so I could look at some of the birdlife that populates the lough, but I found myself simply training the glasses over the water, looking for land on the horizon that I still could not see. We weren't on the water, but we were over it, and the weir creaked and stirred beneath our feet like an uneasy boat.

Lough Neagh, Co. Derry, 17 September 2004

~DUBLIN~

MEN WHO COULD CATCH HORSES AND RABBITS BY RUNNING AFTER THEM

The Schools' Folklore Collection, or Schools' Scheme, was carried out during the academic year of 1937–8, and then extended to run for a further four months, to December of 1938. It was a simple but brilliant idea organised by the then Irish Folklore Commission: to encourage children to collect and record both true and hearsay stories from older family members and neighbours, under a number of topics.

Every primary school in the State was invited to participate voluntarily. The Six Counties of Northern Ireland were not included in the scheme; something which archivists on both sides of the border must surely regret today. The procedure in primary schools in the State went like this: teachers were sent guidelines on how to implement and supervise the scheme; a list of fifty-five topics which they could choose from to give to their sixth-class pupils to write about; and a large, bound manuscript notebook.

Children were instructed to collect stories, based on the list of topics, from family members and neighbours. They first wrote the material into their school copies. The best were then chosen by their teacher to be formally written by each selected child into the large manuscript book supplied by the Folklore Commission: books which were later bound with two or three others from neighbouring parishes. All the school copy-books, including those from children whose work was not written into the book, together with the special manuscript book, were to be returned to the Folklore Commission by the teacher.

The fifty-five set topics were: *The Leipreachan or Mermaid; Hidden Treasures; The Care of the Feet; Bird Lore; Strange Animals; Emblems and Objects of Value; A Funny Story; A Collection of Riddles; Weather Lore; Local Heroes; Local Happenings; Severe Weather; Old Schools; Old Crafts; Local Marriage Customs; In the Penal Times; Local Place-Names; Local Cures; Home-Made Toys; Lore of Certain Days; Travelling Folk; "Fairy Forts"; Local Poets; Famine Times; Games I Play; The Local Roads; My Home District; Our Holy Wells; Herbs; The Potato Crop; Proverbs; Festival Customs; The Care of Our Farm Animals; Churning; The Local Forge; Clothes Made Locally; Stories of the Holy Family; The Local Patron Saint; The Local Fairs; The Landlord; Food in Olden Times; Hurling and Football Matches; An Old Story; Old Irish Tales; A Song; Local Monuments; Bread; Buying and Selling; Old Houses; Stories of Giants and Warriors; Local Ruins; Religious Stories; The Old Graveyards; A Collection of Prayers; Historical Tradition.*

This inspired project – one that surely should have been replicated for the millennium – was overseen by a man who devoted his life to recording Irish folklore, stories, songs, customs and traditions, the famous Seamus Ó Duilearga, who was the Honorary Director of the Irish Folklore Commission. His right-hand man was Sean Ó Suilleabháin, archivist to the Commission.

Although participation was voluntary, there was a huge

response. More than five thousand schools participated in the scheme, which resulted in 1,128 bound manuscript volumes and 1,124 boxes of loose copies. About fifty thousand children in total took part. For some years, the material was held at Earlsfort Terrace. During the Second World War, fearing possible bomb damage in central Dublin, the manuscript notebooks were moved to a rented room in a house near Rathfarnham and stored in big wooden boxes. Ó Suilleabháin personally cycled out there every week to check that they were still safe. The boxes of copies stayed in Earlsfort Terrace, stored under the stairs there; traditionally a structurally safer place should bomb-damage be suffered.

In 1949, the manuscript notebooks and copies went to the Irish Folklore Commission's new headquarters at 82 St Stephen's Green. They remained there until moved to the newly created Department of Irish Folklore at UCD in Belfield in the early 1970s. They are still there.

When I had found out more about the archive, I did a few sums with ages and dates, and wrote down a list of my very small immediate family. I called my parents. Did they remember this scheme? Had they by chance participated in it? Yes, they remembered it and, no, it hadn't been the right year for either of them. "But," my mother said thoughtfully, "I think Máine did it."

My aunt Máine and her sisters, my mother Catherine and my aunt Noreen, who died when I was thirteen, all attended primary school in Ardeevin National School near Glenamaddy in Co. Galway in the 1930s. I called Máine. Yes, she said, she remembered the project. And she had participated. Did she remember what she had written? She laughed down the phone. "It was a hundred years ago!"

It wasn't a hundred years ago, but it was a long time to be re-membering anything you'd done back then: sixty-seven years ago.

The archives and library of the Department of Irish Folklore at UCD open 2.30 p.m.–5.30 p.m. Monday to Friday, apart from August. I called the library when they re-opened in September to find out if, by any chance, they could locate my aunt's contribution. I was asked for her name and the name of the school, barony, parish and county. I could only supply some of this information with certainty. Barony? I didn't even know what that meant. But even so, the information I had given had been enough.

Amazingly, within half an hour of calling the library, my phone rang. It was archivist Emer Ní Cheallaigh. Not only had she found my aunt's copy-book from Ardeevin National School, but she had also discovered that Máine had been one of the children chosen to write in the manuscript book. So she was there on record twice over. And some of the pieces she had written down had been collected from Lucas Ó Ciaráin. Do you know who that is? Emer asked. I did and I didn't. Lucas Ó Ciaráin – or Luke Comer, as he was always called – was my maternal grandfather.

All four of my grandparents had died long before I was born. I had seen only one tiny black-and-white photograph of Luke, which my mother had kept in an old gold locket until it was stolen. He was dressed in a suit, standing formally beside my grandmother Helen, squinting into a camera on the small road opposite their north Galway farmhouse in Knickanes in the townland of Cloonminda. That was the only image I had of him. But now I knew something of him survived in another form.

The Folklore Library at UCD is on the ground floor of the Arts Block, or the John Henry Newman Building, as it is officially called. I was shown into a room at the right-hand side of the long corridor, where there were shelves crammed with box-files and where Emer and a couple of silent researchers were working away, taking notes on their laptops. For conservation purposes, you must wear white gloves to handle the material, use acid-free paper as bookmarks and write notes in pencil.

The file that I wanted was Number 18A. The county was Co. na Gaillimhe; the school, Scoil Ard Aoibhinn; the parish, Gleann an Madadh; and the mysterious barony was Béal Átha Mogha. The filing boxes are grey, with labels on their wide spines. Emer put the relevant one down on the desk in front of me, along with the gloves and a reminder not to use any writing instruments that contained ink.

In the box-file were thirty-seven school copies. My aunt Máine's copy was a faded orange colour. It had her name on the front cover. The words *College Exercise Book* were in capitals on the front, printed over a drawing of the Dame Street entrance of Dublin Castle. On the back cover were tables of weights and measures. I handled it with astonishment; excitement; incredulity. How often do you get this chance: to press your face so closely against the window of the past in general and of your family's past in particular?

Along with the manuscript notebook, each school was sent a small, teal-coloured book of instructions, entitled *Irish Folklore and Traditions*, with a little stylised image of a fir-tree in a pot on the cover.

The first paragraph of the foreword reads:

> The collection of the oral tradition of the Irish people is a work of national importance. It is but fitting that in our Primary schools the senior pupils should be invited to participate in rescuing from oblivion the traditions which, in spite of the vicissitudes of the historic Irish nation, have, century in, century out, been preserved with loving care by their ancestors. The task is an urgent one for in our time most of this important oral heritage will have passed away for ever.

Even to look at the list of fifty-five topics in 2005 is fascinating. Presumably, they were drawn up to try and represent a broad social context of life in 1930s Ireland. In the late 1930s, the consequences of the Famine would still be only a generation away, illustrated by the fact it had its own two topics: *Famine Times* and *The Potato Crop*. Food and food production figured several times: *Churning*; *Herbs*; *Care of Our Farm Animals*; *Food in Older Times*; *Bread*. Some, seventy-odd years on, have a new relevance in our modern society, such as *Buying and Selling*. And *The Landlord*. Seventy years ago, a landlord would have likely been an outsider; in 2005, you may well be a landlord yourself.

In the little booklet of guidelines issued to the schools, each topic was allocated a list of suggested approaches.

Local Heroes

Accounts of local men who in former times or even recently won fame in some field of activity. Swift runners. Feats they accomplished. Distances run. Races between human beings and horses. Men who could catch horses and rabbits by running after them.

Severe Weather

Accounts of great storms of former times given by old people. Are any accounts available locally of the Big Wind of 1839? If so tell how it affected your district. Heavy snowfalls. Portents.

The Care of the Feet

At what ages did people begin to wear boots in former times? Are there accounts of people who never wore boots or shoes? Do children at present go barefoot in summer or all the year around?

The Leipreachan or Mermaid

By what name or names is the little Leipreachan known locally? How tall is he? How is he dressed? Where does he live? What is his usual occupation? Shoemaking? What else? Are stories told of local people who caught him and endeavoured to get him to give up his gold? Did they succeed?

The mermaid. Are stories told about the mermaid in your district? What description is given of her? Has she human faculties such as speech etc? Has one ever been brought ashore? What happened to her? Are any local families connected in any way with mermaids?

Famine Times

Have the old people stories about the Great Famine of 1846–47?

Local Poets

Give the names of any poets who lived in your district formerly. Did poets compete with one another in song-making or did they attack one another. Could they read and write? Were great powers attributed to poets? Did they ever try to banish rats from a house? How did they attempt this? Did they succeed?

Everything my aunt had written was in Irish. My Irish is woeful. I was both ashamed and frustrated. I turned the pages of the big manuscript book, looking at the names at the bottom of each piece to see whom the stories had been collected from. To my delight, there were also a couple of pieces which my aunt Noreen had written.

You are permitted to photocopy only twenty manuscript pages. I worked out what the various headings on the pieces were and then made my choices. I sent the photocopies off in the post to Máine, who had offered to translate them for me. A couple of weeks later, a little green spiral-bound exercise book arrived in my pigeonhole at work, filled with Máine's beautiful copperplate writing in wide-nibbed black ink.

The guidelines for *Hidden Treasure* were:

There is scarcely a district in Ireland in which stories of Hidden Treasure are not current. The wealth may have been hidden for many years or may date from quite recent times. Where is the treasure supposed to have been hidden? By whom placed there? Why? Have attempts ever been made to unearth it? By whom? With what result? What does the buried treasure consist of? Gold or silver or valuable vessels? What is the supposed value? Has buried treasure ever been discovered in your district? Give an account of this. What traditions are connected with the Dames in regard to secret hoards, or with the "fairypeople"? Have people ever been enabled to see this hidden wealth by eating certain food? With what result? Are animals or supernatural guardians supposed to safeguard this hidden treasure? Give an account. Any other treasure stories? Many tales of this character current in Ireland are of great antiquity, and when many hundreds of such narratives are recorded (and their exact location given) an important source of scientific investigation will be made available.

Máine had written:

> It is said that there is a gold treasure hidden in a small garden in Knickanes. The garden is called St Brigid's garden and it is said that two green or black cats protect it. One night when a person was going past the place he fell on the road and broke his head and his back. The fairies were dancing on top of him and him dead. The man was named as Patrick Brady. Every single person is scared to go past this place after midnight ever since.
>
> It is said that there is another gold treasure under a little tree called The Rich Tree. It is said there is a thousand million pounds hidden in it. Three white dogs defend it. It belongs to the fairies.

She had collected these tales from John Kirrane, a neighbour who "was a great man for the stories". The Comer sisters used to go there on their way home from school to visit and eat rhubarb tart. John Kirrane, Máine thinks, was "about seventy" at the time he gave her the stories.

Marriage Customs

Straw boys come to the wedding house asking for a drink. If they get one they are quiet and they dance with the bride. Should they not get a drink they are cross and break things. When the people are going to the wedding feast they bring sweet cake or butter with them. After the marriage ceremony is over the new wife goes in the door of the house, goes down on her knees and an oaten cake is broken over her head. In olden days when people were poor and money was scarce instead of a wedding ring the man used to have a steel key or an iron key to give to his wife.

Máine got this from John's son, Roger, probably at the same time as she talked to his father. She can't recall what age Roger would have been, but thinks he was about thirty.

Special Days

Nobody throws a match or a *cipín* into the fire in New Year's Day. New Year's Eve is the last day of the year, and it is also called the Night of the Big Conflagration. It is also said that if a person ate his fill that night, he would have sufficient to eat to the end of the following year.

In the olden times a fine big cake of bread used to be made and it used to be thrown against the door and during this time the thrower said the following: I order Famine or hunger to the land of the Turks for a year from tonight and tonight included. At the mid hour of night everybody used to be anxious to see how the wind was blowing. If it was blowing from the West, the Irish people would have a prosperous new year; but if it was blowing from the East it is the British people who would have the prosperity.

Máine got this from Luke Comer, my grandfather, in his late fifties at the time. It made me wonder if he had ever personally seen anyone throw bread at a door and incant the saying.

An Old Story

The old people have a lot of stories about the return of the dead. Some of the old people say that the dead people return to this life to do something that they failed or neglected to do when they were alive.

I heard a story about a young boy who returned to this life to pay a debt of six pence to another boy. He was only eighteen years old when he died. This is how he came back. He knew the boy well to whom he was returning. Every evening when the youth was coming home from work he met the ghost of his dead friend. The ghost of the boy never spoke to him. The ghost used to be there every evening when the boy was coming home.

One night the boy spoke to the ghost. The ghost could not speak to anybody until that person spoke to him first. He asked him to pay the few pennies debt. He said that he was ready to enter Paradise if he paid the few pence for him.

He disappeared then and nobody got tale or tiding of him ever since. The boy paid the debt and he is still alive. He is living near my aunt's house [Nora Kearney] in Kiltullagh.

This was written by my aunt Noreen and collected again from my grandfather. Noreen was a tiny lady, who sent us a goose in the post every Christmas from the farm. She was kindness itself and died far too early, at fifty-five. The first time I travelled anywhere by myself was on the bus from Galway to Knickanes, on my tenth birthday, to stay with my two cousins, Mary and Felicity, and aunt Noreen and uncle Larry on their farm for a fortnight. I had my mother's homemade fruit-cake in my bag and was under strict instructions to hand it over immediately on arrival. I worried about missing where I should get off, but Felicity was at the top of the Knickanes road with her black bicycle, waving the bus down. I was ten, and Noreen was the same height as me. She was all warmth and sort of weightless. Years later, when I was researching an article on falconry, I had a hawk land on my wrist and was astonished at how it seemed so strong and powerful and yet was actually so lightweight. It made me think of Noreen, then dead for twenty years.

The Land Lords

The Land Lords were here for approximately seventy years. A Land Lord was a person who was in charge of a certain large amount of land – a parish or two. They divide up the land into parcels and receive a large rent from the tenants.

Desmond Mac Donnell was the Land Lord of Cloonminda, Stone Town, Bush Town, Classaroe and other small villages around the area. It is said there was never a Land Lord in Knickanes and the people believe this. It is said that when the Land Lord was measuring the Knickanes land that a man called Michael Morgan broke the chain measure and the people in this small village were delighted. The Land Lord died in the 1926 storm because there was a lot of snow. Michael was respected and honoured because of his intervention. He died about ten years ago (in 1928). Clonlara's Land Lord was Tadhg. He was very hard on the people and on account of this they did not like him. They thought up a plan to kill him but he was dead before they were ready.

This too was collected from my grandfather, who lived in the area all his life.

*

My aunt Máine was utterly astonished to receive the photocopies of stories she had written in her childhood. She read the manuscript of what she had written as if it had been written by a stranger. And then the stories came back to her; she remembered them; she remembered the people who had told them to her. She asked to keep the photocopied pages.

The original manuscripts of this truly forward-thinking scheme may be in UCD's folklore library, but every county library has their own particular county's contribution on microfiche. Anyone can go looking for the past at their local library; go looking for what grandparents or great-uncles and great-aunts or aunts and uncles, fathers and mothers wrote, and be surprised by what they find.

UCD Folklore Library, Dublin, 4 October 2004

～ MAYO ～

EVERYTHING IS AN EVENT
ON AN ISLAND

Living in an island country, I've become very interested over time in our other, smaller islands. Over the years, I've visited what I thought were quite a few of Ireland's offshore islands: the three Arans, Inishbofin in Galway, Clare, Cape Clear, Sherkin, Arranmore in Donegal, Tory, Rathlin, Skelligs. I had thought I was reasonably well-up on my knowledge of our islands. That was until I looked at the 2002 census statistics for population of inhabited islands off the Irish coast and was astonished to discover that there were literally dozens of tiny islands I had never heard of, each of them with people living on them.

The census for some of these islands recorded just one occupant, such as the woman who lives on Deer Island in the Shannon Estuary. And Inistravin and Illaunmore in Galway, which both have only one man each on them. And Island More in Mayo, also with one man. What, I wondered, must it be like to live on an offshore island all on your own? What would have brought you there? What would keep you there?

The more I studied the 2002 census statistics, the more intrigued I became. Galway has eighteen islands. Cork has fifteen, Mayo twelve, Donegal eight, Kerry seven and Clare, Limerick, Sligo, Dublin City and Fingal have one each. Being census statistics, you can see the breakdown of population by sex. When applied to a tiny island, it seemed almost too intimate to know that Deer Island's sole inhabitant was a woman. Or that Inishbofin in Donegal had twelve men and only four women. Or that Collan More in Mayo had only three men and no women.

Many of the islands, such as Clynish (three men, two women), Inisraher (two men, two women) and Inishnakillew (three men, two women), I couldn't even find on my *Ordnance Survey Road Atlas of Ireland*. True, it's a map more concerned with roads than water, but still, it was strange to see the existence of so many of these islands denied. I had to stand in the tourist office on Suffolk Street one lunchtime and search my way through their collection of county ordnance survey maps to locate these sparsely populated islands.

I decided to try and visit one of these islands and interview whoever would talk to me about their lives there. Having had the idea, I was a bit stumped for a while as to how I would go about it, since I had no names or contacts to go on. In the end, I chose an island at random, Inishlyre (four men, two women) in Clew Bay, and wrote a letter addressed to "The Residents of Inishlyre", explaining that I was writing a book and asking if it would be possible to visit. I had very little expectation of a positive reply, especially since this was my second attempt: an earlier, similar request to visit a different island had been politely, but very firmly, turned down.

But to my surprise, one morning shortly after posting the letter, I turned on my computer at work and found an e-mail from Rhoda Twombly of Inishlyre. Yes, was the answer. She and some other islanders would talk to me. There was no public ferry service, but if I let them know in advance when I planned to come, someone would meet me at Rosmoney pier and bring me across. I was even invited to stay in her house for a couple of nights, should I wish.

At the end of October, I travelled to Mayo with a friend, Brian McIntyre. We left the car at Rosmoney pier and called Rhoda to say we had arrived. Tom Gibbons came in his boat some twenty minutes later, waving up to us as he approached. We were the only people on the pier.

On the way out, Brian and I tried to guess which island was Inishlyre. It was not easy to distinguish the different islands. They are drumlin islands, small grassy knolls like drowned fields. From the water, they change places and fox the eye. Some look stuck together from certain angles. Others look like part of the mainland. And then the boat moves further and you see the sea around each one, before the next sightline arrives to confuse you. Tom pointed out Inishlyre to us when we got nearer. There was a big trawler drawn up on its stony beach, and a brand-new month-old pier, where two people were standing waiting for us: Rhoda and Sheila Keeley.

We went to Rhoda's house. There are only four houses on the island, all of them on the shoreline facing the pier. Rhoda and her partner, Joachim Gibbons, live in one, the furthest house to the east. Sheila and her husband, George, live beside them. Tom is next to Sheila and George. John Gibbons is at the western end of the quartet.

Joachim was away. Tom and George preferred to keep their own counsel. Rhoda, Sheila, John, Brian and myself sat around the kitchen table with mugs of tea, chatting, taking our ease. It was too soon to turn on the tape-recorder and start asking questions. Then Rhoda's dog suddenly got up and started barking furiously. The door opened and a man with intensely blue eyes came in. It was Sean Jeffers, who had heard I was coming and had taken his boat across to Inishlyre to see what was what. I thought of something Brian had said to me in the car on the way down: *Everything is an event on an island.* Sean, now seventy, lives alone on a neighbouring island, Inishgort. Rhoda told me later that, although she has been living on Inishlyre for seven years, she has never been to visit Sean on Inishgort, even though it is only ten minutes away by boat.

Inishlyre is some forty-five acres and it takes half an hour to circuit the island. Sheila was born and reared here. She lived in New York for ten years and then returned with her American husband. "It's home. I always wanted to come back." Tom is her brother. John has lived here all his life. Rhoda came here seven years ago to be with Joachim, who is from Inishlyre.

Sean was one of six children on Inishgort. Apart from his siblings and parents, the only other family was the four who lived at the island's lighthouse. The lighthouse keeper was his grandfather. The lighthouse is long since automated. All his siblings emigrated or left. He never did. "I'm there all my life, thank God," he said. And later, "Someone had to stay and mind the father and mother." Sean's father died first. When his mother died in 1998, he remained on the island. He never married. Listening to his story, it was not difficult to understand why: he had virtually no opportunity, ever, to meet a potential partner. And now, aged seventy, he has seen over his lifetime the island's population drop from twelve to one.

Does he ever get lonely? "I never get lonely! It doesn't come into my vocabulary at all," he said, quite vehemently. He shot the words out before I had even finished asking the question and stared hard at his mug of tea.

Inishlyre has been populated for about two hundred years. In 1909, there were only four houses on Inishlyre, and there are still only four houses on the island that are lived in. In the 1960s, nineteen people lived on the island. Neither John nor Tom have married, and they both now live in their old family homes, where they lived with their parents until, like Sean's, they died.

"It changes when the parents go," Sheila said. "Home doesn't seem like home any more. In Tom's house, I'd walk in and instinctively look for the two chairs where our parents used to sit. Now they're empty."

"The boatman is the island baby," Rhoda quipped when I asked if there were any children living on Inishlyre. The primary school closed thirty-three years ago.

Everyone goes to Westport to shop. They all have their own boats and cars on Rosmoney pier. "You can get days where the weather would be so bad you couldn't leave the island all right," Sean said.

Sean knows all about the weather and when you can and can't take the boat out. For thirty years, he was the postman for the seven populated islands in Clew Bay. When he retired in 1998, John took over. He goes out three times a week. There are fifteen houses to deliver to, between the seven islands. Sometimes, depending on the tides and on which island there is post for, it can take John more than six hours to do his round. "If it wasn't for doing the post and getting out, I don't know how I'd cope living here," John admitted frankly.

Sean has had a phone since 1970, but he only got electricity and water in 2000. He had a generator, but it was usually only turned on at night. He mostly used paraffin lamps – "Aladdin lamps" – and candles for lighting. Cooking was done on gas or on fires. John and Sheila's mother always cooked on the open fire. Sheila still cooks meat on the fire. Until the water system was installed, all the islanders collected rainwater for drinking and washing.

Would any of them ever think about going to live on the mainland? There was a short silence. "There are days you might think about it," John said, with a half-laugh.

"I'd want to see the tide anyway. I'd want to see the tide," Sean said, several times, very quickly and with great urgency. From his house on Inishgort, he has woken up all his life seeing the sea and its litany of tides. He could not begin to think of a life lived that was not in sight of the sea.

"If I'm out somewhere and surrounded by land for more than a day, literally, I can feel a change in my mood," Rhoda said.

"You'd need to see the sea," Sheila said. "If you got up and didn't see it, it would be very weird."

What did they value about living on such small islands?

"You know what to expect, because you know everyone living around you," said Rhoda.

"Privacy," John stated.

Afterwards, I thought how contradictory those two statements were. In a way, you couldn't be less private anywhere than on an island where you can walk around it in half an hour; where only six people live, including yourself; and where all four houses are in sight of each other.

As there is no public ferry service, they never get tourists, apart from the odd passing sailor who is invited ashore for tea. There are no holiday homes on Inishlyre: John owns half the island and Tom the other half. With only six permanent residents, even one holiday house would be a huge invasion. They are not planning on selling part of their land any time soon. Sean owns Inishgort.

After we had finished talking around the table, Rhoda and Sheila walked up with me to the highest point of the island, where you can look out over the other islands of Clew Bay. It's lovely up there, calm, peaceful. You can see the mainland but it feels very far away. Sheila pointed out Inishgort to me, Sean's island. The lighthouse is on a spit of land to its west, as you look across from Inishlyre. Sean's house is painted lime-green, and even from a distance it stands out, as if declaring: yes, someone lives here.

As we stood on the top of Inishlyre, chatting, I saw a boat coming into view round the side of the island, heading to Inishgort. It was Sean. He had slipped away and I had not had the chance to shake his hand or thank him for his time. I was dismayed. I shouted his name, but it got lost in the wind. Then I waved and kept on waving. Suddenly, Sean looked up, saw me and waved back.

Inishlyre, Clew Bay, Co. Mayo, 30 October 2004

~LONGFORD~

LOOKING DOWN

An airport in Longford? When I first heard about this, I was impressed and also somewhat incredulous. I think of airports as portals; places you arrive at and disappear into, to exit at the other mysterious side of a journey. Alice falling down the rabbit hole. Possibilities. I love airports. I love everything about the process of travel. I love the mechanics of getting somewhere, the hours spent between one place and another, which I realise is vaguely unusual, since so many people I know seem to feel exactly the opposite about travel. They like being there, but not getting there. For me, getting somewhere is an integral part of being somewhere. For most of my life, I never drove, and so spent years at stations and on platforms and hitching at the side of the road, on trains and buses and in other people's cars, looking out the window. When I first learned to drive, the strangest thing was not the actual driving, but looking around and realising there was nobody else in the car with me. I thought I would hate driving, but I love it: that purity of choosing your own way after a lifetime of following the set timetables and routes that public transport dictates.

At airports, I love the arrival and departure boards, flashing up their litany of beyond: Moscow, Tashkent, Tokyo, New York, Beijing, Bangkok; an ever-changing atlas of elsewhere. Delays don't much bother me. I love mooching round international airports, that strange, fantastical no man's land where the people who brush past you in the queue for a security check, or sit opposite you in a restaurant, or catch your glance in a bathroom mirror as you absent-mindedly brush teeth or re-do a pony-tail, will be thousands of miles away within hours. Airports are full of temporary displacements. As a child, I used to lie on the grass of our garden in Ennis in summer and watch the planes from Shannon flying overhead on their way to America. From the grass, I watched the jet trails in the sky fade away slowly. I wanted to be in those planes, going somewhere, anywhere, looking down instead of always looking up.

The airport in Longford is on the outskirts of Abbeyshrule. Teddy McGoey of the Rustic Inn in Abbeyshrule is both the airport manager and part-owner of the place. The airport, he told me, is owned by a Longford aviation company. There has been an airport at Abbeyshrule for over fifty years. The original site was north of the village, but there was an accident in 1976 and the runway was moved. Recently, the runway was extended from 600 metres to 799. It didn't occur to me at the time to ask Teddy if there was a reason for the new runway being just one metre shy of 800. Superstition, perhaps? It seemed a strange, ragged figure for it to stop at.

In August every year there is a Fly in Weekend, where visiting planes and jets from abroad come and do those showy things with flips and somersaults. Over the years, Abbeyshrule has seen Tiger Moths, Pitts Specials, Zlins, Robins, Stampes, Falcos, Hawker Hunter Fighters and Spitfires. An Aer Lingus

747 made a low pass once. You can learn to fly at Abbeyshrule – Cessnas, Ultralites or Microlites. There are some thirty planes based there and three different flying groups. Visitors use the airport too: fishermen and golfers fly in, paying landing fees to do so. Originally, I had thought about having a flying lesson. But I changed my mind, figuring all my attention would be on the control panel in front of me rather than on looking down at Longford from the air, and decided instead to go on a short flight over the county.

You turn into the road leading to Abbeyshrule airport through a red gate with a propeller on it and then rattle your way down past the Inny river. There are a couple of hangars and small planes behind bars in some of them, like exotic caged animals; privately owned planes that are kept here.

Omar Whelan is a flying instructor at Abbeyshrule, and I had called ahead and arranged to go up with him for half an hour's sightseeing flight, for €50. I do admit, when I clapped eyes on the plane I had second thoughts about viewing Longford from the air. The plane was a white two-seater Lambada, with a perspex hood. It was tiny. It looked fragile. I left my handbag beside it for a few minutes and the bag looked gigantic: the comparison was disconcerting. I watched Omar fill up the plane with fuel from a blue canister and seriously considered getting back into my car and heading off.

"Where do you want to go?" Omar asked, all businesslike and ready for action. We couldn't go a long distance in half an hour, but Longford county is not that big. I took out my map and we looked at it together. I wanted another perspective on a county. To look at somewhere from the air, particularly a county that was not famous or known for its aerial scenery in the way Clare would be, or Kerry, or Galway, or Donegal. Longford is flat, surrounded by bog. But I still wanted to see it from above. We settled on a route: north over Carrickboy and Ardagh to Longford town and back on the Longford side of Lanesborough.

Omar manually pushed the Lambada out towards the runway. I signed a form. I think it was an indemnity form, but I was too distracted to look at it properly, worried I'd be afraid in the air, in the tiny Lambada, and unable to take notes or concentrate on anything. He showed me how to climb in over the wing, and I scrambled in awkwardly and folded myself into the narrow seat. I was still considering getting out and leaving the airport when Omar closed the hood down and we set off for the runway. Too late.

"You could go to France in this plane!" Omar informed me cheerfully over the noise of the engine as we took off. *Note to self,* I thought silently, *never go to France in a Lambada.*

But once we were up, it was wonderful. I stopped fretting. I loved the perspex hood over our heads; we felt closer to the sky, more open. I looked down onto Longford. What instantly struck me was the bog. How it dominated and shaped the flat landscape. How much of it there was and how far it extended.

You don't fly high in a small plane. We were never higher than fourteen hundred feet. It was a dull day but we could still see for miles. Omar told me that on a clear day you can see Croagh Patrick. We couldn't see Mayo that day, but it was Longford that interested me. You notice things from above you miss on the ground. Small things in themselves, but reminders of what a place is about: where it is, what defines it, how it is changing.

At Ardagh, I looked, startled, at the graveyard. How much space the dead occupy. In the surrounding fields were bales, sheep, sheds: features of a rural-farming Ireland that is slowly disappearing. At Longford town, I was amazed to see so many new housing estates. They looked so symmetrical and orderly, completely at odds with the huge, dark spreading stain of the bog that lapped like water so close by. I tried to look at other things: the sawmills, the power-station at Lanesborough, the long, straight, bright Royal Canal, the crossroads where bars and petrol stations stood on opposite corners, like dancers waiting to make a cross at a ceilí.

But it was the bog that kept drawing my gaze back. There was so much of it. I could see how it would begin to define the consciousness of a place. How some people would hate and feel trapped by it, and how others would love it. You could only work the bog. It wouldn't work for you: no houses will endure built on bog. Looking down at where water winked up from the bog, I thought of the old apocryphal stories of people drowning in bottomless bogholes. Maybe what they are really about is that it is sometimes possible for people to get lost in the wrong place, to fall in and stay when you should go, strike out, leave.

Abbeyshrule, Co. Longford, 6 November 2004

~CLARE~

PUFFIN BILLY

The railway and bus station was located directly across the road from where I grew up on Clonroad in Ennis. Over the years, I came and went regularly as a passenger from the station, usually on the bus. Train services on the line stopped in the early seventies. Until the branch line to Limerick opened again, the only passenger trains I recall as a child leaving the station were specially chartered ones laid on for matches, school tours, vigils to Knock and the Pope's Mass in Limerick in 1979. Cargo trains still ran frequently on the line, which kept it open.

As a small child, I was fascinated by Ennis railway station. It was forbidden territory (roads to cross to get there, cargo trains that might kill you), but I naturally snuck off there whenever I could. It didn't matter that trains carrying people hardly ever arrived or left. The tracks themselves were almost enough. Like a river, I knew they led somewhere. I sometimes walked out along the tracks to Clare Abbey, went exploring among the arcane ruins there and then went home and lied about where I had been, as all children do at some stage.

I loved the station house with its leaded windows and the old cast-iron bridge that spanned the tracks at the station. I don't know why I liked scampering up and down the metal steps so much and leaning over the bridge to watch for trains that never arrived, but I did. But what I loved best was the beautiful engine that stood on a covered plinth close to the stone railway bridge that spanned the road to Quin.

I called the engine Puffin Billy: I have no idea why. It might have come out of some book I was reading. Puffin Billy was on a concrete plinth and sheltered by a canopy that was supported by slender poles at the four corners. When I knew it best, in the mid 1970s, the long-decommissioned engine seemed to be in perfect condition. It was painted grass-green, with red trim. You climbed onto the plinth, then held onto the rails that were either side of the engine, one-two-three, swinging yourself up. There was a wheel to the right you could turn and back and front areas to explore. There was a hole for coal and various wheels that moved and metal chutes that opened, their function mysterious. The round conical top of the engine was in front, which you could sit on top of by letting yourself out of the engine proper and inching along the high ledge that overhung the wheels. For a child, it was the most fabulous object to play on.

My stand-out memory of Puffin Billy as a child is the time I was there with my sister Cáitríona when the tour bus stopped. We were scrambling around happily, jumping up and down off the engine. At one point, when we were both on the grass at the bottom of the plinth, Cáitríona tugged my sleeve and pointed. We looked up together. Stopped on the stone bridge above us was an American tour bus. And most of them were taking photographs of us and the engine through the windows of the bus. Several waved. We were astounded, but waved back. The traffic on the Ennis–Quin road must have been considerably lighter than it is now, because a number of them actually got off the bus and leaned over the bridge to take more pictures. Some of them called down to say how much they loved my red hair and would I stand by the engine so they could take my photo. It was a John Hinde moment before I was ever aware of John Hinde.

Bizarre as it is to imagine now, when Cáitríona and I were playing on the engine, aged about twelve and six respectively, I don't recall anyone ever taking a photograph of us who wasn't either my mother on summer holidays or my uncle Gerald Bruen, who always had a camera with him. Photographs in our family in the 1970s were strictly for holidays in Bunavalla, near Derrynane, only. My mother's Box Brownie came out briefly then.

The memory of those photographers on the American tour bus on the bridge never left me. The idea that something so utterly familiar to me was worth photographing by strangers amazed me. I couldn't puzzle it out. After that day, I started noticing the John Hinde Giant postcards that were on sale in our tiny local sub-post-office on O'Connell Street. Every time I went in with my mother, I examined the postcards, displayed on a rack on the right-hand side of the door. There were cards of Bunratty, with wolfhounds and lassies in velvet dresses; there was the one that became famous as a classic image of Ireland at its most wonderfully kitsch, the little red-haired boy and girl with the donkey and turf; there were the Cliffs of Moher; and there was Puffin Billy, with children in the foreground.

The first time I noticed this card, I was convinced the children in the postcard were myself and Cáitríona. But there were three children in the card, not two, and the image never changed: disappointingly, it was always the same three children.

It was only over time I became aware that Puffin Billy was the last surviving piece of the West Clare Railway. Like so much of childhood, you simply take what is around you for granted. When the new library opened in Ennis in the mid 1970s, a small museum of local history was attached to it in a converted church, which I liked wandering around after I'd chosen my books. The most interesting bit of the museum was the spiral stairs that led to a little mezzanine. The only display up there was a huge glass dome. In it was a carved door, which had come from one of the Spanish Armada ships that had foundered off Clare, and a wheelbarrow with a silver spade sitting in it. Parnell had used the spade to cut the first sod of the West Clare Railway, at Miltown Malby on 26 January 1885, and there was an elaborate engraving on the spade to this effect.

I knew the Percy French ballad, snatches of which my mother sometimes sang.

> You may talk of Columbus's sailing
> Across the Atlantical Sea
> But he never tried to go railing
> From Ennis as far as Kilkee ...
>
> And as you're waiting in the train,
> You'll hear the guard sing this refrain:
>
> "Are ye right there, Michael, are ye right?
> Do you think that we'll be there before the night?
> Ye've been so long in startin',
> That ye couldn't say for sartin,
> Still ye might now, Michael, so ye might!"

The very odd time, in the rush across the grass to get to the engine, I stopped to look at the small triangular bronze sculpture that stood, seemingly placed at random, close to the station's entrance. There was an image of the engine on it, and I vaguely knew it had something to do with Percy French, but when you had the real engine to play on, its two-dimensional image came a very uninteresting second in terms of getting my attention.

I grew up, moved away from Clare. For years, I didn't drive, so the first thing I saw every time I came home to Ennis was Puffin Billy, out the windows of the bus or, later, the train. Over time, I noticed changes. The canopy disappeared. The engine began to look weather-beaten. I still climbed onto it the odd time and was dismayed to find rubbish in the coal hole, graffiti scratched into the paint, bits and pieces damaged or missing. Then I came home one day, looked out the window and stepped off the bus, transfixed with horror. The engine was painted black. All of it. Thick, relentless black. It was completely unrecognisable from the lovely green, red-trimmed, pristine Puffin Billy I had once known. It looked dead, as if it was in mourning for itself. The paint job – apparently some marvellous weather resistant stuff – was the result of some woefully tasteless Fás project. I could hardly bear to look at poor Puffin Billy after that.

And then I came home about ten years ago and the engine was simply gone. Vanished. There was nothing left but the empty plinth. The station looked all wrong without the engine. I had hated the black engine, but no engine at all was even worse than the sad travesty it had become.

It had been all over *The Clare Champion*, my parents told me. A group of entrepreneurs in west Clare wanted to reconstruct a bit of the old railway and had acquired the engine to be the prize exhibit at Moyasta. One local businessman in Ennis was so enraged at the removal of the engine from the town that, in protest, he climbed aboard on the day it was due to be moved and refused to leave. The engine duly arrived in Moyasta – with him still aboard. He eventually returned to Ennis, but Puffin Billy stayed in Moyasta.

On St Stephen's Day in 2004, I set out to try and retrace the route of the old West Clare Railway. I wanted to end up in Moyasta, where I had never been and where there was now a museum dedicated to the railway. I had a notion about climbing up on Puffin Billy once again. I had read it had been restored and two miles of tracks had been relaid. I wasn't at all sure that the museum would be open on Stephen's Day, but their web site, www.westclarerailway.com, assured me it was open all year. I called the number on the web site about a week before Christmas to inquire and got a recorded message. It said: "Hello, this is Percy French of the West Clare Railway." I rang it twice to be sure I was listening to someone who purported to be a man who had died in 1920.

Stephen's Day was clear and chill and blue. My aunt Máine came with me for the spin. I started by driving across the road from my parents' house to Ennis station. The plinth that the engine once stood on is still there. It looks strange and redundant: a stage for a performance that never happens. I stood in front of it and studied the bridge behind, where the American tour bus had stopped all those years ago. The trees had grown up all along the boundary wall and partially overhung the bridge. You wouldn't be able to see through the trees now to look at the engine, even if there still was an engine there.

I walked across the grass to the little memorial. I hadn't looked at it closely for years, possibly decades. It was a small triangular bronze on a tall square plinth. It was charming: a three-faced piece, signed Kieran Kelly and dated 1964. Each face had the roman numerals of a clock. The middle one depicted a quill, the other two depicted scenes from the Percy French ballad. One showed Puffin Billy all set for action, the guard's flag down. The other showed people pushing the engine.

> "Are ye right there, Michael? Are ye right?
> Do ye think that ye can get the fire to light?
> Oh, an hour you'll require,
> For the turf it might be drier –
> Well it might now, Michael, so it might!"

When the West Clare Railway opened first, the trains were powered by steam and fuelled by coal. When there was a shortage of coal, turf was used. Turf simply didn't have the same energy, and thus the train was always running late, giving rise to the song. Diesel was used in the 1950s, until the line finally closed in 1961. The narrow-gauge line opened in 1887 and ran from Ennis to Miltown Malby. Five years later, it was extended to Moyasta Junction, where the line split, and you could go on to either Kilrush or Kilkee.

I had with me a map and a sheaf of articles written by primary-school children in Clare as part of a millennium project. Trawling on the Internet, I had discovered a wonderful interactive map of the West Clare Railway, at www.clare-education-centre.ie, which had been produced in 1999–2000. Children at primary schools in towns and villages along the line had written short local histories of the line as it had been when it went through their home places, and what now remained of it. You clicked on the names of the places along the route to see what each school had written.

The Ennis section had been written by children from my old primary school, the Holy Family: Darren, Gary, Christopher, Katie and Noreen of Room 6.

> The address of our school is Station Road, Ennis, Co. Clare. Ennis train station is at the top of our road, and the West Clare Railway began its journey from this station ... The journey from Ennis to Kilkee was 54 miles. The West Clare Railway was used by many people and one time trains of that famous railway came and went at least five times daily ... One of the most famous engines of the West Clare Railway, the *Slieve Callan*, has been preserved and was on display at Ennis Railway Station and bus depot until 1994.

The *Slieve Callan*. I had never known that was the engine's correct name.

We drove out of Ennis, past the Maid of Erin, out the road to Corofin. I missed the turn off to Ruan, where the railway had passed through and had a station on and off during its history. There was snow in the fields and the lakes had the dull gleam of pewter. A small child and her grandfather stood in their garden and waved to us.

At Corofin, there were horseboxes and people in hunting jackets on the main street.

> They find out where the engine's been hiding,
> And it drags you to sweet Corofin
> Says the guard, "Back her down on the siding,
> There's the goods train from Kilrush comin' in."

I went the wrong way, through the village, and then had to turn back and go over the bridge again. There was a tiny winding road to Clouna, with frost in the middle of it. Somewhere on the back roads between Corofin and Ennistymon, I saw a building by the side of the road that looked on the point of dereliction.

In faded letters on the white gable wall were painted the words "The Station Bar", with a faded but accurate mural of Puffin Billy on it, in green. I stopped the car and walked back to have a better look. The place was empty, and the road it was on was empty also. I'd seen very few houses for a while.

There was something truly exciting about seeing that empty, isolated building that had once been called The Station Bar. It told me that the line must have run nearby. I had felt, setting out, that I was looking for something akin to an underground river. Virtually none of the tracks survive. But here was proof that the West Clare Railway had once passed near to this building. I got back into the car, buzzing, delighted.

A little further on, there was a railway bridge. It was a rusty, crude affair, but as we passed under it, I whooped. No trains now crossed that bridge, but they once had, and that was enough for me. The West Clare Railway began to feel real.

By Ennistymon, the sun was so bright and stern I had to put on sunglasses. In the village, I saw a B&B called Station House, and there was a row of newly built houses not far away called Station Terrace. The names endure to tell of what passed before.

We parked the car on Lahinch front and went for a walk on the glittering beach. There were lots of surfers in the water and people on the beach with their children; more people than you sometimes see in the summer, and this was 26 December. One child tried to rollerblade on the sand with no success. Another hit a tennis ball too smartly with a hurley and sent it out into the ocean, from where it did not return.

At Lahinch the sea shines like a jewel.

"Like diamonds," Máine said. We marvelled at the blue cold day and the number of people in the water. We did not know it then, but at the other side of the world, tens of thousands of people on beaches and in fishing villages had lost their lives that morning in the tsunami that devastated so many coastlines of South East Asia. We walked happily on Lahinch beach, innocent for a few more hours.

Outside Lahinch, there is a caravan park where the freight

shed used to be located. A couple of miles outside Lahinch, we passed under another bridge. This one is called the Major's Bridge, after Major George Studdent, who once lived in nearby Moy House, now an exclusive small hotel.

Miltown Malby is where Parnell turned the first sod of the railway. On the way into Miltown, we passed its original station. It has also been converted into a B&B, but even without the name, Station House, you'd know it had railway connections. The old wooden veranda with its fluted canopy and cast-iron pillars that abut the house look like, well, look like the platform that it once was. There are no tracks, but the veranda is pure Victorian railway-station platform. We walked up to the house and the veranda. There were cars parked right up to it, in between the cast-iron pillars: two eras of transport lined up beside each other.

At Kilkee, the surface of the crescent-shaped bay was still and calm. There was nobody out on the streets at all.

> Kilkee! Oh, you never get near it!
> You're in luck if the train brings you back,
> For the permanent way is so queer, it
> Spends most of its time off the track.

Kilkee had been a branch line from Moyasta, a few miles east. We headed east. Time was getting on, the light was beginning to fade in the early winter day and we were expected back for dinner. My very old (frankly, ancient) VW Polo, which had carried me round and round the country countless times, would pack up for good in less than a week, although, obviously, I didn't know that right then. I did know that on Stephen's Day the heating wasn't working, for the first time ever. Both of us kept our respective coats and jackets on all day. It was, literally, colder inside the car than outside. I drove to Moyasta, shivering, my hands stiff and awkward on the wheel. Stalwart Máine was wearing a coat, two scarves, a hat and gloves and still admitted politely to being a lot less than warm.

Moyasta, like a lot of Clare, is flat. It's a wee village. I wasn't sure what I was looking for, but as soon as I drove in, I saw a big painted sign with an image of Puffin Billy on it and the words

West Clare Railway Co. There were tracks going across the road. I parked and looked for an entrance. Not seeing it, I scrambled over a wall and walked along the tracks towards the little station hut I could see in the distance. A building beyond that looked like a station house and I could see carriages on tracks, but nothing else. Nothing that looked like an engine, anyway. The Moyasta page of the interactive map I had found had informed me that the engine was in England being restored and would be back in Moyasta in two years. That had been dated 1999–2000. We were now on the brink of 2005. Where was it?

There was a platform, two green-painted carriages that looked like reproductions and a station box a bit away from them. I started walking towards the station box and was startled to see someone on the other side of the platform: a man of a certain age, who had a magnificent white beard that extended all the way up his sideburns to his hair, which was equally white.

This was Jacky Whelan. Jacky bought out the West Clare Railway Company consortium that had originally had the idea to revive the station at Moyasta Junction. He seemed entirely unperturbed to see a stray visitor on a Stephen's Day afternoon (there was absolutely nobody else even in sight). The old station house, he explained, is now a museum. There is also a decommissioned national railway carriage in which teas are served. The two reproduction railway carriages bring tourists out along the two miles of track. They had fourteen thousand visitors in 2003. And the engine? I could see it wasn't on the platform, but I still hoped it might be in a shed somewhere. Now I was here, I badly wanted to climb up on it again. This is the way I had wanted to end this quest, hauling myself up those well-remembered cast-iron steps and looking out over Clare.

The engine, Jacky told me, was still in England. In Ross-on-Wye, still being restored. They thought it might be back in late 2005, but were not sure. I was so disappointed I could hardly speak. I had imagined, foolishly, a moment of epiphany perhaps: a connection of past with present; an understanding of something. But things don't happen that neatly in life. There was no engine waiting for me.

Whelan pointed northwards. "That's Slieve Callan," he said. A small but distinctive hill. I'd never been to Moyasta before; I'd never known the name of this hill was Slieve Callan.

The little museum inside the old station house still has its original ticket office. Displayed on the walls are maps, railway posters and lots of photographs. Behind one wall of glass, I found the old John Hinde postcard so familiar to me from childhood, with those three children: taken at Ennis station when Puffin Billy was still pristine, under its canopy, and when the trees had not yet grown up to obscure the view of a bus stopped on the railway bridge.

Ennis, West Clare, and Moyasta, Co. Clare, 26 December 2004

~ LAOIS ~

No Television, No Cards, No Singing

Un-PC or sad as it might sound, given our abysmal track record with alcohol as a country, it is nonetheless a fact that some of the best nights of my life have been spent in pubs in Ireland. When I was twenty-five, I spent three months hitch-hiking around the entire coast of Ireland to research a book. I tried to stick as closely as I could to the coastline and followed rural roads wherever I could. Since it was winter when I was doing this – October, November, December – and I was often staying in quite small places, I ended up spending a lot of my evenings in the local pub, as nothing else tended to be open. I started drinking later than most of my peers – at twenty – and was out of Ireland most of the years between twenty-one and twenty-five, so my hitch-hiking winter was a bit of a personal odyssey through Irish pubs. That winter, I discovered the pubs I liked best were small and old and simple with a clientele that included sometimes quite elderly people, whom I particularly liked talking to and listening to their stories.

Some months ago, I was in one of those Dublin superpubs, meeting an old friend for a drink. While we were there, a few of her office colleagues joined us. One of them asked us for our orders on her way to the bar. I said Guinness. She looked blank. "*Guinness? A pint?*" I agreed that this was what I would like, helpfully holding up my glass by way of an additional clue as to its size and contents. I thought she hadn't heard me properly the first time because it was so loud – ear-splitting music being played over the loudspeakers that were lurking behind every potted palm in the place.

It turned out I was, apparently, a) only the second woman whom my friend's colleague had ever seen drinking a pint of Guinness and b) the first woman she had ever ordered said pint for. She told me this as she handed over the glass. The result of her sharing this information with me was that a) I felt very, very old and b) very, very gobsmacked. Ever since a brief period of drinking gin and tonics in my last year as a student, I have always drunk Guinness in pubs. As have many of my friends, of both sexes. (And no, nobody belonging to me works for Guinness, in case this all sounds like a large ad.)

The woman who had just bought me the first pint of Guinness she'd ever bought another woman was from Wicklow. She'd been living in Dublin for four years. She loved superpubs, cocktail bars and hotel bars. When in them, she and her friends drank bottled lager, wine, cocktails, flavoured vodka. What age was she? Twenty-five. She had never touched Guinness. Why? Because it was an old man's drink. I looked around me with new eyes to see what everyone else was drinking. I was indeed an anomaly: I was the only woman in the vicinity with an old man's drink.

For all the debate about how Ireland has changed so much in the last decade, our mad property situation, the shambles of the health system, the traffic, the new cars, new money and newly acquired permatans, blonde hair and so on, to me, nothing quite illustrated the changes in our society like that exchange. I still haven't worked out exactly *what* it says, but I know for me it was the moment I realised how fundamentally Ireland had changed since I was twenty-five: in many subtle ways as well as the more obvious ones, including generational.

It did set me thinking, though. We spend a hell of a lot of time in bars in Ireland, and, obvious as it sounds, the bars we choose to drink in these days, when there is such a variety, must say something about us. What do I hate in pubs? Music. Television. Eejits. Junk on the walls. When they're too big. When everyone there is the same age. Themed spaces. Quite a lot of things, actually. My ideal pub is old, small, unruined by being renovated, has an open fire, a mixed clientele and an atmosphere that belongs exclusively to that space. If I had to pick my favourite pubs in Ireland, they would be: Bridie Keating's close to Derrynane beach in Kerry, Tigh Neachtain's in Galway, Tynan's Bridge Bar in Kilkenny and Morrissey's of Abbeyleix in Laois.

Morrissey's is one of the great old pubs of Ireland and one of the few that has not been destroyed by "modernisation". There has been a bar on the site for some three hundred years, and the current premises, which was rebuilt in the late nineteenth century, remains unaltered. It stands on the main street of Abbeyleix, the front painted black. Within is a very grand version of the traditional Irish grocery–bar. Most surviving grocery–bars are quite modest in scale: a counter at the front, with rows of shelving behind the counter, then a simple bar in either an adjoining room or further along the same room, which is almost always low-ceilinged.

Morrissey's is large, high and grand, although the bar side retains that dim light so crucial to atmosphere. A bar-counter runs round the perimeter of the room, with plenty of snugs and corners and walls for punters to disappear behind, thus giving the large space intimacy. Everything looks old because it *is* old:

the dark wood of the counter, the shelves that once held many kinds of groceries, the cast-iron stove, a calendar from 1933, the wall of biscuit tins – Marietta, Jacob's USA, Goldgrain – the framed documents that detail the names of the grocery assistants over the centuries: *John Ryan, 1850*; *Ann Phelan, 1988*.

Morrissey's was always family-run, and its last but one owner, Paddy Mulhall, worked here for sixty-eight years. He sold the place in 2001, since he was then in his eighties, but he still lives in Abbeyleix and comes in every day for tea or a bite to eat and a chat. We sat together at the table beside the old cast-iron stove, which has a pipe leading from it that "heats the whole place". About a century ago or so, according to Paddy, a local ironmonger came and added a cast-iron cat to the top of the stove where it sits yet, keeping warm. He started in 1934, when he was fifteen, working in the shop for his aunt, Mrs Morrissey. That first year, he was paid four shillings a week to wash glasses and bottles – Morrissey's bottled its own ale and Guinness, in common with many other pubs of the time.

"We would open at 9 a.m., as we were a shop, and close at around 10.30 p.m." Paddy progressed from washing glasses to weighing sugar and tea into pound bags for customers. Once he started serving customers, he wore a white coat – a tradition those who work behind the bar still follow. At that time, there were six people working behind the bar and two men in the yard, as well as two bakers. "The bakers came in at four in the morning. They baked pan loaves, turnovers and Madeira cakes at Christmas." The premises also had an undertaker's attached to it, with a horse-drawn hearse. Does he remember that? "Remember it? I *drove* it." Paddy recalls a time when the pints of Guinness he served up were eight pence. Their time of biggest demand was during the town's monthly pig-fair, when farmers converged on Abbeyleix. Bacon was always a big seller in the grocery part of the shop.

For as long as Paddy had Morrissey's, there was no television. "Or cards. Or singing," he added sternly. Paddy sold the place to the man who had already been leasing it from him for some time. There have been virtually no changes. Apart from the television in a small back-room, separate from the rest of the bar.

And having been a barman and worked in such a famous pub for sixty-eight years, what was or is Paddy's own preferred drink? "Oh, I never drank at all!" he said, laughingly. "I never broke my confirmation pledge." So that knocks two clichés on the head: not all old men drink Guinness, and not all Guinness drinkers are old men.

Morrissey's is the kind of bar that people who commission Irish-themed bars abroad are always trying to copy by hanging road-signs, St Brigid's Crosses, bicycles, cream-cracker tins, fiddles, bodhráns, old maps, whiskey jars, washboards and a million other bits and pieces on the walls of their foreign bars. Individually, they all have some element of integrity to them as objects one might associate with Ireland, but stick them all up together ad hoc on a pub wall abroad and what they create collectively is something fake. Because to be in an Irish bar, you have to be in Ireland: it's as simple as that.

*

Paddy Mulhall died in July 2005.

Abbeyleix, Co. Laois, 3 January 2005

~ MEATH ~

THE *FAR EAST*

Once a month at my primary school, the Holy Family in Ennis, we read the *Far East* in class; the religious magazine published by the Columban Missionaries. It was a diversion from lessons, but never an easy or entertaining one. I remember very clearly the glossy smell of the paper. The photographs all seemed to be of Africa, and sometimes the Philippines; hot-looking places even in black and white, full of missionaries and nuns in dark clothes. It could not be true, but as I remember it, very many of the articles were about leprosy. Men with leprosy sitting under trees, looking straight at the camera. Leprosy was a kind of nightmare word in my life as a child. I knew more about leprosy than I did about cancer: I certainly heard the word years before I ever heard the words cancer or Aids. When I discovered as an adult that leprosy is curable, I was utterly astonished. As a child,

I had thought it the worst disease anyone could ever have. It had not crossed my mind for a second that you could have leprosy and survive. I had assumed all those *Far East* photographs of lepers – as they were described in the captions – were of the living dead.

The only light relief in the *Far East* was a page called Colum's Corner, which we were allowed to read when we had read the rest of the magazine. I understood perfectly well that the *Far East* was not a jolly journal in the way my weekly comics – *Jinty*, *Whizzer and Chips*, *Mandy* and *Bunty* – were, but it was clear to me that Colum's Corner was a very bad token attempt at entertainment. The main part of it was a diary – or 'diry' – written by an unfunnily illiterate boy named Pudsy Ryan. Pudsy Ryan's diary was never convincing, even when I was a child. Nor was Pudsy's name. *Pudsy*. Who did you ever know who was called that? Fatso Ryan, maybe, but not a wimpish excuse of a name like Pudsy. Even as a child, it was obvious to me that it was written by an adult who just didn't get it: get the true perspective of a child.

The *Far East* is still published. As explained on the contents page, it is published eight times a year by the Missionary Society of St Columban to: "promote an awareness of the missionary dimension of the Church among readers; report on the work of Columban priests, sisters and lay missionaries; seek spiritual and material support for missionaries". The January/February 2005 edition contained, among other things, an article by a Columban seminarian on the community spirit in Yanaoka, Peru; one on Brazil; a column by a nun about an uplifting experience she had had in Pakistan; an article by a Columban priest about eco-farming in the Philippines; a religious-themed short story; and Colum's Corner. There were no pictures of lepers.

Pudsy Ryan's Diry still endures.

> We were doin a reedin lessin when the inspectre kame in. He is a littil short man, big in the middile and wee at the ends. He seed to sister pawl I happent to be passing by and I thawt I wud drop in for a minnit. Sister pawl

sed mister dolan iss a grate pleashure to see you but thass
not what her face sed when he cum in. Mister donal sed
well now that I am heer I mite as well do sum work,
What are you doin at the moment childrin and we sed
togethir pleez sir reeding. He assk mayr healy to reed an
the lessin was bout war and she reed out the word
katastrofay. The inspectre sed do you know whot that big
wurd mean? Mary said yessir it meens a hole lode of
kats. He sed nonsins duz annybody kno? Our noreen put
up her ole han she sed pleez sir it means when sumthin
awfil kums unexpektedly. He sed thass eksellint, who can
giv me an eggsampil? I sed pleez sir you.

I picked up the magazine from a table in the lobby of Dalgan
Park. Dalgan is the administrative headquarters for the Columbans as well as a home for its retired missionaries. Since 1995,
the Columban Mission Awareness Centre is also here: an
interpretative centre which explains the history of the work done
abroad by its missionaries.

I grew up taking entirely for granted the presence of missionaries. I was not of the generation familiar with giving pennies for
the black babies in Africa, but I was certainly aware of a culture
of mission. It was announced sporadically from the altar in
Ennis when someone in the parish was being posted abroad to
do missionary work. Our chaplain at boarding school had been
a missionary priest in Africa who had to return to Ireland after
suffering repeated bouts of malaria. And, of course, there was
the *Far East*, through which we were updated regularly about
what was happening in the world of mission.

Since the foundation of the Maynooth Mission to China in
1918, over fifteen hundred Irish Columban missionaries have
gone overseas. They were not the only Irish missionaries:
Roscrea, for instance, is a Cistercian mission house. It struck me
as remarkable that – to my knowledge – not one of these literate,
educated Irish men and women, who must have had quite
extraordinary experiences in the Far East in the early part of the
twentieth century, had published a memoir. Certainly not one
well known and published by a mainstream press, as opposed to

a private printing. It is a missing, unrecorded story and one that is as much a part of our social history as our spiritual history.

I was interested in Dalgan Park for two reasons. One was that, when I had started doing some research on the place, I had discovered there were five rooms filled with artefacts from countries where the Columbans had been missionaries: Burma, China, the Philippines, Korea and Japan. Five tiny museums, if you like, full of artefacts, all of which were open to the public. It seemed fantastically exotic to me to think of treasures collected long since from the Far East in rural Meath. I wanted to see them. I also hoped to look at paper archives, should there be any: to read some letters or diaries kept by missionaries decades ago.

I first read about these rooms in the 1992 edition of the *Reader's Digest Illustrated Guide to Ireland*. Not for the first time, I discovered both the advantages and disadvantages of consulting elderly guidebooks. When I subsequently phoned to inquire if I could indeed see the five rooms, I was told that only one room now remained, the Chinese room. The others had been dismantled in the early 1990s to make way for the Mission Awareness Centre.

I also discovered that, while there is an extensive paper archive of the Columban missionaries, it is not held at Dalgan. The intention is that it will be moved there eventually, but for the moment it is held at the Columbans' house on Grange Road, at Donaghmede in Dublin.

Dalgan is not far from Navan, set off the road in a vast estate. It was bought by the Columbans in 1926. The college there was built in 1941 to house and train the missionaries. There is a dairy farm on the estate, a nature reserve, rivers, a forest of fifty thousand trees and a large graveyard, where deceased Columbans are buried. The public are invited to walk in the grounds, while observing the fact that the area is a place of retreat. Dogs are not allowed. Nor is cycling, rollerblading, sunbathing or picnicking.

The college itself is an enormous building, almost the size of a university. When I drove up the avenue, I was staggered at its size and spent a few minutes staring at the expansive

Hiberno-Romanesque-style limestone façade before I got out of the car.

Ger Clark is development officer for Dalgan's Columban Mission Awareness Centre. He arrived to greet me as I was finishing reading Pudsy's Diry in the lobby. Ger's office is without doubt the most unusual office I have ever set foot in. It is not so much an office as a small museum. When the Burmese, Japanese, Korean and Filipino rooms were dismantled to make way for the new Mission Awareness Centre, which Ger set up, quite a lot of artefacts that couldn't be housed elsewhere in Dalgan ended up in his office. Fighting for space with his desk and filing cabinet were: a silk parasol from Burma with landscapes hand-painted on it; a gong hanging from two arched ivory horns; a panama hat; lacquer boxes from China; Filipino musical instruments; a scabbard; elephants made of different kinds of wood; feathered arrows with metal tips; Fijian tree-bark paintings; a military uniform; embroidered bags; wooden figures of Burmese tribes; a bugle; and a painting of Burma's most famous temple, the solid-gold Shwedagon Paya. There were literally dozens of other objects; in glass-fronted cabinets, stacked on the floor, hanging off coat hooks and piled on top of cupboards.

Ger took me to meet Father Pat Raleigh and Michael O'Sullivan. Father Pat is a former missionary who was in the Philippines from 1968 to 1977 and then in Pakistan from 1982 to 1993. He is the Columbans' mission, justice and peace co-ordinator. Michael is the education officer of the interpretative centre and, like Ger, is a lay worker at Dalgan.

Father Pat filled me in on some background information. At Dalgan's height, from the 1940s onwards, vocations to mission life were many. The seminary could, and did, hold 180 students at a time. The training period was seven years. When a seminarian had completed his studies, he was called to a meeting in one of the five museum rooms to be told where his posting was going to be. "You knew by what room you were called to where you were going," Father Pat explained.

Times changed. By 1977, there were only thirty missionary

vocations at Dalgan. It was deemed impractical to keep such a large seminary open for so few, and the remaining students were transferred to Maynooth. In 2005, there are no Columban missionary students at all in Ireland. Dalgan operates now only as an administrative centre and a retirement home. There are sixty retired priests here. Many are very elderly: in their eighties and nineties.

When we came out of the room the four of us had been talking in, we started walking down one of Dalgan's many long corridors. You could practise the hundred-metre dash on the quadrangle of parquet corridors at Dalgan. At intervals along the corridors, there are beautiful, enormous, glass-fronted oak cabinets. Each one is different, and each one contains artefacts from the Far East. They are a mixture of souvenirs and gifts from the local communities. They have been arranged with a good eye. Each cabinet is utterly intriguing. One contains only small ivories, which look like snowflakes from a distance. Another contains only painted wooden figures of different Burmese tribes. Another has blue and white Chinese plates. I tried to write down inventories of different cabinets and had to give up, because I didn't know what some of the objects were or which country they were from: there were few labels or hints at origins and provenance. I only knew they were beautiful and unfamiliar and lovely. For one cabinet I wrote: *peacocks carved from mother-of-pearl shell. Framed butterflies under glass. Lots of ivories of work scenes – drawing water, ploughing, threshing, fishing, boating. Two gold ceremonial-looking helmets decorated with semi-precious stones.*

The Chinese Room is the only remaining room of the original five themed rooms. It is painted yellow, with the same parquet floor as in the corridors. There are specially built cabinets that display ivories and jade, teapots, teacups, chopsticks, a woman's shoe for a bound foot, mah-jong, calligraphy tools, Chinese lacquer and bowls. Four pink armchairs stand in front of a marble fireplace, and there is an oval dining table and chairs. Beside the door is a huge carved wooden trunk, painted gold.

Over it hangs an exquisite silk embroidery of a path through a forest of tall, thin, leafless trees. It is worked almost entirely in silver, grey and white thread, and is as delicate as an etching; a very beautiful piece of superb craftsmanship. Once I had noticed it, I found myself unable to look at anything else in the room: it commanded it, in the way only truly striking works of art can.

Walking around the enormous building, it struck me very forcibly that Dalgan had been built big: built with big assurance and big confidence for a developing and enduring future. It must have seemed unthinkable in 1941, when the seminary was completed, that the day would come so soon when Dalgan's 180 missionary students had dropped to literally nothing. And that now the place contained only missionaries at the end of their lives, instead of those at the beginning. You didn't need a Mission Awareness Centre at all, I thought. The whole place had become a kind of living museum itself.

Ger offered to show me Dalgan's chapel. It is a lovely place, and much of the interior comes with a story. The monstrance is a replica of the one designed by Michael Scott for the Honan Chapel in Cork. The jewels in it were a gift from Ruth Nicholls, who was a frequent contributor of short stories to early issues of the *Far East*. The pulpit was given as a gift from the child readers of Colum's Corner. The benches are of African mahogany; the floors are of Burmese teak. In fitting out and decorating the chapel, the Columbans tried to reflect the places they worked in and the people who worked with them.

Ger also showed me the sacristy that had been used by the seminarians. Priests are supposed to say mass once a day. To facilitate the large numbers once at Dalgan, when the church was built so too was a large sacristy, with two wings containing seven little rooms, each with an altar. They were once used on a rota. The retired priests at Dalgan still come here to give their daily private mass. I walked through one wing. The altar-rooms are all interconnected: a corridor runs through them. A window faces each room, and each windowsill has a candlestick and a box of matches placed neatly beside it.

In the sacristy, Ger pointed out a piece of furniture to me. It was a kind of cabinet, consisting of a specially built series of little drawers, like pigeonholes. Each drawer had a slot for a name-plate. Ger opened one of the drawers and showed me what was inside. A single perfectly ironed and folded white handkerchief. This is what the priests use to dab their lips after they have tasted the wine and bread during mass. Each priest has their own designated drawer and their own handkerchief, with their name on the drawer. Most drawers now are empty and have no names on them. When a missionary priest dies, their hand-kerchief is removed, as is their name, and the drawer remains empty. There will come a day when all the drawers are empty. Afterwards, I found myself unable to get that cabinet of drawers, with all its blank name-plates, out of my head.

The Columban archive that is held at their house in Donaghmede in Dublin is not open to the public, but after I had been to Dalgan, my request to visit was accepted by the archivist, Father Pat Crowley. When I arrived, I wasn't sure what I was looking for, as I didn't know what was held there, but I knew I wanted to try and find original material: letters, papers, anything that would give me a flavour of missionary life in Asia several decades ago. Father Pat is seventy-eight, a courteous, kindly, dignified man, with perfect manners, who still works full-time as editor and archivist for the Columbans. He worked in Japan between 1952 and 1960 and later in Australia and New Zealand. "Call me Pat," he insisted after a while.

Pat showed me into his domain: his library. Two walls were filled neatly with box-files, floor to ceiling. They were arranged by country. I took out one file on Burma. In that file alone were drawings of Burmese landscapes, letters from missionaries, cor-respondence to Burma from Ireland, copies of long-ago visa applications, newspaper articles, the typescript of an unpublished memoir and maps. My difficulty was finding a focus. Every country had rows and rows of similar files, all containing material relating to the missions that had been based there. I decided to concentrate on a couple of the Burmese files and took two more of them to study at the library's desk.

The earliest archival material of foreign Columban mission

dates from 1920, when the first missionaries went out to China. The Burmese archive runs from 1938 to 1979: the Columbans have only had a couple of people posted there since. When I went through that first file I had pulled out, I was astonished to discover one of my own articles: a piece I had written for *The Irish Times* about the month I had spent in Burma in 2003.

The Columban mission in Burma was based in Bhamo, north of Mandalay and not far from Katha, where George Orwell set his searingly dark novel *Burmese Days*. Reverend Daniel Treanor recorded the story of his time in Bhamo on seven pages of a copy-book, the staple holding them together now rusty. He entitled it *Burma 1946–1977: I Was There*. It opens:

> On a late Sunday evening in September 1946, eight of us disembarked at Rangoon full of enthusiasm as we took our first steps on the soil of Burma, the land and people that must be awaiting our arrival for the good news of Christianity. We were ushered off to the clergy house were we spent the night and there our ardour died – the sand-built castle began to tumble into nightmares – veni, vedi, but we had no return ticket.
>
> Eventually we reached Bhamo and there got another glimpse of the war destruction – no town, no church building, no anything except hope, much sunshine and very warm welcome from the Columban veterans who were on the spot to greet us.
>
> By January 1947, with little or no Kachin, I got my first appointment to assist Father Devine at [indecipherable]. There I was soon to learn that we were on a disputed site and a few influential Baptists were pushing the authorities to have a hospital rather than a Catholic centre.

Father Daniel Treanor was from Emyvale in Co. Monaghan, born in 1918. He stayed in Burma until 1977, when the Columbans withdrew their mission there. On return to Ireland, he was appointed curate in Coalisland, Co. Tyrone. He died after taking ill while hearing confession. He is buried in Dalgan.

In the same file was a letter dated 25 April 1945, sent from

Mandalay by Father John Howe. The Columban missionaries in Burma were interred by the Japanese for the duration of the war. They spent most of the time being held at St Joseph's Leper Asylum in Mandalay. The letter is a very long one, describing what had happened in the previous three years, when it had not been possible to get any post out of the country.

> Towards the end of October they packed us off to Mandalay ... That trip to Mandalay was a memorable one. There were 26 of us altogether, 19 priests and 7 boys. The boat we travelled on was already hopelessly overcrowded when we went onboard. The journey should have taken about two days but it was the dry season, the river [Irrawaddy] was low and the boatman incapable, so it took us 12 days. We sat on every sandbank of the Irrawaddy and on one for four days ...

On arrival in Mandalay:

> That night when we lay down on the floor the boards seemed to us like an Odearest mattress, so hard had been the iron sheeting on the boat ...

The Japanese also interred Franciscan priests. Commenting on this, Father John wrote:

> The Jap never gave any solid reasons for his action but from his questioning it was apparent that he considered them either fools or spies for staying behind and in either case, the jail was a fairly safe place to have them. They knew of the Catholic Church of course, but they looked upon it as mainly a westerning influence which should be curbed in the greater Asia co-prosperity sphere ...
>
> About my precious belongings in Rome, if they are still there I would be glad to have them whenever the road to Mandalay is made open to the public. I imagine it will be quite a long time before the first group of priests come out here ...

Bishop John Howe was from Ballinakill, Co. Galway. He went to Burma in 1941. After being released by the Japanese, he was appointed bishop of Myitkyina. He returned to Ireland in 1988. He died in 2000 and is buried in Dalgan.

One of the papers in the file was a typed carbon copy of "Statistics for Mission, ended 30 June 1941". They read:

> Priests – 26
> Paris Foreign Mission – 1
> Burmese priests – 1
>
> Population [of parish] – total, 500,000
>
> Catholics – 4,201
> Buddhist – 340,000
> Animist – 150,000

At the bottom of the page was a hand-written note in copperplate from Father Patrick Usher.

> My dear Doctor O'Dwyer [Father Austin O'Dwyer, from Duniry, Co. Galway, had a doctorate in Canon Law and was working as professor of Moral Theology in Dalgan at the time this letter was sent. He died in 1975, and is buried at Dalgan],
>
> Make what use you please of these statistics. We are not harking for publicity for them. They represent what God enabled us to do; the work, I think, was honest and hearty.

Father Patrick Usher was born in 1899 in Tullyallen, Co. Louth. He led the first Columban mission to Bhamo. He went out to Burma in 1936 and remained there until he died suddenly, in 1958. He is buried in Bhamo's Christian cemetery.

The library also holds an entire bound set of *Far East* magazines. I took out 1974: a year I would have read when at primary school. A year's subscription then cost forty pence. The May issue that year had a cover picture of the Basilica at Knock, which was still under construction, with scaffolding around it. Among the articles inside was one on the new basilica, which ended by asking for donations towards the costs still to be met. There was a piece by Father Dan Moriarty from Lima; another called "China's Challenge to Christianity"; and one about a missionary sister trailing her peer in Korea, called "Catching Sister Zita". Pudsy's Diry began: *Sistir gongezaga tole us that a man was kumin with a kamera to take picktures for the papers …*

Inside the front cover, along with the list of contents, was – literally – a mission statement.

> The *Far East* is absolutely essential to our work. It still is, as it has been for 56 years, our chief means of com- municating and advertising. In common with other mis- sionary magazines, it has a part to play in educating our people to the mission and arousing in them an awareness of the mission.

The Columbans had also placed their own ad in the *Far East*. There were headshots of thirteen students recently arrived in Dalgan. Underneath was the headline, "There Are Places for More".

> Last September, the students above came to St Colum- ban's College, Dalgan Park to begin studying for the priesthood. There have been years in the past when over three times as many came to Dalgan in one year. Is the decline because priests are no longer needed for missionary work? If the Society of St Columban were to meet all its commitments for the next three years it would need 80 more priests. The number available will be less than 50, not allowing for deaths and illness. But the purpose of a missionary society is to push ahead, not just to "meet commitments". The labourers will always be few.

When I was leaving and Pat was walking me to the bus-stop, he told me he hadn't slept the night before for worrying he wouldn't be able to help me; that I would find his library – his meticulously ordered and documented library – of no use. I told him there are entire books that could be written about what is to be found in the extraordinary archives at Donaghmede. I hope he believed me.

Dalgan Park, Navan, Co. Meath, 17 January 2005
Columban House, Donaghmede, Dublin, 31 January 2005

~KILDARE~

DAN DONNELLY'S ARM

Odd as I now realise it is, given it is one of the most famous things in Kildare, I'd never heard of Donnelly's Hollow. Or his arm. Until December 2004, when I was having Christmas drinks in Ennis, and Colin and Bridget Doyle enlightened me.

On a filthy Saturday in January, I drove to the Curragh. Or rather, through the Curragh. I'd never been right in it before, although I spent my childhood staring across it from the back window of the car on our regular trips to Dublin. Or later, from the windows of the westward trains.

It was a day that was dim even at 1.30 p.m., when I was leaving the house. I had to switch the headlights on as soon as I set off. On the Curragh, the gorse glowed through the mist. I went the wrong way first and ended up in the little Curragh camp village itself. It was deserted, rain soaked. I peered through the rain at the period buildings, opened the window and shivered in chill air.

I drove back across the road through the empty fields and took a right to Kilcullen. I wasn't even sure what I was looking for, but I reckoned a sign would show up somewhere. It did: a brown sign on the crest of a hill, on the right-hand side of the road. Donnelly's Hollow.

I parked a little further on, in front of the school, and walked back. When you stand by the sign and look down, you see a perfect bowl-shaped hollow, scattered with gorse bushes. In the centre is a stone obelisk, with severe-looking railings around it. I slid down the muddy slope and went over to it. This marks the spot where Dan Donnelly fought and won a famous bare-knuckle fight with Englishman George Cooper on 13 December 1815. At the foot of the obelisk is a plaque which reads:

> Dan Donnelly born in Dublin in 1786 was trained in the art of bare-knuckle boxing by Captain Kelly of Maddenstown of the Curragh of Kildare. He beat Tom Hall from the Isle of Wight on this spot before 20,000 spectators on September 14 1814, For prizemoney of 100 sovereigns on December 13 1815 before a greater crowd he defeated the famous English pugilist George Cooper for prize money of 60 sovereigns. On July 21 1819 he beat English champion Tom Oliver of Crawley Hurst, near London when £100,000 of wagers changed hands. He was knighted Sir Dan in a tavern immediately after the fight, by the Prince Regent (later George IV). Sir Dan died penniless on February 18 1820 aged 32. Buried in the Bully's Acre, his grave was robbed, his body sold to Surgeon Hall who dissected and preserved his right arm which is on display in a Kilcullen tavern, the Hideout.

I transcribed this clutching an umbrella with one hand, cursing myself for forgetting to bring my tape-recorder. I could hardly read the writing afterwards, my hands were so cold and clumsy. It must have been freezing in December, fighting with bare fists. I looked around, trying to guess how many people had squashed into the hollow itself and how many had crowded on the lip above, roaring and shouting. Twenty thousand! They must have literally been shoulder to shoulder. The noise alone must have been tremendous in such a small space. *Erected by public subscription, 1888*, was written on the obelisk. I walked around the hollow, trying to imagine it then: the crush, the noise, the intensity. It was totally silent.

The famous fight lasted eleven rounds, and began soon after 10 a.m. Donnelly had come to symbolise the national struggle for independence. Probably like football matches two centuries later, where, whether we like it or not, the most ferociously followed games are those between Ireland and England – each crowd roars for their own. By the eleventh round, Donnelly was the winner, breaking Cooper's jaw.

He went on to fight other men, notably Tom Oliver – a marathon which lasted thirty-four rounds. But like sporting heroes of every century, he went astray with his own success, drinking far too much and allowing himself to be swindled out of all his money. He died at the shockingly early age of thirty-two, in 1820. His funeral was enormous.

Donnelly was not destined to lie in peace. His body was dug up and stolen by medical students. Somehow, they got away with it. Donnelly's arm was bought from them by a Dublin surgeon, a Mr Hall. Hall removed Donnelly's right arm. He wanted to dissect it and examine the muscle structure, to try and see what had made him so strong. The same thing happened to Charles Babbage, inventor of the world's first computer, who died in 1871. His brain was removed after his death, split in half and studied, to try and solve the mystery of what made his particular brain so astonishing. To this day, half of it is still on display in the Royal College of Surgeons in London.

Donnelly's body, minus his right arm, was re-interred. The arm was carried by Hall to Edinburgh, to be displayed in a medical school there. At some point, it was then acquired by a circus, who used it as a curiosity and put it on public display. This was, after all, the era of freak shows: lobster boys, bearded ladies, giants, dwarfs.

Hugh McAlevey, a northern Irish bookie and boxing fan, either went looking for the arm or was offered it. It was displayed in his Belfast pub, McAlevey's, for some years. When he died, it went into the possession of a Tom Donnelly, a wine merchant, who presented it in the early 1950s to Jim Byrne, who owned the Hideout in Kilcullen. The arm remained there, in a glass case, until 1995, when the pub was sold.

I went back to the car and drove the couple of miles onwards to Kilcullen village. I was looking for the Hideout. I knew Dan Donnelly's petrified arm was no longer in the bar, but I still wanted to see the place where it had been on public display for some forty years.

The Hideout is on a corner on the main and only street of Kilcullen. Inside, a fire was burning in the right-hand alcove. You can see it has been done up several times, but it still retains some vestige of character. There are comfortable stuffed armchairs and various nooks around the bar where you can settle in. The prints on the walls are mainly of horses. There are several glass cabinets, displaying sporting memorabilia, mostly racing and golfing, as well as odds and ends: old weighing scales, pastry-cutters in different shapes, vases, ornaments.

On the front of the cigarette machine is a facsimile of a poster of Dan Donnelly. It depicts him in period fighting gear – odd long-john-type trousers. *Donnelly's Arms were the longest in the history of pugilism! He could button his knee-breeches without stooping!!* it declares. There is a little inset picture of the obelisk at Donnelly's Hollow, but it is incorrect: the railings in the drawing are circular, whereas the ones I saw made a rectangle. *Specially drawn for Hugh McAlevey of Belfast, Ire, by Joe Carney, New York, USA, 1934*, read the words at the bottom. Joe Carney must have worked from a description. He probably never saw the monument himself. *The only monument ever erected to a prize fighter on the site of the fight!* The railing represents the ring made by the spectators. The stone is on the spot where Donnelly and Cooper fought.

Framing the main drawing, a sentimental-looking depiction

of Donnelly, is a ballad about the fight. It ends: *Now one and all/ Who would recall/ This great fight of the past/ Step into McAlevey's pub/ The Duncairn Arms, Belfast/ And in a glass case on the wall/ You'll see it hanging there/ The arm of bold Dan Donnelly/ Who fought upon Kildare!*

I stood by the fire and thawed out. A waitress came over to take my order. I asked her where Donnelly's arm used to be displayed. She didn't know. "I've never seen it myself," she said. "It was before my time. But it's amazing the number of people who still come in, wanting to see it and not realising it isn't here any more. I don't know where it is now."

Dan Donnelly's arm is actually less than a hundred metres away from where it was displayed in the Hideout for four decades. Des Byrne is an undertaker, and also owns the Esso garage in Kilcullen and the little shop that goes with the garage, which sells newspapers, confectionery, ice-cream and basic groceries, such as milk and bread and tins of beans. He used to own the Hideout too, the pub which his father and grandfather had both run in their day. He sold it in 1995 and took the arm with him. "I was afraid that if the pub got sold again, the arm would vanish," he explains. "And I wanted it to stay in Kilcullen." The Hideout has changed hands since Byrne sold it and has been done up each time, so the decision appears to have been a wise one. And after all, it did belong to him.

Dan Donnelly's arm now lies flat on a piece of white curtain lining on a table in Des Byrne's pretty sitting-room. On the day that I was there, the arm shared the table with a pair of binoculars and a golfing-themed pen and clock desk set. The pen-holder was full of pens. On the window-sill behind were various china ornaments, including four pieces of Lladro.

Two things struck me instantly about the arm: it was extremely long, and it was quite scarily arm-like. I'm not sure what I had been expecting to see. If I had thought about it, it was as a skeletal arm, all bone. But it's not like that. The arm is like a cross between an anatomy lesson in dissection – the muscles are all clearly exposed – and a piece of petrified wood.

It's brown all right, but full, not like the flat, leathery-looking limbs of bog people. And its fingers are cupped, extended, as if in a gesture. The fingernails are long, long as a woman's, and they were all intact. I stared at the fingernails, mesmerised. Afterwards, I remembered that hair and nails are supposed to keep growing for a time after death.

I asked Des if he had ever measured it. He hadn't. I laid my own right arm down beside it on the table and guessed Donnelly's arm was at least eight inches longer than mine. I glanced up and noticed that one of the Lladro ornaments on the windowsill, a woman with a dog, was missing an arm. A *right* arm. It was a truly surreal moment.

Every few years, someone calls him up and asks to see the arm. "You wouldn't believe the number of relatives Dan Donnelly is supposed to have had!" Just before he sold the pub, ten years ago, the most famous and prestigious sports magazine in the US, *Sports Illustrated*, came and did a big article on Donnelly and his arm. It's the *National Geographic* magazine of sport, in terms of its international impact. "I still get letters arising from that article. Even now. The feedback was just unreal."

Des wants Dan Donnelly's arm to go back on public display in the Kildare area, but hasn't figured out where, partly due to concerns about security. "My difficulty is where to put it. You can't insure it. It's a one-off. I will have to put my mind to it again," he declares. Then he says, wryly, "It sure wouldn't look too good in a glass case in my shop, over the milk."

Donnelly's Hollow and Kilcullen, Co. Kildare, 22 January 2005

~CAVAN~

THE ONE THAT DIDN'T GET AWAY

The summer I left college, I worked as a barmaid. For years as a child, my family had rented a chalet at Bunavalla, near Caherdaniel, a place we all loved. My brother David loved it so much he went back there to live permanently. I went to live with him for that happy summer, in between the end of formal education and the beginning of adventures new. David fixed me up with a job in Ted's Bar in Caherdaniel, a bar I had run in and out of as a child, with bottles of 7-Up and bags of Taytos. Now I was the one serving another generation of children their minerals and crisps, and pouring pints and gins and tonics for their parents.

I had a party trick in the bar that I played on new visitors. Among all the usual paraphernalia of interior decoration of an old seaside pub – a huge lobster over the door, lifeboat moneyboxes on the counter, posters advertising trips to Skelligs from Derrynane, paintings of seascapes – was a small black-and-white framed photograph in a corner of the bar. It was this that I used to draw new punters' attention to when talk slackened off. I would point them in the direction of the photograph, wait while they examined it and read the caption, and then wait for the spontaneous reactions that would come tumbling out after the silent examination, like a time-delay conversation on a long-distance phone call.

The photograph in the corner of Ted's Bar depicted a classic line-up of three fishermen, all proudly holding their various day's catches. One was a pike, a true whopper of a beast, two-thirds the length of the man who had caught it. The fisherman who had caught it was beaming at the camera, a day's work well done, his hand firmly hooked into the pike's mouth. The caption underneath read: *Seconds after this photograph was taken, the pike revived, and took the fisherman's hand off.* There was, of course, no way of knowing if this was true, but at twenty-one it bred in me a healthy respect for the jaws of a pike and those who went after these apocryphal hand-biting fishes. It also never failed to kick-start an animated new conversation.

Cavan is reputed, very conveniently, to have 365 lakes. It's fishing country, this county, and specifically pike-fishing country. I wanted to find someone who had landed a big pike in recent years; a pike that was now on public display in some bar or restaurant in Cavan. I e-mailed *The Irish Times'* angling correspondent, Derek Evans, looking for a lead. He came back to me with a contact, which I followed, and which led on in turn to someone else, in the way leads do.

One Saturday afternoon in January, I met Paul Sheridan and his son Niall at the Crover House Hotel, which overlooks Lough Sheelin in Cavan. The Sheridans live in Killycannon, Cavan, and Paul is a life-long dedicated fisherman. His teenage son is less convinced of the merits of sinking a line in a lake or river. "It's very boring," he says, almost, but not quite, rolling his eyes. His dad just laughs and shakes his head.

Paul has been fishing since he was about eight, going out with his father. He started off by fishing for perch. Their next-door neighbour had a boat, and nearly every weekend they took the boat to Lough Gowna or to Lough Sheelin and spent the day on the water. What makes a good fisherman? "Patience," Paul answers instantly. "You have to be very patient. You might spend six hours out on a lake and not get so much as a touch."

What does he like about fishing? "How do I explain it? Out on the boat, it's eight hours of tranquillity. That it's enough just to be there, sitting in the boat, waiting for the rod to bend. It's a wonderful feeling when the rod bends. That's when the adrenaline starts going. I go out with my brothers a lot. It's so *relaxing*, out there in the boat. Then coming ashore somewhere and making a fire, boiling the billy for tea, cooking sausages – and trout, if we've caught any. You think, 'Isn't this heaven?' I wish I could do it every day."

On 29 May 1994, Paul was out in a boat on Lough Sheelin with his three brothers, John, Alan and Enda. They had been out about eight hours and dusk was just beginning to fall. They were thinking of food and of heading in to shore, finishing up for the day. Then Paul's rod suddenly bent almost in two.

"I knew I was on to a big fish, the way the weight was on the rod. Pike are cute. They go to the bottom of the lake and hide in the reeds. When you hook them, they try going under the boat, so you're at the wrong angle to reel them in. They are trying to get off the hook. You have to play with them and leave enough of the line slack, so that if they bolt suddenly, they won't break the line. I've had that happen to me. You want to try and keep them from going under the boat at all. If you had a pike on the line, you'd have a fair idea that'd be the fish it was, but until it lands in the boat and you see it, you don't know for certain."

For half an hour, with his Celta Spinner, Paul played the fish, which was sitting at the bottom of the lake and resisting all attempts to reel it in. His brothers were rowing and keeping the encouragement up as he tried to tire out the fish, which he suspected was a pike. Then he reeled in again, and this time the pike came thrashing furiously into the boat, to the cheers of all four brothers. "I was shaking, so I was," Paul recalls. "Me arms were hanging off me."

The three of us walked down to Lough Sheelin, and Paul pointed in the direction where the boat had been that day. Lough Sheelin is a big, wide lake

The brothers were sure it was a specimen fish. For pike, a fish weighing more than thirty pounds qualifies as a specimen fish. According to the Irish Specimen Fish Committee, who keep the official records, the Irish record for a pike caught in an Irish lake is forty-one pounds, set in 2002 at Lough Ross in Crossmaglen. The record for a pike caught in a river is forty-two pounds: this record has stood for a long time – that pike was caught in 1964, in the River Barrow.

Paul's pike had to be weighed on calibrated scales to record an authenticated weight. It was too late to find anywhere at that time of night, so Paul brought the pike home to their mother's house, where he was staying at the time, and put it in the bath. "Just to keep him fresh." It was late by the time they got home, and Niall, then a small boy, was already in bed. Next morning, he came running into the bathroom and discovered the huge pike with its rows of scissor-like teeth looking up at him from the bath. He screamed the house down. "I was afraid of my life!" he admits frankly.

Paul took out photographs of the pike to show me. There is one of Niall lying alongside the pike on the grass. He has his eyes closed and his face scrunched up in a mixture of horror and disgust. His entire body is recoiling away from the pike, and his fist is clenched tightly. The pike, dead by then, is quite a bit longer than the child, and just as broad.

Paul called in a favour from a friend whose father owned a bacon factory in Cavan town. He took the pike there to be weighed. It came in at thirty-one pounds and six ounces: a specimen fish, as he had guessed. He took it off right away to a taxidermist, Jim McGurran, who stuffed and mounted it for £300. "It was a once in a lifetime catch. I know rightly I'll never get one like it again. It's what you dream of when you start fishing."

Once stuffed, Paul wasn't sure what to do with his mighty pike. His wife wasn't terribly keen on it – in fact she hated it – and banished it to the top of a press, out of sight. "It was a bit big to put up in a house, right enough," Paul admits, slightly regretful. He did offer it to the Crover House Hotel, since it had been caught in Lough Sheelin, which the hotel overlooks. They turned it down, but he wasn't really surprised. Pike don't have the romantic association of a fish such as salmon, with our folk-tales about the Salmon of Knowledge.

"Well, Lough Sheelin is known as a trout lake. The hotel mightn't like to be advertising the fact to other fishermen that the lake also has big pike in it. Because pike eat trout, of course. They eat anything, even each other."

In the end, Paul sold his big pike to Seamus O'Reilly, who owns the Drumlane Bar in Milltown, Co. Cavan. I drove there from Lough Sheelin. Milltown is a tiny village in the north of Cavan. I arrived there as darkness was falling. Seamus O'Reilly was the only person in his honest-to-God bar, in the middle of lighting a fire. I looked around, but could see no pike on display. When I had explained myself, Seamus told me he was getting a new glass case made for the pike, which was almost finished. It would be up on the wall within the month. He showed me where he intended displaying it, opposite the bar, between two windows and over a banquette of seats.

Would I like to see it? I had assumed the pike was with the person making the new glass case for it, but it wasn't; it was upstairs in the Drumlane. Seamus brought it down for me to have a look at. It was mounted on a board and was the size of a small shark, with jaws that stretched for an eternity. It looked as if, when alive, it would happily have taken a hand off, if a hand had been foolish enough to come its way.

Lough Sheelin, and Milltown, Co. Cavan, 29 January 2005

∽ LOUTH ∾

HOW GOES THE WEATHER AT GREENORE?

On my old *Educational School Map of Ireland*, there are twenty-four routes marked in red, signifying sea routes from ports in Ireland. Even though at nine, when I got the map first, I had never been on a plane or a ferry other than the twenty-minute Killimer–Tarbert car-ferry that ran between Clare and Kerry, I knew with certainty I wanted to see as much of the world as I possibly could, and I was always studying the routes which might lead me there. My favourite sea route on my map was the unlikely seeming thin red line that led from Moville in Derry to New York, 2860 miles away.

Although we never once went abroad together as a family, for some reason my father kept stacks of holiday brochures in his study. He renewed them every year. From early childhood, I spent hours and hours looking through the pictures in the brochures of elsewhere. The wider world looked as if it was composed entirely of beaches and swimming pools, of hotels and formal dining-rooms, cocktail bars and palm trees. The sky, I was eternally impressed to see, was always blue. So was the ocean. I loved those holiday brochures. The world beyond Ireland seemed so glamorous and exotic; full of sunlight and people eating dinner by candlelight out-of-doors (out-of-doors!) served by waiters in white coats; where there were blue blocks of swimming pools shimmering everywhere, where there were palm trees, bright pink bougainvillea, and where everyone looked happy. There must have been other pictures, but I don't remember a single cultural image or street-scene or a landscape from any particular country. All I remember from the brochures now are the white-painted hotels, the glittering turquoise sea alongside them and the intense blue of the empty swimming pools. Thus, as a small child, my notion of abroad was composed solely of beautiful seaside hotels, and I badly wanted to go there; to go to wherever those places were.

One of the sea routes on my map that led out of Ireland was from Greenore in Louth to Holyhead, a distance marked as seventy miles. No passenger ships have left there for several decades now.

Greenore is at the far end of the Cooley Peninsula. It is a lovely location, surrounded by mountains that turned blue and amber and then back to blue again as I stood on the shoreline, looking out over Carlingford Lough and the rushing clouds above. The water shirred black and grey in the wind and glowed dark-green where the occasional arrow of sunlight sped across it.

There is a plaque on the wall close to the gates at the entrance to the port. It reads: *This fort and railway were opened for public traffic by his Excellency, Earl Spencer K.G. Lord Lieutenant of Ireland, April 30th 1873.* Behind the port gates is a large old red-bricked building, four storeys high, with several chimneys. Some of the windows were boarded up or missing. It looked as if it had once been a very grand building, and I wondered what it could have been. The building was overhung by cranes. A yellow gantry stood close by. There were piles of industrial-looking equipment behind the walls; iron rods and sheets of metal. Inside the port's white-painted stone boundary wall was a small and lovely old lighthouse. It had an iron balcony running the width of it, just under the light itself. It had been domesticated. There was a weather vane on top of it and coloured glass in some of the panes through which the light would once have shone.

"I lived in that lighthouse for eleven years," Vanessa Price told me, at her home not far from Greenore. Vanessa is the granddaughter of Aodoghan O'Rahilly, who bought Greenore Port in 1954. He bought it from its owners, British Rail, for £12,000. However, as he disliked golf, he passed up on the chance to buy the adjacent golf course, the asking price of which was then £4,000. In 1951, there had already been an auction of the rest of Greenore – the entire village was owned by British Rail – including the shops, church, post-office and row of red-bricked houses where employees had once lived.

Greenore Port remained privately owned by the O'Rahilly family until it was sold after Aodoghan's death in 2000. He was ninety-six when he died and still involved in the day-to-day running of the port. The large red-bricked building I had seen behind the port gates was once a hotel. The railway line had run out to Greenore from Dundalk, where it connected with trains from both Dublin and Newry. "The idea was that you stepped out of the train and into your bed," Nuala Price, Vanessa's mother, explained. The railway tracks led right up to the hotel, in the tradition of Victorian railway hotels of the era, such as Charing Cross and Paddington in London, and the Irish railway hotels, like the Great Southern Railway Hotels of Killarney and Galway. There was an underground tunnel beneath the hotel by which livestock and mail were transported, out of sight of the travelling public.

Aodoghan had stayed in the hotel in the 1930s when it was in its heyday. It was famous then for its dances and was known to have a marvellous chef in the dining-room. The port and railway dated back to the 1860s. There was a lift in the hotel, which Vanessa thinks is reputed to be the first lift in a public building in Ireland. There was also a billiards room. By the time Aodoghan bought the port and hotel, nothing much was left of the interior furnishings, apart from the billiards tables, marble fireplaces and wash-basins. Nuala remembers the billiards tables being auctioned off and the interest they stirred because of their flat, true slate surface. She took a double wash-basin for her own home, where it still is. When Vanessa moved into the Greenore Lighthouse, she put in two fireplaces that had come from the hotel.

When I had been looking at my school map back in the 1970s, Greenore Port was still privately owned, surely the only Irish port to be thus owned in recent times. By all accounts, Aodoghan O'Rahilly, Nuala's father and Vanessa's grandfather, was a remarkable man. He certainly had a remarkable father: his father was Michael O'Rahilly, the only leader of the 1916 Easter Rising to die in action. Michael O'Rahilly was shot on the last day of the Rising as he led a charge against the army barricades in Moore Street.

As he lay dying in a laneway, he wrote a note to his wife:

Written after I was shot –
Darling Nancy I was shot leading a rush up Moore Street and took refuge in a doorway. While I was there I heard the men pointing out where I was and made a bolt for the laneway I am now in. I got more than one bullet I think. Tons and tons of love to you dearie and the boys and to Nell and Anno [his sisters]. It was a good fight anyhow.
Please deliver this to Nannie O'Rahilly, 40 Herbert Park, Dublin. Goodbye Darling.

A soldier took it out of his pocket when he was dead and duly delivered it to Herbert Park. The document is now in the possession of the State; it was given as a gift by Nancy O'Rahilly, his widow.

In April 2005, a plaque containing the text of this note was erected on the site where he died, on the laneway now called

O'Rahilly Parade, off Moore Street. What the plaque does not include, however, is the text on the reverse of the note. When he was shot, Michael O'Rahilly already had a note in his jacket pocket. The bullet went through the paper. It was the only paper he had on him, and it was a message from his twelve-year-old son Aodoghan, which read:

> 26 April 1916
>
> Dear Dadda
>   I got your [word missing in bullethole] letter. I heard from Nell and Anno that the Volunteers are winning. I don't suppose they will ever get the GPO for as long as you are in command. Father O'Mahony told us that up in Portobello Bridge there were two soldiers killed and twenty-four wounded. We had Father O'Mahony down here last night with Anno and had a grand talk about the whole thing.
>
>   With best love
>   From Egan [his family nickname]

It was on the other side of this note from his son that, two days later, Michael O'Rahilly wrote his dying message to his family.

O'Rahilly's death stirred the imagination of many, including the poet W.B. Yeats. Yeats wrote a four-verse poem about him called "The O'Rahilly", which is a stirring response to O'Rahilly's death. It also details the manner of his dying, and each verse ends with the same line: *How goes the weather?*

Under Aodoghan, container cargo plied between Greenore and Holyhead. Some hundred people were employed at the port. He had a special container cargo-ship built for the route. When Vanessa went to work for him, she moved into the then-decommissioned lighthouse, where she lived until 2002, when the arrival of her daughter prompted another move, to a more conventional house.

The port was sold when Aodoghan died in 2000, and it moved out of family hands. It is now owned by Dublin Port and the Irish Agricultural Wholesales Society (IAWS). The chief trade now is in steel and animal fodder. Vanessa still works there. It is only recently that her office was moved out of what was once the railway hotel building. She misses her grandfather and misses living in the lighthouse at the port, but she knows times change and things move on. "It's a different rigour now, working for new people," she admits. Nobody lives in Greenore Lighthouse now. The lantern from Greenore Lighthouse is held at the Commissioners of Irish Lights' museum at Dun Laoghaire. Vanessa hasn't been to see it yet, but she plans to go there one day to show it to her daughter, Greta, and tell her about her famous great-great-grandfather and the great-grandfather who once owned Greenore Port.

Greenore, Co. Louth, 30 January 2005

~WATERFORD~

A STILL POINT

"Have you been here before?" asked the elderly monk in the reception area who gave me the keys to my room in Mount Melleray's guesthouse. I said I had not. "I suppose I'd better show you where to go, so." He came out slowly from behind the desk he was sitting at, crossed the foyer, opened the door and pointed right. It was almost dusk. The Knockmealdown mountains beyond were dark stains on the horizon. "You go down there," he said. "There is a door in the wall. One key opens it. The other is for your room." I said that I would hurry, as Vespers was in ten minutes. The monk looked at me, startled. "It's a fine long walk to the guesthouse!"

I fairly scampered in the direction he had pointed out, crossing in front of the long chapel and towards the boundary wall, where an arched wooden door stood shut and locked. I was hurrying, yet it took perhaps two minutes, three at the most, to get there. A fine long walk? What had he been talking about? But as I put the key in the door, I tried to forget the long car journey from Dublin, when I had kept getting hopelessly lost as I attempted short-cuts on unsigned back roads; tried to forget the boundaries and scale of my world; tried, in short, to remember where I was: in a monastery, where there was a self-contained world and where a short walk to an outsider can in fact be one that takes in a quarter of the complex of buildings the residents live in. A fine long walk.

The first Cistercian monastery in Ireland was Mellifont Abbey, founded in 1142. The Cistercian ideals, then and now, are: authenticity in monastic observance; simplicity and poverty in everything; solitude; austerity of life and of work; and conformity to the rule of St Benedict. By the time of the Reformation in 1539, there were thirty-four Cistercian mon-asteries, all of which were outlawed. Mount Melleray was the first monastery in Ireland to be founded after the Reformation, almost three centuries later, in 1832. The sixty-four Irish and English monks that formed the new community had been taken from their abbey in France and jailed, being under suspicion by the government simply for being foreigners. They were allowed to choose the country they wished to be sent to: they chose Ireland and set about searching for a site for a new monastery.

The monks were offered 470 acres of what was then poor, isolated land by Sir Richard Keane of Cappoquin, which they accepted. The same day, they were given a cheque for £100 by the Duke of Devonshire in Lismore, which they used to build a temporary wooden chapel. When local clergy heard of the arrival of the monks into their mountain wilderness, they appealed to their congregations to assist with building and land clearance. The first visit was from the parish of Modeligo: four hundred men turned up with spades and started making a wall. Others followed, and the monks themselves started reclaiming the land, slowly building up their monastery. "It is the work of God and consequently he will assist in completing it," said Dom Vincent Ryan, first abbot of Mount Melleray.

During the Famine, the monks, although they had so little, did not forget their wider community who had helped establish them. Up to seven hundred people a day came to the abbey, seeking food. "From morning till night there was a strong Brother with a knife, cutting bread under a shed ... And a strong sturdy secular man beside him with a wattle to prevent the strong from snapping the bread from the weak," reads part of an undated memoir by one of the Mount Melleray community in the 1840s.

The monks have been accepting guests at Melleray ever since they were established there. The monastic tradition of hospitality is ancient: in medieval Europe, monasteries served as hostels for travellers. Daniel O'Connell came here for a week-long retreat in 1838. Eamon de Valera came frequently. You can write or phone the Guest Master and tell him when you would like to come. The best time to phone, you are advised, is between 10 a.m. and noon, as at almost all other times the monks are praying, working or sleeping. There is no fixed fee for your room and meals, but you are expected to leave a donation, the amount of which is up to yourself.

My guestroom, Number 7, overlooked a large, pretty garden, which had a Victorian summer-house at the end of it, all lovely gothic arches and french doors. It was a sizeable square room, painted white, which was plain except for a Celtic cross on one wall. The furniture was utterly functional: MDF wardrobe, desk, bedside locker. There was a reddish carpet, thick curtains, an armchair in front of the window and a single bed. But everything was thoughtfully selected in that room: the table was the perfect height to sit and write at; there were two proper reading lamps, one on the table and one over the bed, which are becoming more and more difficult to find in hotels and guest-houses; the radiator was old, but it kept the whole room warm. The bathrooms were down the corridor. I found myself wondering which room Daniel O'Connell had occupied and if the place had changed beyond recognition in the intervening centuries. I had hopes for the front door being original. I liked to think of him walking through the same door from the garden as I had done.

Vespers are the evening prayers in a monastic day that is defined by a timetable of prayer. The Melleray church is long and high and narrow. It is very simply furnished and decorated, which makes the large Harry Clarke window over the altar all the more astonishing; a jewel-coloured butterfly on an utterly plain white wall.

Lay people sit behind a low wooden wall at the back of the church. There are five pews aside, with four seats in each. There were a few other people there. We looked at each other briefly, nodding our acknowledgements. I sat in my seat, listening to the bells ringing to signal the start of Vespers, and slowly registered how very cold it was in the church. It is such a high space – you would be financially ruined if you attempted to heat it for eighteen hours a day, every day, which is how often it is in regular use.

The monks enter the church by a separate door to those used by lay people. They filed in in their white habits and went to stand facing each other in long pews that run down the side of the walls. Two things struck me instantly: how little of the pews their numbers filled and how many of them were white-haired.

Aside from rituals, such as weddings and funerals, I am rarely in a church, although, occasionally, I will go into an empty one of any denomination and sit for five minutes or so. Vespers is a short service, perhaps twenty minutes. Prayers are sung; sung like chants. It is peaceful and mesmeric. My mind flew away like a kite. There were spoken prayers also, including one for us, their guests. When it finished, I sat there for another few minutes, after the monks had filed out quietly. I had tried counting them as they left, but some left by a different door to the one they had come through, and I was distracted and lost count.

After Vespers, the guests gather for supper together in a room with four square tables, opposite the reception area where the elderly monk had given me my keys. The tables were laid for seven people. We introduced ourselves as we came in. Apart from me, only one person was there for the first time. He had come from Dublin for a week. "To sort my head out. There are lots of things happening in my life right now: too many things." Nobody pressed him on what those things might be.

There was a man from Lismore who comes often at weekends. He did not say so in so many words, but I got the impression that he came as much to escape his family as he did to seek retreat. There were a mother and grown-up son from Kilkenny who come four times a year. There was a man from Dungarvan who comes about three times a year. There was a woman from Cork who wore several holy medals on a chain prominently around her neck and who comes regularly. They all knew each other from previous visits. "It's mad busy in the summer," the woman from Kilkenny told me. "You'd be hard pushed to get a bed here then." All, except the Dubliner, newly arrived like me, had been there for some days already.

The others knew the run of the place. They waited by the hatch that led into the kitchen, from which a monk handed out plates, aluminium pots of tea and flasks of hot water. Both teapots had colourful hand-crocheted cosies. I found myself wondering who had made them. Had they been a gift? Had the monks made them? The table was set very simply with white ware. The placemats were ones depicting various John Hinde scenes; mine was of Bunratty Folk Park. We all received a plate with a fry: sausages, rasher, egg, tomato, white pudding. There was jam in little green plastic bowls, white sliced pan and pats of butter. We poured each other tea and passed plates of bread. It felt old-fashioned in a good way, all of it.

When it emerged over supper that I was staying only one night and that I was not a practising Catholic, there was surprise on both counts from most people. Why, so, had I come? I was fairly surprised myself at the reaction. I had thought it would be quite acceptable in 2005 that anyone, no matter what kind of religion you had – or hadn't – was equally welcome in a place of retreat, provided of course that you behaved respectfully as a guest in return; that it was something unremarkable in modern Ireland.

I went to my room for the hour before night prayers and sat at the desk, writing notes, taking stock. On the desk was a copy of *The Psalms* and a piece of paper that detailed the timetable for guests.

7.00 a.m.	Rise
7.15 a.m.	Morning prayer (Lauds)
7.45 a.m.	Mass in community church
8.30 a.m.	Breakfast
9.30 a.m.	Midmorning prayer
12.15 p.m.	Dinner
2.15 p.m.	Afternoon prayer
5.45 p.m.	Evening prayer (Vespers)
6.15 p.m.	Supper
8.00 p.m.	Night prayer (Compline)
8.30 p.m.	Guesthouse doors closed
10.00 p.m.	Retire to rooms

It is important to be in time for meals.

"It's the only thing they are fussy about," I had been told at supper. "Come and go as you like, but let them know if you will be around for meals or not. They hate wasting food."

I picked up the copy of *The Psalms*. The book fell open on a page where the spine had been creased. It was "The Prayer of an Exile":

> Like the deer that yearns
> For running streams,
> So my soul is yearning
> For you, my God ...
> Deep is calling on deep,
> In the roar of waters;
> Your torrents and all your waves
> Swept over me.

I had looked at the guestbook in the hallway before coming up to my room. Many of the addresses of those who had signed were in England. I wondered if someone in exile, homesick, back in Ireland on holiday and staying in Mount Melleray for whatever reasons for a few days, had found this psalm and read it so often the book now opened on it.

I wore another layer of clothes to Compline, night prayers. We went to the chapel through the connecting buildings this time, instead of leaving the guesthouse and going round a longer way outside. Bells rang again. I watched carefully as the monks came in, but again, counting them eluded me. I guessed there were maybe twenty-five, but I wasn't sure.

Again, there were sung prayers, reading, chanting. Nothing was expected of us, the guests. We did not have to make responses of any kind, or sing, or even kneel. Most of the time, the monks were facing away from us, intent, absorbed. We were at Mount Melleray for our various reasons, simply observing their daily and nightly rituals: bearing witness. I valued the fact that I could just sit; watching and listening and thinking. There was no right or wrong way to be there: it was enough simply to be there.

After Compline, we gathered in the guesthouse common room, in front of the gas fire. I went to put the kettle on in the adjoining kitchen. Seven mugs were set out and seven spoons, a pint of milk, a canister of tea-bags and a tin of Lincoln biscuits. I was struck by the fact that one of the monks had gone to the trouble to put the exact number of mugs and spoons out for us, when we could so easily have rummaged in the press and found them ourselves. It was only a small detail, but it was an attentive one, a thoughtful one.

At 4 a.m., I woke to the sound of the bells calling the monks to vigils. Their day had begun fifteen minutes previously.

3.45 a.m.	Rise
4.00 a.m.	Vigils
5.15 a.m.	Breakfast, prayer and reading
7.15 a.m.	Lauds
7.45 a.m.	Eucharist
8.30 a.m.	Reading and study
9.30 a.m.	Terce, followed by work

12.15 p.m.	Sext
12.30 p.m.	Dinner, followed by rest and reflection
2.15 p.m.	None, followed by work
5.00 p.m.	Tea
5.45 p.m.	Vespers, followed by prayer and reading
8.00 p.m.	Compline
8.30 p.m.	Retire

When I was woken by the bells, I had been dreaming about being in a boat with no oars, watching cats' paws on the water. I read for a while, listening to the sound of the rain on the window, then went back to sleep again, until my own alarm woke me.

It was a damp morning. I walked to the chapel for Lauds through the guesthouse garden, where everything was dripping and misty. The previous night, the Dungarvan man had told us over tea and biscuits how he had once come across one of the older monks in a corner of the guesthouse garden, standing perfectly still while a blackbird ate out of his hand. The patience and time you would have to have to build up enough trust with a bird like a blackbird for it to land on your hand. I had thought of Seamus Heaney's poem "St Kevin and the Blackbird":

And then there was St Kevin and the blackbird.
The saint is kneeling, arms stretched out, inside
His cell, but the cell is narrow, so

One turned-up palm is out the window, stiff
As a crossbeam, when a blackbird lands
And lays in it and settles down to nest.

I sat for Lauds in another happy, empty state of mind. I had studied the monks' timetable in my room the previous night and realised that, apart from when they were asleep, there were no more than two or three hours between chapel prayers each day, every day. The pews, I guessed, would fit perhaps two hundred. This time I counted correctly: there were thirty monks in the chapel. I looked again at the rows of white heads and wondered about the future of the order.

"It is a concern," the Guest Master monk admitted with frankness when I was leaving. The community at Melleray has dropped from 145 to 30 over the last half-century. Whereas once they needed a chapel, a roof over their heads, food and a way of maintaining their monastic lives, they now face the irony of having a huge estate, a large dairy farm and far more buildings and land than they need. What they lack are new monks joining and regenerating the community. In 1834, only two years after the monastery was established at Melleray, the abbot had to turn away novitiates. In the last fifteen years, twenty-five men have come to Melleray to test their vocations. Only one stayed.

"You had a short visit," the Guest Master said as I returned the keys. But my visit didn't feel short: it felt like a long time, a long, rich time. And it has stayed with me. I've found myself occasionally, as I glance at my watch, working out what part of the day the monks of Mount Melleray are at in their rituals. It is oddly satisfying, reassuring. It is like having a touchstone; a knowledge of a rare fixed and still point in an ever-turning world.

Mount Melleray, Co. Waterford, 5 February 2005

⌒TIPPERARY⌒

A THOUSAND-YEAR-OLD SECRET

When I was nine, my class from the Holy Family Primary School in Ennis, Co. Clare, went on a school tour to Dublin. We left on a special 6 a.m. train from Ennis. I can honestly say that never before or since have I covered so much of Dublin in a single day. We were taken to the public viewing gallery of the Dáil, the sole time I have been there; to Kilmainham Jail, which I only realised was a museum when we got there – I had thought we were going to be visiting prisoners; to Trinity and the *Book of Kells*, which impressed nobody; to the Zoo, where we were instructed by the nuns to eat our packed lunches, several of which, in those more irresponsible days, got thrown to the monkeys and orang-utan; to Roches Stores for shopping, although few of us had any money; to the GPO to see Cuchulain's statue and where the Proclamation, which hung in every corridor in our school, had been read from; and to the National Museum, where we were marched past the Ardagh Chalice, the Tara Brooch and the artefacts in the 1916 room, where my strongest memory is of the Bible which had been hollowed out inside to conceal a gun.

In 1980, when I was in secondary school, the Derrynaflan Chalice was discovered in a bog in Tipperary. I knew a bit more about the Irish treasures in the museum by then and owned a postcard of the Ardagh Chalice, bought on a later, solo visit, as I liked the shape of it so much and the fact the bowl had been beaten from a single piece of silver. I had even tried writing a poem about it. The news filtering down from art teachers that another ancient chalice had been found in a bog made a strong impression on me. I wondered what it had felt like to be the person who had discovered it: who had, literally, found treasure. And what, I wondered, had it looked like when it came out of the bog, after being hidden there for so long?

In 1980, I was at boarding school in Athlone. We didn't have much access to communications or media back then. I don't think I'd even heard the word computer at that point. There was one payphone between 119 of us boarders, located, ironically, in an old church confession-box under the main stairs. We rarely saw the news. We were allowed to watch television on weekdays between 7 p.m. and 8 p.m. at night only; the undisputed highlight of the week being Thursday's *Top of the Pops*. Radios were confiscated if discovered, although we all had them and listened to Radio Luxembourg and Radio Caroline with earphones after 10 p.m. lights out. There were no newspapers unless you were a sixth year: at the initiative of the school's brilliant and inspirational English teacher, Josephine Maloney, an *Irish Times* arrived daily to the sixth-year common room. I wasn't in sixth year then. Unsurprisingly, I never saw any coverage of the Derrynaflan find at the time it was made.

Almost twenty-five years later, I spent an hour or so one afternoon in the library of *The Irish Times* searching through microfiche, looking for the newspaper that had first recorded news of the find. I knew that Michael Webb and his son, also Michael, had found the Derrynaflan hoard on 17 February 1980, but that the news had not broken until some weeks later. The reels of microfiche whirred as I pressed my way through weeks of papers. The story broke on Thursday, 6 March 1980 and was carried on the front page. There were no photographs available of the artefacts at that stage.

Archaeological find of the century in Tipperary, was the headline on Geraldine Kennedy's report.

> A chalice similar to the Ardagh Chalice and a number of other gold, silver and gilt bronze objects have been found in Co. Tipperary in what is regarded as the most significant Irish archaeological and historical find of the century ... it is understood that the chalice dates from the eighth or ninth centuries and is from the same period as the Ardagh Chalice. Experts from the British Museum have already examined the chalice to ascertain that it is of old silver ... The discoveries are regarded by experts as the most exciting and significant in this country in the twentieth century, but no further confirmation of them could be obtained last night because the information was said to be subject to the Official Secrets Act. The Ardagh Chalice is one of the major artefacts of the early historic period in this country ... The chalice was discovered by a farmer digging potatoes in his field in the village of Ardagh, Co. Limerick, in 1868.

The same day, the paper carried a report that said: "CIÉ's proposal for a rapid rail system for Dublin has been opposed by a new group, 'Stop the White Elephant Campaign'." One of the letters was from an Eileen Hewson, who complained that: "The Irish roads are a national disgrace, giving a seedy and rundown appearance to a country supposedly booming in the Common Market." The editorial was entitled "Protest": "The excremental protest at Long Kesh may be the source of many learned theses in years to come, in much the same way that the sexual mores of the Irish since the Famine have been fertile ground for sociologists, psychiatrists and followers of allied disciplines ..."

The following day, 8 March, the first photograph of the chalice was published on the front page, with a long accompanying report. Geraldine Kennedy wrote:

> The treasure trove of the century was unveiled in the National Museum in Dublin yesterday after being discovered by an English amateur archaeologist with a metal detector in the bogs of north Tipperary 2½ weeks ago. The hoard consists of a chalice similar to the Ardagh Chalice, a strainer and a large tray or paten together with the stand. The objects will be on view to the public in a single glass case in the central court of the museum from 10 a.m. today for a month ... the finder of the items will be awarded compensation by the State in due course, though Mr Ryan [Michael Ryan, the museum's Keeper of Irish Antiquities] would neither put a value on the hoard nor the amount of compensation yesterday.

Almost a quarter century to the day after the discovery of the Derrynaflan hoard, I sat and waited in the Horse and Jockey pub in Horse and Jockey, Tipperary, for Michael Webb Senior to arrive with his partner, Mona Croome-Carroll. After the Webbs found the Derrynaflan hoard, there was a seven-year, high-profile court case with the State over compensation. Unhappy with the money originally offered to them, the Webbs took a High Court case, which found that they were entitled to either keep the hoard or the £5.5 million it was estimated to be worth. The State then appealed the ruling to the Supreme Court, which subsequently found that, under ancient medieval law, the State owned the treasure. It was a law that had not been tested in living memory, since the last significant finds of museum-quality artefacts had been in the nineteenth century. The Webbs were awarded costs and a fraction of what the hoard was worth, and the hoard legally became the property of the State. The case resulted in the introduction of a new National Monuments Amendment Act in 1994. "Oh, it was all great fun," he had said laconically down the phone to me on one occasion, although it was clear from the way he had said it that it had been anything but.

I had arrived good and early, but even so, I beat Michael and

Mona to our meeting spot by only a couple of minutes. They insisted on buying me lunch before they took me to the site nearby, where the hoard had been found. I found out later Michael had given up watching the Ireland–Italy rugby match that day to keep our long-arranged appointment. When she discovered I had not brought any boots, Mona loaned me an extra pair that they kept in their car to wear across the bog, assuring me that I would need them.

After lunch, we piled into Mona's car in the Horse and Jockey car-park and headed down a labyrinth of side roads, which turned into potholed bog roads, which turned into no road at all. We left the car where the bog road ended and pulled on boots and jackets and coats. From where we left the car, there was nothing to be seen on the horizon.

The others led the way, through barbed wire fences and across fields. Mona was right: we did need boots. We squelched through the bog, ankle-deep at times. The wind cut through my coat and we had to call loudly to hear each other. It was wild and lovely bogland, exposed and lonely-feeling, framed by a huge sky and ever-changing light. We climbed the slight incline and saw more. On the horizon were silhouetted two ruined buildings, quite close to each other. One, Derrynaflan church, had the unmistakable look of an early Christian church, with its high gable and long wall. The other was in a much more advanced state of ruin, really only a few broken walls. They were the only structures in sight for miles.

In 1980, Michael Webb had come walking across the bog-land here with his son Michael. Michael Senior was in a flying club, and the Derrynaflan church was a landmark from the air he was well used to seeing. They decided to explore the site more closely, from the ground, with their metal detectors. They each had one. Father had given son a metal detector as his Christmas gift in 1979 and, home from boarding school for the weekend, they had decided to try it out for the first time. Why had he given his son a metal detector? "Because he had that inquiring sort of mind," Michael explained. "It was very fashionable in those days. You don't hear much about them now, do you?"

We walked closer to the ruined church. The sun came out from behind the clouds and swept across the bog like a search-light, briefly turning the green a luminous golden colour, before the clouds rushed over to close the gap and the light faded again.

When the Webbs arrived at the site, they split up and started wandering around between the ruins with their metal detectors. No more than twenty minutes after arriving, Michael Senior's detector suddenly gave a strong and unexpected signal. "So I called Mike over and asked him to try it. And he said, 'Yes, that's it, that's a good signal!'" When they got the signal, they started digging. They had only one trowel between them, so they took turns digging with their hands. "It was quite hard work. It took an hour and a half to dig down, to expose it."

What the Webbs saw first was the bronze bowl that had been placed over the hoard to protect it. "And the bowl got bigger and bigger and went on and on. And we were delighted. It looked as if it was in the corner of an old building." When they lifted off the bowl, thinking that that was all they had found, they saw, dumbfounded, the silver ninth-century chalice underneath, with its gold filigree and amber ornamentation.

"We saw the chalice. And I *knew* what it was. I knew *exactly* what it was. I'd seen the Ardagh Chalice in the museum. The paten and the stand were leaning against the chalice. Mike lifted out the paten and the stand. I couldn't move. I just couldn't. I just could not believe it. I lifted it up and then it hit me that was a chalice and I was so shocked. I heard Mike from a hundred miles. He was saying, 'Dad, Dad, are you all right?' It was absolutely wonderful. It was absolutely *wonderful*. The making of a dream come true, to see this. It was just unbelievable. And he was saying, 'Dad, Dad, are you all right?' And I tried to speak to him, and I couldn't. My whole face was frozen."

We stood over the exact place the hoard had been concealed for a millennium. It was close to the ruined church, located between the church and the stubs of walls remaining from the other building. The bog had long since closed over the space again, having yielded up the secret it had kept for so long. I looked around me and tried to imagine the people who had hidden the pieces there; what time of day had they put them into the bog? Why did they hide them? Why did they choose this particular spot? Did they ever think, even for a second, that it would be a thousand years before they would be discovered again? The paten predates the chalice – it is eighth century. Made of hammered silver, cast gilt-bronze and knitted silver and copper wire with glass studs, gold filigree and stamped gold foil ornaments, it is from the same period as the Ardagh Chalice and may even have come from the same workshop. Fascinated, I walked across the site of the hoard over and over again, where past and present had fused a quarter-century ago. Two days previously, I had gone at lunchtime from work to look again at the Derrynaflan hoard in the Museum. It is displayed in the middle of the Treasury Room, right between the Ardagh Chalice and the Tara Brooch; the Treasury's new trinity of must-see artefacts.

The land around Derrynaflan church had never been fertilised, which undoubtedly saved the hoard. Nitrate on the surface of the bog would have seeped underneath, corroding and destroying the metal. What had the chalice looked like when it came out of the ground?

"Beautiful! Oh, that bluey-green copper sulphate blue! And streaks, where it looked a little bit greener. And then, through all that, the silver was shining though, dull and black. And the gold was just as bright as the day it went down. We were shattered. We were absolutely shattered. And we were running out of time because it was getting dark by then. We put the soil back and gathered everything up and took it back with us. It's difficult to know *what* I was thinking. I can't remember what I was thinking about. I was so excited, really excited. I've never felt like that before. The *elation* was absolutely wonderful."

Michael Webb recalled all this into my tape-recorder as we stood leaning on the fence that now stands at the front of a tidied-up Derrynaflan church. When the Webbs found the hoard, the ruined church was totally abandoned, with trees growing inside it and ivy over the walls. There are now neat pebbles flooring the bare interior and a sign with a drawing of the hoard and text explaining that it was found in the vicinity and is now in the National Museum. When I played the tape back later, I had to listen hard to hear our voices under the wind that had blown stronger than I realised that day, but even so, the excitement in Michael's voice as he recalled the find was unmistakable.

The Webbs gathered up the chalice, paten, stand and strainer and went back over the bog, as the February light was fading, to where they had left their car. They carried the hoard in one of their anoraks. It was a Sunday and both the Webb children had to be returned to boarding school. Michael drove his daughter to her school with the hoard lying hidden under the anorak on the back seat of the car. He did not tell her what they had found. Mona returned Mike to his school, still unaware of what they had found. Afraid that opportunists would descend on the site if the word got out before the authorities could excavate the site properly, Michael had instructed his son not to tell anyone what had happened that day. It must have been a difficult secret for a teenage boy to keep, especially away from home, for the three weeks or so before the story broke, even though his father wrote regularly to update him on what was happening.

That evening, Michael phoned a friend of his, Elizabeth Shee, who was an archaeologist. He told her he had found something she might be interested in seeing. "I took just the chalice up to her, wrapped in newspaper. And she nearly died when she saw it. She did what I did: she was mouthing. I said, 'Is it genuine?' And she said, 'Absolutely.' And then I told her there was more, a ladle and stand and other things ..."

When Elizabeth Shee had recovered from the shock of her career, she put a call through to the National Museum, and arrangements were made for the Webbs to travel to Dublin first thing next morning with the hoard. The Derrynaflan Chalice, quite possibly for the first and only time in its existence, spent a night beside a bed. During the night, Michael Webb reached out from time to time to touch it. "I didn't sleep. I kept looking at it, to see it was still there. That it wasn't a dream."

The Webbs brought the hoard to the National Museum the next morning, which opened specially for them, as, then and now, the museum is closed on a Monday. There followed an authentication process. Archaeologists were dispatched to Derrynaflan. Rumours started circulating locally in Tipperary that something had been found, but no news broke formally until the hoard was deemed to be genuine and the site had been properly examined.

The unrestored hoard went on view to the public for a month. I found an archive black-and-white photograph by Tom Lawlor in *The Irish Times* library of the first day's viewing. A crowd of people are leaning over the ropes that cordon off the showcase where the hoard is displayed together. A uniformed museum guard is inside the ropes, hands on hips, keeping an eye on things and preventing the public from leaning in too far. Everyone is completely focused on the glass case. There are old ladies with woolly hats and headscarves leaning right in to look; there are men with thick overcoats, scarves and trilbys standing intently. There is a nun, with a long black veil, just disappearing out of shot. Three men each hold a hand to their chin, as if they are thinking. Nobody is looking at the photographer, who is on the gallery above the central area of the museum, where *Ór, Ireland's Gold* is now on display. To a man and woman, they are all staring at the newly discovered treasures; staring with a curiosity and interest that leaps right out of the photograph.

It took a year for the artefacts to be restored. The Webbs went to the National Museum when they went back on public display. For both Michael and Mona, the chalice was less beautiful when it was pristine and gleaming than it had been when it had stood beside their bed, encrusted with age and stained with greeny-blue copper sulphate. "It was so sad. But it had to be done, it had to be restored. I mean, it looked fabulous all cleaned up, but it was different ..." Michael said.

We walked back over the bog towards the car. I looked back one last time to the ruined church on the brow of the small hill. "When they cleaned the chalice," Mona said suddenly, "it was like all its secrets disappeared."

Littleton Bog, Co. Tipperary, 6 February 2005

~CARLOW~

THE TEMPLE OF ISIS

Growing numbers of people are discovering their love for the Goddess. At first, this love may seem to be no more than an inner feeling. But soon it develops; it becomes a longing to help the Goddess actively in the manifestation of Her divine plan. Thus, one hears such inquiries as, "How can I get initiated into the Mysteries of the Goddess? How can I experience a closer communion with her? Where are her nearest temples and devotees? How can I join the priesthood of the Goddess? The Fellowship of Isis has been founded to answer these needs. [From a leaflet I was given at Huntingdon Castle, Clonegal, where there is a Temple of Isis in the basement.]

"There has always been a tradition of eccentricity in these houses," explains David Durdin-Robertson, whose aunt, Olivia

Robertson, is the High Priestess of Huntington's Temple of Isis. Parts of Huntington Castle date from the seventeenth century. It is a huge, rambling place, full of such diverse objects as the head of a crocodile David's grandmother Nora Robertson shot in the 1920s; a vine that reputedly came from Hampton Court when Henry VIII was on the throne; and antique Bedouin wall-hangings, which now cover every inch of the dining-room walls.

The Temple of Isis and Huntington Castle are open to the public in June, July and August for guided tours. David and his wife, Moira, once had a visitor who was very disappointed and surprised to discover, on inquiring, that the crocodile had not been shot on the Huntington estate.

In the 1970s, David's father and Olivia were among the small group who co-founded the Temple of Isis. "Isis celebrates the feminine side of deity," explains Moira, as they show me around the castle. "They wanted to be in tune with nature and healing forces. When I was a girl, I would have called it looking for positive vibes." David and Moira are very, very polite about the Temple of Isis, which is in the basement of the castle they live in, but they go to some trouble to point out to me that it is Olivia's territory and that they really have virtually nothing to do with it. Olivia, now in her late eighties – nobody seems to know exactly what age she is – lives in Huntington with David and Moira.

> Membership of the Fellowship of Isis provides means of promoting a closer communion between the Goddess and each member, both singly and as part of a larger group. There are hundreds of Iseums and thousands of members all over the world, since the Fellowship was founded in 1976 by Lawrence, Pamela and Olivia Durdin-Robertson. Love, Beauty, and Truth are expressed through a multi-religious, multi-cultural, multi-racial Fellowship. The good in all faiths is honoured.

"Olivia's parents were friends of W.B. Yeats'. She was taken to tea with them as a child. I think that influenced her greatly," Moira says. It is possible that Olivia, left to her own devices as children often were in those days, overheard quite a lot of interesting things when she took tea with William and George Yeats: the couple famously intrigued by automatic writing, seances and the esoteric. "Olivia has continued their mystic tradition."

> The Fellowship respects the freedom of conscience of each member. There are no vows required or commitments to secrecy. All Fellowship activities are optional: and members are free to resign without question. Membership is free.

Between them, Olivia and Lawrence wrote many books. Some of Olivia's books include: *The Call of Isis: Spiritual Adventures*; *Urania: Ceremonial Magic of the Goddess*; *Sophia: Cosmic Consciousness of the Goddess*; *The Rite of Rebirth*; and *Maya: Goddess Rites for Solo Use*. Lawrence's books include: *The Goddesses of Chaldea, Syria and Egypt*; *The Vital Elements*; *Priestesses*; and *Idols, Images and Symbols of the Goddesses, Egypt Part I: Isis*.

As I understand it, from my *Brewer's Dictionary of Phrase and Fable*, Isis was the principal goddess of ancient Egypt. The cow is sacred to her, and she is identified with the moon. There is supposed to have been a statue of her that bore the inscription, *I am that which is, has been, and shall be. My veil no one has lifted. The fruit I bore was the Sun* – hence, *Brewer's* explains, "to lift the veil of Isis is to pierce to the heart of a great mystery".

The Temple of Isis is located under the castle, reached by a white-washed stone stairway, in an area that once used to be cellars, dungeons and storerooms variously. Moira told me that there are twelve separate shrines, one for each sign of the zodiac. I have definitely never seen a basement of a residence so odd as the one at Huntington. As I wandered around looking at the twelve shrines, trying in vain to distinguish one zodiac sign from another, I thought that perhaps the reason it looked so strange to me was that it came with no point of reference. It literally didn't look like anything I'd ever seen before. And yet, pieces of it were familiar individually.

> The Fellowship reverences all manifestations of Life. The God also is venerated. Nature is revered and conserved.

> The work of the Order of Tara is for conservation of
> Nature. The Rites exclude any form of sacrifice, whether
> actual or symbolic.

The basement ceiling is made of rafters in part and in part is
painted blue and decorated with gold stars. The floor is stone.
We could all see our breath. It must be absolutely glacial in the
Temple of Isis in winter. I was there in early March and even
then it was like being in a fridge. Visually, it is a very busy space.
There are a lot of colours and textures and everything is
glittering and shining and demanding your attention. I did not
know where to start looking. It was overwhelming.

> The Fellowship accepts religious toleration and is not
> exclusivist. Members are free to maintain other religious
> allegiances. Membership is open to all of every religion,
> tradition and race. Children as "Children of Isis" are
> welcome, subject to parental consent. We have The
> Animal Family of Isis enrolled through members.

"Everything here has been slowly accumulated over the last
thirty years," Moira explains. "And people bring gifts." There are
about fifty "hard-core" members of the Temple of Isis in Ireland,
and some ten thousand worldwide. They meet regularly, and the
big date in the calendar is the summer solstice.

> The Fellowship believes in the promotion of Love, Beauty
> and Abundance. No encouragement is given to asceticism.

No asceticism is present in the Temple of Isis. It contains
every colour. The shrines were all laid out roughly the same way,
with an altar in an alcove. In the centre of each altar was a
depiction of a woman, either as a statue or a painting, and on
each altar were laid very many objects. One shrine alone
contained: gold and purple cloth; an Egyptian papyrus painting
of four women; a decorated plate; a bronze figure of a woman
with her hand up, her clothing picked out in metallic red; vases;
Chinese-looking boxes; candles in brass vases; some ceramic
object that looked like an egg; more pictures, more cloths and
two tin pencil-boxes in the shapes of Egyptian sarcophagi.

The Fellowship seeks to develop friendliness, psychic
gifts, happiness, and compassion for all life. The Druid
Club of Dana develops Nature's psychic gifts.

There are also many objects in the Temple that were salvaged
from an old church in Bunclody, particularly candle-holders. I
wandered around with my notebook and my head began to ache.
There was too much of everything, and none of it made any
sense to me. I wrote: *tiaras, crystals, lions, elephants, fake flowers,*
Holy Mary, Egyptian goddesses, native Indian dolls, Hindu
goddesses, Indonesian-looking goddesses, shawls, cats, owls, gold
bowls, gold teapots, glass box, scrolls, ankhs, stars, moons, suns, angels,
Celtic images, butterflies, St Brigid's Crosses, fake lilies, bells, masks
with peacock feathers, goblets, African carved antelopes, spinning
wheel, tilly lamp, fleur-de-lis. Collectively, what did it all mean?
To lift the veil of Isis is to pierce to the heart of a great mystery. I
couldn't lift the veil.

The College of Isis has been revived after its suppression
1,500 years ago. Like Aset Shemus, the Fellowship of Isis
itself, it has always been alive in the Inner Planes. It is
from these Inner Planes that its return has been inspired.
Magi degrees may be conferred through Lyceums of the
College. Correspondence courses are offered. There are
no vows nor secrecy. Fellowship of Isis homepage
www.fellowshipofisis.com.

I had hoped that I could talk to Olivia, High Priestess of the
Temple of Isis. She appeared briefly on the corridor to say hello;
an old lady with a steely eye. She had to rush, she said apolog-
etically, because she had to watch *Star Trek.* She thrust a leaflet
into my hands, invited me to come to a future ritual and disappeared. I stared at the door through which she had vanished.

"*What* did she say she was going to watch?" I asked David.

"*Star Trek*," he confirmed with an indulgent laugh. "She's
a Trekkie."

Huntington Castle, Clonegal, Co. Carlow, 5 March 2005

~WEXFORD~

THE DARKEST MIDNIGHT

At 10 p.m. on New Year's Day 2005, I broke down on the motorway approaching Dublin from the west. It was not, as it happens, the first time my car had broken down that evening. En route from my sister's house in Galway, the engine had started steaming and gasping near Horseleap at about 6 p.m. I know nothing about cars, but even I knew from the sound of things that something possibly fatal was happening under the bonnet. I went to a nearby house to ask for water, and the kind man of the house fetched a torch and came out with me. We surveyed the damage. A burnt-out hosepipe poured water.

The AA came and I was instructed to drive a mile or so back the road to a garage to be patched up. By about 8 p.m. I was on the road again, but edgy now, anxious that something else might happen to the car; already thinking ahead to the next day, calculating distances and time.

Between Lucan and my right-turn off home along the Grand Canal from the motorway, the car flashed red on all its dials and drifted slowly to a halt. It was dark, cold and horribly busy on the motorway. The engine hissed and groaned and, yet again, steam flew from under the bonnet. My lights still worked, though, and I switched on the hazards and called the AA on my mobile for the second time that day.

This time, there was nothing to be done. It was a distinct possibility, the AA told me, that a head gasket had blown. In fact, it was virtually certain. I wasn't surprised. My fourth-hand VW Polo was fifteen years old. The clock on it had gone round three times. The car was pronounced undriveable. I was towed home the last ten miles or so, right to my door, in my lovely old car that had suddenly become functionless and redundant. It was never to go anywhere again, apart from being transported on a truck to the scrapyard. *All racehorses retire in the end*, one of my friends e-mailed me later. Yes, but I had hoped my horse wouldn't collapse on me in the middle of a race.

For over three hundred years, six men of Kilmore parish in Co. Wexford have sung carols, unaccompanied, during the Twelve Days of Christmas. There was a time when these carols, known now as the Kilmore Carols, were sung across south Wexford: at Lady's Island, Piercetown and Drinagh. For some unknown reason, they have long since died out everywhere except the tiny village of Kilmore. Possibly they were suppressed over time by local clergy who felt the words of the carols were too dark and too uncomfortably pagan-like. Even in Kilmore itself, there have been priests who disliked the carols and tried to stop them being sung, without success. One nineteenth-century priest who tried to suppress the singers was himself got rid of: the bishop transferred him to another parish when the local people stopped attending the church in protest. In more recent times, one Kilmore priest who declared early in the year that the carol singers had had their last December with the carols died in November. The carols were sung as usual that year.

The carols are sung only during the Twelve Days of

Christmas, and there is a different carol for each significant day. The cycle starts at Midnight Mass on Christmas Eve, with "The Darkest Midnight", and continues through Christmas Day, with "Christmas Day Has Come"; St Stephen's Day, "A Carol for Holy Innocence"; "A Carol for the Feast of St John" on the 27th; "A Carol for Saint Sylvester's Day" is sung on one of the Sundays that falls between Christmas and Twelfth Night. The carollers sing on New Year's Day and then, finally, on Twelfth Night, the Farewell Carol is sung, the "Carol for the Twelfth Day". Followed by a session in Quigleys. Since I was spending Christmas in the west, there was no way I could get across to Kilmore for the first days of the carols. My opportunities to get to Wexford within the carol cycle were very limited. By Twelfth Night, a Thursday, I would be back at work. My plan had been to attend the 10 a.m. Sunday morning mass in Kilmore church on 2 January: the Sunday in-between the beginning of the cycle and Twelfth Night.

The tow-truck left me to my door after 11 p.m. I had intended getting up at 6 a.m. and driving south to make the 10 a.m. mass. I went on the Internet, looking for Bus Éireann's timetable, thinking that perhaps I could get to Wexford or New Ross and then get a cab onwards. But the Bus Éireann web site was frustratingly down, and when I looked at the train time-table, still a Sunday timetable because of New Year arrange-ments, there was nothing that would get me anywhere vaguely near the area on the a.m. side of noon. By then it was way too late to go calling friends and pleading for a return lift across the country at the crack of dawn next morning on a day that was still holiday-time for most people. I took a deep breath, cut my losses and went to bed. This time, my quest for the essence of what was local wasn't going to happen. What was local in Wexford was definitely staying local.

In the morning, I called Father Denis Doyle of Kilmore church to apologise and explain why I couldn't make it down as arranged that day, to listen to the carols at mass and interview the carollers afterwards, but that I hoped to come later in the year. I had still not heard any of the carols I was hoping to write about, as I had wanted to hear them first sung in the church at Christmas, in real time. This wasn't going to happen now. Was there, I asked, a CD of the Kilmore Carollers that I could buy, so I could familiarise myself with the music in advance of a future trip?

"They're awful shy people," Father Denis said down the phone. "People are always asking them to record the carols and they won't." So that was that. I considered giving up on the story altogether but it still fascinated and intrigued me: that such old carols were still sung, sung only in this one tiny parish in one part of the country, and had been sung in an unbroken tradition for over three hundred years.

Two months and one new-to-me car later, I sat in Father Denis Doyle's kitchen in the parochial house at the back of Kilmore church while he made tea and cut apple tart for myself and Liam Sheil. The oil for the heating had run out the day before, and he fretted that we would all be cold, but in fact, the early spring sun shone through the window like a prism. Liam is sixty-eight and has been one of the six Kilmore Carollers for many years. His son Jimmy is also a Caroller. The other four are: brothers Martin and Pat Bates; Robert (Robbie) Whelan, whose father and uncles were Carollers; and Richard (Dixie) Devereux.

All the Kilmore Carollers are special, but Dixie Devereux (sixty-two) has the distinction of knowing that a Devereux has been part of the sextet of singers for over three hundred years. When Dixie's father, Johnny, died, Liam asked him to take his place. "I wanted my eldest son, Robert (Bobby), to sing them because he has more years in him than me. But he was too busy with football at the time," Dixie told me later down the phone. "So I did it, and since I've started, I've really enjoyed it." He is proud of the fact the men in his family have been singing the Kilmore Carols for three hundred years in an unbroken line. "To tell you the truth, I wouldn't like to see it broken. As long as I'm alive, I won't refuse to sing them, and that's the truth."

"It's a privilege to be asked to sing the carols," Liam says. "I was listening to the carols all through my schooldays. That helps. You get used to hearing them. It takes maybe three or four years of singing for your voice to come out, to be heard. The carols used to be sung in two groups of three, but now we all sing them together, all the time."

Small things have changed over time. The singers have moved round the two-hundred-year-old church. They used to sing from the gallery, upstairs. At the back of the church. At the front of the church, their backs to the congregation. When Father Denis arrived in the parish, he decided he would ask the Carollers if they would stand and face the congregation. He didn't need to ask, as it turned out: the Carollers decided themselves they would sing in a new direction for a new priest and faced out to the congregation of their own accord his first Christmas.

In 1684, Luke Waddinge, the Catholic Bishop of Ferns, published a pamphlet of Christmas songs called *A Small Garland of Pious and Godly Songs*. He had written them himself, although the airs they were set to were traditional. Later, in the mid-eighteenth century, when Father William Devereux was parish priest of Drinagh from 1730 to 1771, Devereux himself published a collection of carols. Devereux's book (perhaps in deference to Waddinge's title for his book) was called *A New Garland Containing Carols for Christmas*. The book contained some of his own carols, as well as some from Waddinge's *Small Garland*.

Devereux's book became popular, and the tradition of singing these carols in south-west Wexford churches started round this time, although some of Waddinge's had been sung even earlier. The carols now sung in Kilmore were, at one point, hand-written into a leather-bound book. The book has since gone missing, but it is known to still exist and is thought to be somewhere within Wexford county. Father Denis hopes that someday it will be returned to Kilmore church, where it should rightfully be, since the book belongs to the community.

Nobody knows why the Kilmore Carollers have always been men. Possibly because when the tradition first started men were more to the forefront of society in general, and as the centuries passed, the tradition remained. Some things you don't change. As Father Denis had told me on the phone in January, the current Kilmore Carollers have never made a CD. Other musicians and broadcasters have come to Kilmore to listen and record, but the Carollers themselves have never recorded their carols. Liam, speaking for all the Carollers, feels very strongly about their reasons for choosing not to do so.

"There were people who came down here and took away tapes. And they just didn't sing them the way they should have been sung. When we heard what they done, we were highly disgusted. They jizzed them up and they just didn't sound right. They didn't sing them to the right airs. The trouble is if you change something like that, it's gone."

"We were thinking of doing a CD, but I can sense they are not over-enthusiastic," Father Denis said. "But what struck me very forcibly, when poor old Johnny died [Johnny Devereux, who had been a Caroller for over sixty years], it would have been lovely if we would have had something recorded with him singing on it that we could have played at his funeral that day."

"I like the idea of …" I began.

"Having a CD so you have the carols for posterity?" Father Denis suggested.

I drank some tea and thought for a while, in a comfortable silence. "No," I surprised myself by saying. "I actually like the idea that if you really want to hear them, you have to come here to hear them. That you can't buy the music; that you have to experience it first-hand instead, in the place it has always been sung." Then I asked Liam, "Are you happy that the carols stay in the church and are not recorded?"

"I'm a believer that the carols should stay as they are now," he stated firmly. "As near as they can to the way they have always been done. And when one of us drops out, there will always be someone else to pick it up. And no, not recorded. Just leave them unrecorded."

The Carollers start rehearsing in mid-November. They take

turns going to each other's houses for practices, usually six times in total before Christmas. They rotate the carols, singing different ones at each practice.

"It's a big commitment, because at Christmas most people like to be free to go wherever they want," Father Denis says. "The lads are bound here, over the Twelve Days of Christmas."

"Well, we do that for the sake of what we're doing. I'd hate someone to miss hearing the carols. I'd hate someone to come into the church here over Christmas and not hear the carols."

The Kilmore Carols are the least jolly and conventional carols imaginable. They are dark, brooding and haunting, using language that is dense with potent imagery. "Song for Saint Sylvester", for instance, contains these lines:

> Eleven million of stout marchers
> The rage of tyrants stood
> And sealed the heavenly testament
> Of Jesus with their blood
> Which still increasing the faithful for three hundred years
> Nothing was left for Christians
> But torture death and fears …
>
> Till Constantine the great
> A pagan emperor too
> His predecessor stepped resolving to pursue,
> Was struck by the Almighty
> With the most filthy sore
> And that with scabs and leprosy
> Infects his body ore.
>
> The bath of infants' blood
> By witches was contrived.
> This deed of hell was ordered
> For him to be revived
> Like another Herod those harmless babes would slay
> Had not our Saint Sylvester
> Cured him a better way
>
> This Pontiff by command of heaven
> Brought from his cave here before the emperor,

Undaunted, stout and brave
Reviled his black design,
His magic art condemned
And told him the only cure
Was to make God his friend.

Witches. Torture. Pagans. Scabs. Leprosy. A bath of infants'
blood. Black designs. Magic art. When I looked through the
words in Liam's carol book, I could understand a bit better why
some priests were concerned about such potent language and
images being used in their church. It's strong stuff: aeons away
from decking halls with boughs of holly and benign Good King
Wenceslas looking out on the feast of Stephen.

The first carol of the series to be sung is "The Darkest
Midnight", at Midnight Mass on Christmas Eve. "'The Darkest
Midnight' is a very heavy carol," Liam says. It opens:

The darkest midnight in December
No snow nor hail nor winter storm
Shall hinder us for to remember
The babe that on this night was born.

"The most of us have a favourite – but it's not because we're
finishing up," Liam stresses. "It's the last carol, the Farewell
Carol, 'The Carol for Twelfth Night'."

It wasn't fair to ask Liam to sing solo, without the others, but
I asked anyway. I was beyond curious to hear for myself how
these words were sung; to hear how they had been sung for
centuries; to get a sense of it at least, even though there was only
one Caroller present.

Liam sang the first verse of "The Carol for Twelfth Night",
his eyes closed, his head moving in time to the slow tempos.

Now to conclude our Christmas mirth
With the news of our redemption
We will end our songs on our saviour's birth
With one that deserves attention.
Three great wonders fell on this day,
A star brought kings where the infant lay,
Water made wine in Galilee
And Christ baptised in Jordan.

Later, I played back my tape over and over again. It was the some of the strangest music I had ever heard. I grew up listening to *sean nós* songs, but the mood and sound of this unaccompanied voice was something totally different. It was dark and haunting and very slow; almost like chanting, but definitely singing. Taking a melody and extending it almost to the point of collapse. And yet everything sounds right. The way Liam sang "mirth", for instance, in the line "Now to conclude our Christmas mirth", denies the meaning of the word. It sounds anything but mirthful. It sounds entirely solemn. But the "wonders" of the "three great wonders" *are* truly wonders. It is a word that goes on forever and sounds beautiful, inspirational.

At the time, sitting in Father Denis's kitchen listening to Liam sing, I wrote in my notebook: *It sounds medieval, dense, primeval. The voice sounds incredibly old, majestic, mysterious. You need time to sing them. It seems like they are about time. Time to practise and sing, time to listen and be still while listening.* When I went back and looked at my notes, I discovered I had underlined the word "time".

Later still, I realised that everything to do with writing about the Kilmore Carols had taken time because of my initial thwarted visit in January. In the end, my car breaking down the night before I was due in the Wexford church seemed apt. There will always be another year to hear the carols sung in Kilmore church. Another year. Another chance. Another time. After all, they have been sung in Kilmore for over three hundred un-broken years now.

Kilmore, Co. Wexford, 6 March 2005

~ MONAGHAN ~

A KITCHEN TABLE

For a long time now, the clichéd version of an Irish house abroad has been the eponymous whitewashed thatched cottage. Usually in a field somewhere. In 2005, a truer image of a representative Irish house would surely be one of the many thousands of new and identical urban estate houses, built in towns such as Rochfortbridge and Mullingar and Drogheda; built as a response to a property market gone quite strange. It is unlikely, though, that these houses in our new commuter towns will be featuring on a John Hinde postcard any time soon.

In the past, houses that did not fit into the John Hinde version of Ireland – simple, small, rustic – never made it onto postcards either. The big, grand houses such as Clonalis in Castlerea, or Ballinkeele near Enniscorthy, or Temple House in Ballymote, or Hilton Park in Clones were everything the Irish thatched cottage was not. They were enormous, they signified wealth and they were entirely remote from the soft-focus image conjured up by the thatched-cottage postcards: of the romanticised Irish peasant-farmer with his thatched roof, turf fire, clatter of red-haired kids and nice fluffy donkey out the front.

Although some of these Anglo-Irish houses were fired during the War of Independence, many of them still remain, scattered all around Ireland. Some have been sold and passed out of the original families. Only a few of the really enormous and long-established houses, such as Temple House and Ballinkeele and Hilton Park, have managed to stay in the same family throughout. It is no coincidence that all three of these houses are now members of Hidden Ireland, a collective of historic private houses that take a small number of paying guests and offer dinner in the evenings. "Our country houses are emphatically not hotels or guesthouses. They are private houses of great character and history, with unusual and interesting owners who enjoy sharing their special homes with appreciative visitors," reads part of the introduction to the Hidden Ireland handbook, www.hiddenireland.com. Taking guests, even for part of the year, is an essential way of maintaining such huge properties. Temple House alone is set in an estate of a thousand acres, and the house is reputed to have close on a hundred rooms.

Hilton Park near Clones is about as large and grand as an Irish country house gets. I drove into the estate via its lesser-used Scotshouse entrance, and for at least ten minutes I had no idea if I was in the right place or not. The potholed road kept going on, through fields and forests. Then, quite far in the distance, possibly a mile to the left, I saw the grey stone of the austerely beautiful house, beyond its lake.

Hilton Park has been in the Madden family since it was built, in 1734. There was a fire in 1803, and most of the house was gutted. For some thirty years, while the new house went up, the Maddens lived over the stables. "The only part of the house that survived," explained Johnny Madden, the current owner, "was everything under the brick-arched ceilings."

"And the furniture in it," Lucy, his wife, interjected. "Including this table."

The table Lucy was talking about was a very long, old pine kitchen table, which would easily seat twenty. Their son, John Frederick (twenty-five), always known as Fred, was sitting on the table. The other three of us were sitting round it, in the basement kitchen, drinking coffee. To me, the almost three-hundred-year-old kitchen table summed up living in such an old family house. That you could have something both so old and so functional, and that it was virtually certain every Madden who had ever lived here had sat round it at some point. Or, like Fred, had sat on it. Old furniture was so familiar to them as to be unremarkable. How many of us have kitchen tables that last even a generation these days?

"In a cupboard, in that room there," Johnny said at one point, gesturing towards a small room off the kitchen, which led into a breakfast room, "we found a carpenter's signature on a piece of wood with 1735 carved on it."

The Maddens left Ireland for England in the fifteenth century and came back in the seventeenth century. One of the Maddens who returned was Controller to the Lord Lieutenant of the time, Sir Thomas Wentworth. By 1734, when Samuel Madden's son, John, was twenty-one, there was enough money for the father to give the Hilton Park estate to his son, on an 80 per cent mortgage. "We reckon it was bought for him as a twenty-first birthday gift." There were originally four thousand acres on the Hilton Park estate; today there are four hundred. Over time, chunks were sold off to pay for the upkeep of the house and gardens.

The eldest Madden son has always inherited the estate. Johnny is now sixty-five. He and Lucy returned to live at Hilton in the 1970s from London. They were living in Hilton with Johnny's parents, John and Nita. "Even in 1974, we knew the house was going to have to pay its way for us to keep it."

In 1978, the estate with its herd of six hundred cows was continually hit by brucellosis. So badly were the herd and associated income depleted that Johnny's father contacted an auctioneer and told him the house and estate were going on the market. It never got as far as being advertised in the media, however. The house was saved by the compromise of selling off some land. "We sold 150 acres of land and, with that, we survived. It made the farm uneconomic, and what was left after the land acts was not enough to keep it going. It was obvious that once the land went, the two families were a drain on the place." The two generations of Maddens continued to live together in the house until 1983. By then, it had been agreed that joining Hidden Ireland and letting rooms to generate income was the only alternative to selling. Johnny and Lucy were all for opening the house. But it was tough for John Madden senior to reconcile himself with the old family home opening its doors to paying strangers.

"Both my parents, but my father specifically, could not envisage having strangers – people he didn't know – in the house he'd lived in for forty-five years, Which I think is understandable. So they left."

"Not acrimoniously," Fred stressed.

"Oh, not acrimoniously, but they were sad to leave," Lucy said.

"There were six months between the decision being taken and them leaving the house. And my father walked around with a camera virtually every day, photographing everything."

Hilton Park opened to paying guests in 1984. There are six bedrooms available, and the house opens between April and September. At most Hidden Ireland houses, guests eat together in the evening round a big table, but at Hilton, guests eat at separate tables in a dining-room that overlooks a parterre and the estate's lake. "When we started taking guests, 80 per cent of our income was from farming and 20 per cent from other sources. Now you could say that 30 per cent is from farming and 70 per cent is from taking guests. And the 'other sources' no longer exist. Whatever they were. My parents. Lloyds."

Johnny took me on a tour of the house. Everything is big –

grand: that was my most lasting impression. From the vast stone-flagged hallway, to the stained-glass windows with the family crest on the stairs that were put in to hide the farm from view, to the chandelier in one of the sitting-rooms, Hilton Park is a house where everything is on a bigger scale and from a different era, a different way of life. Is it hard to heat, I asked Johnny, as he showed me yet another beautiful, huge, high-ceilinged room? "No," he said briskly. "Not hard to heat. It just costs a fortune."

One of the guest bedrooms has a four-poster bed and overlooks the lake. Its adjoining bathroom has an old claw-legged bath. "A much-requested room." It was the wallpaper, though, rather than the view of the lake that caught my attention. The whole room was papered in an extraordinary cobalt-blue, with white flowers and trellises. There was a framed square of the same paper on one of the walls, a much brighter colour blue. "It's 1830s wallpaper. We found an old roll somewhere in the house in 1984 and put up this piece to show what the colour was like in its original state."

Other bedrooms look out over the fields. They are all a mixture of old and new, 1970s bathroom suites alongside beds you needed to either hurl yourself at or use a stepladder to get into. The dining-room has faded 1830s red curtains, which are so fragile they are no longer pulled: the window shutters are closed of an evening instead. "Shabby chic, I understand it's called these days," Johnny said, laughing. "We're fashionable, apparently, without even trying."

One of the drawing-rooms has a rosewood Erard grand piano, covered in family photographs. I had recently read Daniel Mason's novel *The Piano Tuner*, in which a London piano tuner goes to rural Burma in 1886 to tune an Erard grand for an eccentric British officer. I had never heard of Erards before reading this novel, but 355 pages later, I knew a lot more about them. "They were the ground-breakers of piano technology," Johnny explained. "They made their pianos like a piece of furniture, so the cabinet-making was always exquisite." The Hilton piano came into the house in 1865, and Johnny's great-grandfather composed three published tunes on it. Guests are welcome to play it, which must be something quite special if you can play the piano, which sadly I cannot, otherwise I could have definitely delayed in the Erard drawing-room far longer.

The Madden's own private sitting-room is painted cornflower blue and gold; an exotically beautiful combination that only a big period room could carry off. One corner has extensive damp. I noticed that in every room Johnny showed me he instinctively patted walls and examined ceilings with a quick professional eye. A huge house is both your home and your enemy: parts of it are always treacherously attempting to leak or seep or collapse or rot away.

The house is full of its history. Everything has a story, even the doors. The old schoolroom, which now contains a table-tennis table instead of a desk for lessons, also has an old rocking horse, dolls' house, toys and the tiny model cars that Johnny collected. The panels of the doors of this room, as well as four cupboard doors, have all been painted: charming scenes of gorges and rivers, of castles and lakes and mountains. A long-ago governess, from either Switzerland or Germany – Johnny can't remember which – painted them.

Back in the kitchen, I asked if the house had ever been a target during the War of Independence. "My grandfather was in the Ulster Volunteers, and every able-bodied man on the estate had rifle practice every Wednesday, so I was told. It was known that whoever came to Hilton would be met by lead."

"This property was always a bought property," Lucy explained. "It didn't displace people. And the Maddens were never absentee landlords. It was never just a rural retreat for them."

"It was always run by the Madden of the day, never by an agent," Johnny said.

Do they know the families in other Irish country houses? "Not really. We're not particularly sociable. Our social life is our guests, really," Johnny offered.

"We're not at all sociable, any of us. We dread going out," Lucy said brightly.

"Speak for yourself!" Fred countered, looking both horrified and embarrassed.

"We don't do any of the green-welly things either," Johnny said.

"We're not at all county, we don't like horses or shooting or fishing," Lucy said. "We like growing things."

What was it like, I asked Johnny, growing up as the eldest of three sons, knowing that he would inherit the place and all the responsibilities it brought? "Rather frightening. Rather frightening, when I used to see my father's desk and all the papers on it and all the filing cabinets and all the maps and stuff."

Was it not difficult to have two other brothers knowing that, by accident of being first-born, he would inherit? How did they feel about it?

"Because that was the way it was. They were brought up that that was the way it was. The reason being that Samuel Madden, who bought this place, left in his will that Hilton should always go to the eldest son. There was no actual legal entail, but he left it expressly as a desire. And I am quite sure my father didn't regard me as the most suitable son to look after the place."

"Certainly not," Lucy agreed.

"In fact, I would have said that of the three sons, I *might* have been second, but I really might have been third."

"It just shows you can't legislate for the future," Lucy said.

Fred is the youngest of Johnny and Lucy's children and the only son. His sisters are Amelia, Laura and Alice. What was it like for him, growing up?

"The last ten years especially, it was *never* concrete that this place would stay in our hands, in our family hands, and also that I would be the heir. It's always been outsiders who have told me, 'Oh, I presume you'll take over.' But my parents didn't want to put that pressure on me growing up, and my mother doesn't really believe that the male should necessarily be the heir."

"Is that a gut prejudice?" Johnny shot in. He was addressing Lucy. I got the feeling that this conversation had had many previous airings.

"No, not necessarily," Lucy responded. "It's based on sound common sense. It's crazy to say prejudice."

"*I* think it's gut prejudice," Johnny stated happily.

"It's crazy to disagree, Mother. You can't ignore the generations. For three centuries it's stayed in the family name," Fred responded. "Tradition *does* mean something. I tend to agree with you generally, but you can't just …"

Lucy was not for turning, not now or possibly ever. "The world changes all the time," she insisted.

"Not always for the better," Johnny countered. There was silence for a while after this exchange, but not an uncomfortable one, more a silence that suggested this conversation always went the same way and that it was now a matter of both pride and principle that everyone stuck to their own particular artillery.

In July 2004, Johnny and Lucy had a meeting with their four children to discuss the future of Hilton Park. "I put it to them that I was now really reaching a point where it was time to be thinking about handing over to someone else. I'm young enough to remain as a consultant but old enough to want somebody else to do the hard work. And Lucy and I recognise that there's no point in soldiering on in a place like this if nobody wants to come after you. So Fred and Laura said that they were possibly interested in doing something at Hilton and possibly together. Definitely together."

"I don't think any of us want to take it on our own," Fred said. "We're looking at this – myself, Laura and Kevin – as a business primarily. Because we have to look at it like that. I absolutely don't think anyone will really ever reside in this house again. Properly, like we have done."

Laura Madden has returned from Los Angeles with her husband, Kevin, and three children to live on the family estate. They have applied for planning permission to build a house in the orchard. Fred may or may not live in Hilton Park. Or build a house on the estate. He doesn't know. Although Hilton Park is home, Fred is utterly pragmatic about the future of the house and estate. "I've been brought up with my father always emphasising the huge financial pressures of this place and, basically, we need to make a lot of money to keep it going. So the majority of my thinking is based on that. But hopefully we can. We are in a position now where things are still manageable. But ten years down the line, they may not be, if we continue at the same rate of outgoings, which was what my father was thinking about when he discussed with the next generation what to do with the house and estate."

"It's true, you do view this house as a business for the future," Johnny said, admiringly, happily.

"It has to be, otherwise there is no point in us being here."

Among the plans that Fred, his sister and brother-in-law have for the future are creating more bedrooms from rooms currently used by the family and opening Hilton Park all year round. "You can't really complain about not making enough revenue if you're not open all year round."

There are also plans to put up a semi-permanent structure in the garden that would be a venue for weddings. "The premise of a marquee, but with a more architectural edge," as Fred sees it. They showed me a model: a grand circular structure, like a cross between a circus tent, a pavilion and a yurt. "We get a lot of wedding inquiries, but we can't cater for them at present."

The long-term plan is to renovate the courtyard at the rear of the house to create extra accommodation and workshop space. Laura and Lucy, both gardeners, hope to make allotments available to local children. "We want to get children gardening. Develop this into something educational, as we have a lot of unused land here."

Will Johnny and Lucy continue living here once the next generation take over?

"I don't think we're wanted!" Johnny laughed. Then he said, "I will be here for three years regardless, because I have to run the show. But live here forever? Feet first, you mean? Oh no, God no."

"We do envisage a time when we won't be here," Lucy said

Afterwards, Lucy showed me round the gardens with frustrated pride. She looks after them virtually single-handed. There is a herb garden with thirty-seven kinds of herbs; a huge vegetable garden that feeds the house and guests; glasshouses; a parterre; lawns; more gardens. Lucy has written a book called *The Potato Year*, which has 365 recipes for potato-based dishes. Since she wrote it, she has come up with a further 150 recipes.

After the tour of the gardens, we walked back towards the house. Would she miss Hilton when they leave eventually, I asked?

"No," Lucy said firmly. "Well, yes, of course, but no, really not. I'll never have another garden after this one. I've done it all, you see. When you've lived somewhere like this, there does come a time to move on. And I'd be quite happy in a tiny house. Or a caravan, reading books, which I don't have time for now." We approached the east side of the house. A wall of windows three storeys deep glittered in the early-afternoon light. "A caravan. Yes, I'd be very happy in a caravan."

Hilton Park, Clones, Co. Monaghan, 17 March 2005

~ DOWN ~

THE LOST VILLAGE

A complete village is buried in the sand at Ballyvaston. I read this line while going through the 1976 edition of the *AA Touring Guide to Ireland.* That was it, nothing more. There was no further information given about this buried village. Only that one line. But it was still enough to fascinate me.

I had once seen a newspaper wire photograph of a church spire sticking out of a lake near Pately Bridge in north Yorkshire. It was during the drought in 1995, and the church was part of a village in a valley that had been drowned to create a reservoir forty years earlier. It had never been visible since. I had looked at the photograph and wondered about the people who had once been in that church: who had been married there, or christened there, or been at funerals there. I wondered also about the things under the water you couldn't see: the houses and shops and schools and post-offices, the paths and streets and laneways. I had wondered what it would feel like for those people who had lived in the village to come back and stare across the surface of the reservoir to look at the church spire; to try and remember the way things had once been, while realising they could never go back, never recreate their old homes and their old lives. The image had haunted me for a long time.

Albert W.K. Colman lives in Crossgar, Co. Down. Among many other things, he is an expert local historian and, in the fifties, took part in an archaeological dig close to Ballyvaston. After I had spoken to him on the phone, he sent me three photocopied pages from a book he owned that had been originally published in 1744 and a detail of a map which showed the possible site of the lost village, with the townland of Hannastown a couple of fields away.

The magnificently long title of the book was: *The Antient [sic] and Present State of the County of Down. Containing a Chorographical Description, with the Natural and Civil History of the Same. Illustrated by Observations made on the Baronies, Parishes, Towns, Villages, Churches, Abbeys, Charter Schools, Mountains, Rivers, Lakes, Medicinal and other Springs, etc. With a Survey of the New Canal; as Also, A New and Correct Map of the County.* It had been published in Dublin by A. Reilly in 1744. I had never heard the word "chorographical" before. My father looked it up for me in my grandmother Katherine Boland's old *Chambers Dictionary,* which he now has in his library and which was published in 1909. Chorographical: "the description of the geographical features of a particular region". The "New Canal" of the title was the Newry Canal, which linked Lough Neagh and Newry and which was completed in 1742, just two years before the book was published.

The photocopied extract from the book which Albert sent me read:

> The Town Land of Ballyvaston lies on the Shore between Terela and Killogh, on which a remarkable Accident happened about 9 years ago. A strong South Wind setting in on the Land raised the sandy Soil about

10 feet from the Bottom, and thereby overwhelmed, and almost destroyed a Rabbit Burrow, by which the Vestiges of several Cabbins were discovered, and the Hearthstones, and wooden Chimney Frames surrounding them appeared. From these Traces it is manifest, that this Place was formerly inhabited. Besides, it is marked as a Village in Petty's Maps by the same Name, and by Bishop Echlin's Return of the State of his Diocese in 1622 it appears there was a Chappel there, which paid 5s. Procurations; so it is probable the like Accident, which so lately befel the Rabbits, formerly overwhelmed the Village since 1654, when Sir William Petty surveyed this Kingdom. The Place was cloathed with Herbage before this late Alteration; but by the prodigious Quantity of Sand blown in at that Time, a considerable Space of Ground was reduced to the State of a Desert, in which Condition it still remains.

I arranged to meet Albert at Tyrella church one Sunday afternoon. He then led the way onwards to the Dundrum Bay site. Dundrum Bay arcs between Newcastle and the lighthouse at St John's Point. Past Minerstown, Albert pulled his car in and indicated for me to stop.

When I got out of my car, the wind whipped the door from my hand and sent the pages of my notebook flying. You'd need good hard-wearing paint on your house around here, on this lovely but exposed piece of coastline. The site of the lost village is thought to lie here, under this raised beach, between the road and the shoreline, a half-mile or so long and, depending on the tide, a couple of hundred feet wide. We stood on the edge of the site. It was sandy land, with clumps and tussocks and brambles. Closer to the shore, the wet seaweed glittered on the stones and pools. In the distance, the Mountains of Mourne stood up. If you were driving past, you would have absolutely no idea that this is reputed to be the site of a lost village.

Albert reckons the village was here four hundred years ago. His grandfather, George Colmer, was the coastguard for this area, based just beyond the lighthouse at St John's Point, which we could see from where we were standing. His father, also called Albert, was an engine fitter on the *Titanic*. "The morning she was to sail, he had a premonition," Albert said. "He refused to board the ship. He didn't sail. His mate did, though. My father was devastated. Men cried on the streets of Belfast. My father could never come to terms with the tragedy, or that he had lived when so many had died."

Albert is sixty-nine now, and he grew up hearing stories about the lost village of Ballyvaston. "I always heard that the remains of the village were right on the shoreline. The road is new, of course." He waited while the pages of my notebook escaped yet again. "This area was always prone to wind. It would have been badly hit in 1839 too, the Night of the Big Wind." The theory is that the village was hit by a storm. High wind, or big waves. That perhaps people died, making the remaining villagers move to higher land or further away. The abandoned houses were covered over by sand and dunes and sea-grass, only to be discovered in the storm of the 1730s. He indicated the fields on the far side of the road from us, the site which he had excavated in the 1950s. "There is a cluster of ruined houses and a path there. It's a good fishing area, even to this day, which is what would have brought people here. Mackerel. Pollard. Cod. Lobsters."

It is manifest, that this Place was formerly inhabited. Besides, it is marked as a Village in Petty's Maps by the same Name. William Petty completed a survey of Irish estates between 1654 and 1655. Unlike other such surveys, which had been in the form of written information only, Petty's survey were laid down in maps on a large scale. He got the information "down" both literally and visually, hence the maps now carry the name of the "Down Survey".

I got a reader's ticket for the Manuscript Room at the National Library and set about trying to locate Ballyvaston on the Down Survey map. The Manuscript Room is separate to the National Library itself: it is further down Kildare Street, located over the Heraldic Museum. It is a bright, high room, with tall windows overlooking Kildare Street.

Most of the Down Survey maps are on microfiche, but it seems the northern counties were not microfiched, hence being directed to Kildare Street. Since leaving university, I have spent very little time in academic libraries and rather foolishly supposed with excitement that what was coming my way from the stacks were the original seventeenth-century maps of Down. What appeared on my table was a huge green hard-backed book, within which facsimiles of the Down Survey maps of Down, Armagh and Tyrone were collected together. Or rather, "The Counties of Downe, Ardmagh and Tirone".

I spent a couple of hours examining the Down maps. To begin with, I turned the pages swiftly, searching for the sea and thus a marker of where to look. I arrived at the Armagh section, several pages later, not having recognised one thing on any of the pages. The maps are on different scales, some eighty perches to an inch, some forty. They looked like estate maps: where the plots of land were written over as to who owned what. *Unforfeited lands. Irish papist prop. Wooddy Bog. Cabbins. Bogg and loch. River impafsable. A pafse kneedeep. Landes profitable. Lands unprofitable.* After each map, there was a page of text in old writing, where the s's were f's, of a list of what I took to be villages and the names of those who lived in them and paid dues on the lands they owned. I went through the maps several times, but only once did I find one with a tiny corner on the right-hand side, marked simply "the sea". I could not even find Dundrum Bay, let alone Ballyvaston, and whatever about a village getting lost over the centuries, a bay does not.

In the end, I gave up. I tried to find more maps, but drew a blank. The record of the place, as referred to in Albert's book, seemed to be as lost as the village it once recorded. I could find nothing. But who is to say it is not there and will re-emerge in time? The lost village of Ballyvaston, Albert told me, has never been excavated. "The place is a time capsule," he said, as we looked out over the beach that day and tried to imagine roofs, cabins, hearth-stones, people; a village now lost and buried, but enduring yet in stories.

Ballyvaston, Dundrum Bay, Co. Down, 10 April 2005
National Library, Dublin, 16 May 2005

~KERRY~

EVERYONE AT A LIGHTHOUSE
FENDS FOR THEMSELVES

Parknasilla Hotel, Sneem, Co. Kerry

18 September 1910

My Dear Jackson

... Yesterday I left the Kerry coast in an open boat, 33 feet long, propelled by ten men on five oars. These men started on 49 strokes a minute, a rate which I did not believe they could keep up for five minutes. They kept it up without slackening half a second for two hours, at the end of which they landed me on the most fantastic and impossible rock in the world: Skellig Michael or the Great Skellig, where in south west gales the spray knocks stones out of the lighthouse keeper's house, 160 feet above calm sea level. There is a little Skellig covered with gannets – white with them – covered with screaming crowds of them ... Both the Skelligs are pinnacled, crocketed, spired, arched, caverened, minaretted; and these gothic extravagances are not curiosities of the islands: they are the islands: there is nothing else.

The rest of the cathedral may be under the sea for all I know: there are 90 fathoms by the chart, out of which the Great Skellig rushes up 700 feet so suddenly that you have to go straight up stairs to the top – over 600 steps. And at the top amazing beehives of flat rubble stones, each overlapping the one below until the circle meets in a dome – cells, oratories, churches, and outside them cemeteries, wells, crosses, all clustering like shells on a prodigious rock pinnacle, with precipices sheer down on every hand, and lodged on the projecting stones over-hanging the deep huge stone coffins made apparently by giants, and dropped there God knows how.

An incredible, impossible, mad place, which still tempts devotees to make "stations" of every stair landing and to creep through "Needle's eyes" at impossible altitudes, and kiss "stones of pain" jutting out 700 feet above the Atlantic.

Most incredible of all, the lighthouse keeper will not take a tip, but sits proud, melancholy, and haunted in his kitchen after placing his pantry at your disposal – will also accompany you down to the desperate little harbour to squeeze the last word out of you before you abandon him, and gives you letters to post like the Flying Dutchman – also his strange address to send newspapers and literature to; for these he will accept.

I tell you the thing does not belong to any world that you and I have lived and worked in: it is part of our dream world …

George Bernard Shaw

Via e-mail, to the Commissioners of Irish Lights

7 February 2005

Dear folks,

I am a journalist here at *The Irish Times*, and also a writer. I'm currently working on a non-fiction book about Ireland.

I am writing one thing about each county. One of the counties I have yet to cover is Kerry. I know that Irish Lights maintain the lights from time to time, and I wondered if anyone ever spends the night at the light-house while doing so. I am particularly interested in Skelligs, as I went there while a child, and my brothers used to skipper boats out there.

Do you think you could let me know if this might be possible or not?

Many thanks,

Rosita Boland

Via e-mail, From the Commissioners of Irish Lights

8 February 2005

Dear Rosita,

Thanks for your e-mail. We have a maintenance visit to Skelligs Lighthouse planned for about a week from around 6 April. The maintenance team will live at the lighthouse for the week. There is plenty of room at Skelligs Lighthouse and you could stay there too, subject to certain conditions.

Transport to the rock is by helicopter from Castle-townbere, Co. Cork. If there is spare capacity in the heli-copter you could avail of it to fly to the rock; or you could make your own transport arrangements to travel to the rock by local boat for part of the time – irrespective of how you decide to travel the journey will be subject to weather, sea conditions, and other exigencies.

If you wish to go ahead with this please write for-mally to the Inspector of Lights & Marine Super-intendent at this address giving plenty of notice (at least a month). Please mark your letter for my attention.

Best wishes,

David Bedlow

for Inspector of Lights & Marine Superintendent

Text message to my brother Arthur Boland, 8 February 2005

Have been offered trip to Skelligs Lighthouse but not sure if can take it as am running out of time.

Text message reply from Arthur, 8 February 2005

Oh, you must go – think of those monks & what they thought about each morning.

Via letter, to the Commissioners of Irish Lights

4 March 2005

Dear Inspector,

I have been in touch with David Bedlow at Irish Lights and he has suggested that I write formally to yourself re my inquiry.

I am a journalist here at *The Irish Times* and also a writer. I am currently working on my fourth book, a non-fiction book about Ireland. I am writing one thing about each county (no photographs). For Kerry, I am particularly interested in writing about the Skelligs. I have been there twice, the first time as a child of six. The reason I am approaching Irish Lights is that I am hoping to spend a night in the lighthouse there.

David Bedlow has explained to me that a maintenance crew are next due out in early April, and that, in principle, it should be possible for me to join them.

I know this is a long shot, but I am also asking if it is possible for my brothers, David and Arthur Boland, to accompany me. David lives locally, in Caherdaniel. He has skippered boats out to Skelligs from Derrynane many times and has a great personal interest in and knowledge of the place. All three of us knew Ted Butler, now dead, whose family used to own Skelligs. I used to work for him, when he ran Ted's Bar in Caherdaniel. David works on the fish-farm at Deenish and goes to work by boat each day. David is also a member of the Derrynane inshore lifeboat team and is well aware of the demands of life at sea. He was part of the team from Derrynane who recently travelled over to England to bring the new lifeboat back.

My brother, Arthur Boland, writes below:

Dear Inspector,
My sister Rosita has been telling me about her plans to

visit Skellig Michael through the courtesy of the Com-
missioners of Irish Lights and that it might be possible for us,
her brothers, to accompany her on her short trip. I would
relish the opportunity to spend a few nights on the Rock as it
is a place with which I have been familiar ever since my first
trip there at the age of nine. As a teenager, I used to spend all
my summers in Béaltrá and had a summer job working on a
boat bringing visitors out to the Skelligs from Derrynane
harbour. We used to bring milk and newspapers out to the
lighthouse keepers. I used to scheme about bringing a tent out
and staying for a night but never got round to it so this
would be a wonderful chance to realise an old dream. I used
to know Ted Butler well, now dead a few years. His great-
grandfather sold the rock to the Commissioners back in the
1820s. Regarding practicalities, I have a head for heights
and am healthy and fit and well-used to camping and
fending for myself. And St Michael, the patron saint of high
places as I am sure you are aware, will be there to keep an eye
on us!

I understand that my request is slightly unconventional,
but I thought that it was important to at least ask if a
visit by all three of us was possible, given that I will be
there for research and my brothers both have very strong
local ties with the place and a huge appreciation of
Skelligs and the sea. However, if it is only possible for
myself to visit, I will of course understand and I do very
much appreciate the assistance Irish Lights is giving.

I look forward to your reply.

All the very best,

Rosita Boland

Via letter, Commissioners of Irish Lights, 16 Lower
Pembroke Street, Dublin 2

11 March 2005

Dear Rosita

Thanks for your letter of 4 March.

A mechanical/electrical maintenance visit to Skelligs
Lighthouse is planned for the period 6 to 13 April. We

would have no objection to your visiting the lighthouse during that time, subject to the willingness of the Attendant to facilitate you and the availability of accommodation at the lighthouse, and to your acceptance and compliance with the following conditions –

1. *The Commissioners of Irish Lights must be put to no expense or inconvenience.*
2. *Your visit must not interfere with the routine operation of the Lighthouse service.*
3. *The Attendant of the Lighthouse must be present and any instructions, including safety precautions, given by the Attendant, must be complied with.*
4. *The Commissioners of Irish Lights will accept no liability for any damages, claims or costs arising from your visit. The attached form of indemnity must be completed and signed by all the visitors and returned to me in advance. The original form must be returned; a fax or photocopy cannot be accepted.*

There should be no difficulty about accommodation at Skelligs Lighthouse, and we have no objection on principle to your brothers visiting the Lighthouse with you subject to the conditions set out above. However the increased number of visitors introduces complications with regards to our helicopter operations and in these circumstances it would be preferable if you would make your own arrangements to Skelligs by boat from Valentia or Ballinskelligs while the Attendant and maintenance team are at the station.

You will need to bring your own food, drinking water and bedding. Everyone at a lighthouse fends for themselves.

You should phone the Attendant, Mr Richard Foran, in good time to make the necessary arrangements with him. Please note that any arrangements made may have to be changed at short notice if weather conditions or the exigencies of our Service so require.

Finally, I would emphasise that our Attendants are part-time employees and looking after visitors is completely outside the scope of their duties and remuneration. Subject to the Head of Marine, the

Attendant will have discretion to regulate all aspects of your visit to any lighthouse.

Yours sincerely,

David Bedlow

for Head of Marine

*

On the afternoon of 13 April, I stood on the tiny pier of Blind Man's Cove – the "desperate little harbour" as described by Shaw a century before – on Skellig Michael, looking anxiously out to sea. The maintenance trip planned for the previous week had been postponed, as the weather had turned wild and the wind was too dangerous for a helicopter landing. The landing pad at Skelligs is particularly tricky, located as it is on concrete stilts over the sea, the rock-face just beyond it. When the wind blows in the wrong direction, landing has to be abandoned, due to the very real possibility of the helicopter being blown in against the rock-face and smashed to bits. Instead of a week on Skelligs, the team's trip had now been changed to two nights, 13 and 14 April.

For all the e-mails, letters, phone calls and holiday leave arranged from work by the three of us, and all our carefully laid plans, in the end, everything was a mad scramble, defined solely by weather. The previous day, I had collected Arthur in Killarney and we had driven down to Bunavalla, near Caherdaniel, where David lives with his family. The plan was for the three of us to join the Attendant and maintenance team on Skelligs on Wednesday afternoon via a training excercise on the Derrynane Inshore lifeboat, of which David is a crew member. We woke up on the Wednesday to a mean-looking sea and a poor forecast. I accidentally broke a glass while washing up, staring distractedly out the window at the sea. Arthur silently rolled endless cigarettes and also looked out to sea. David phoned me at 9.30 a.m. from the sea, on the fish-farm boat he worked on. "It's feckin' nasty out here," he said bluntly. "We mightn't get out today. And the forecast is worse for tomorrow. If there is a chance for you to get out by helicopter, you should take it."

I had been in regular contact with the Attendant, Richard Foran, who lives in Valentia, and with Donie Holland, who was based at the Castletownbere heli-pad. I called them both. At 10 a.m. Richard called me back to say that the helicopter would pick both of us up at Knightstown in Valentia at 11 a.m. sharp. It is the best part of an hour's drive from my brother's house to Knightstown. I had to leave instantly. My rucksack was already packed, but we had planned on buying our provisions in the village before leaving that afternoon. *Everyone at a lighthouse fends for themselves.* My sister-in-law, Annie, ran round the kitchen, firing things into a bag for me. I threw my stuff into the car and took off, shouting back to Arthur that I hoped to see both himself and David later.

I made the helicopter. While Richard and the two-man maintenance team, electrical technician Mark "Buzz No-Light" O'Connor and mechanical technician Paddy "Crazy Pony" McLeughlin, sorted out their gear in the lighthouse, I went down to the cove to look at the state of the water there. It was OK for a landing, but the sea beyond the harbour was fretful, white-topped. Back ashore, there were discussions. Arthur and David decided they would launch at 3 p.m. I waited by the pier for a couple of hours, feeling ridiculously like Peig, worrying about her menfolk out on the open Atlantic Ocean off Kerry.

When Arthur and David finally stepped onto the pier and waved the rescue boat off on its return leg to Derrynane, Arthur handed David a cigarette. David took it, then laughed as he realised it was pre-rolled. "Did you think you'd get a chance to smoke that on the boat?!" They didn't need to tell me it had been a bone-shaking ride.

There are two lighthouses at Skelligs. One, now abandoned, started operating in 1826. Its light was extinguished in 1870. The "new" lighthouse took over then. Until the 1980s, it was operated manually, full-time. Now it is automated and nobody lives permanently at the lighthouse, although the Attendant visits regularly, and about twice a year a maintenance team also visits.

You access the lighthouse along the narrow path that leads

from Blind Man's Cove, going through various gates along the way. It is a lighthouse where the light itself is surprisingly modest looking, since the elevation of the building is already so high. Downstairs is a control room, the crew's kitchen and pleasant living-room, a telephone room, a bathroom, guest kitchen and guest living-room. Upstairs is a store-room and six bedrooms. The lighthouse is built virtually into the side of the cliff. My room looked right down over wild Seal Cove, the small bay separating the two immense lighthouse headlands, and across at a cliff where the white fulmars and guillemots crowded together in rows along clefts like beads in a pearl necklace. It was a stunning view; without doubt, the most amazing view from a bedroom I've ever had, or probably ever will have. The rooms themselves were simple but more than adequate: single beds, a chest of drawers, a wardrobe and a chair. Lino had been laid over the original floorboards. I shook out my sleeping bag and marvelled again at that fantastic view – although it is true to say that everywhere you look on Skelligs there is an amazing view.

Richard Foran has worked for the Commissioners of Irish Lights for forty years. He started off with a year at Roancarrig in Bantry Bay. After that, he was on the Bull Rock in Kerry for three years; a time when you were on the rock for a month and off for a fortnight. By the time of his next posting, to Tory Island in Donegal for six years, it had changed to a month on and a month off. He then went to Wicklow Head for five years and Mizen Head in Cork for two years. Since then, he has been at Skelligs. He was there when it was automated and his title changed from Keeper to Attendant, since now the light keeps itself. Richard has seen a lot of changes. His old station, Wicklow Head lighthouse, is now available as an upmarket rental through the Landmark Trust. When at Mizen, he was part of the lighthouse team who rescued Charlie Haughey and his friends when Haughey's boat ran aground on the Mizen rocks. The lighthouse at Mizen has now been turned into a fascinating museum, which records the way of life of the past lighthouse keepers. I had been there once with my sister

Cáitríona and had clear memories of the place, from the specially commissioned ware of old Irish Lights plates and egg-cups, to the startling figure of a dummy in an old iron bed in the keeper's room. Richard has been back to see the museum. Was it strange, I asked him, to see the place where he had once worked now transformed into a museum? "Yes," he said. "Especially when I saw that man sleeping in my bed!"

That first evening on Skelligs, Arthur, David and myself climbed up to the beehive huts. We worked out how long it was since each of us had been there. For me, it was seventeen years; for Arthur, eight; and for David, even though he had skippered boats out from Derrynane many a time, it had been, he realised, about twenty-five years since he had left the boat at the harbour and climbed up to the monastery. At the top, we split up and wandered in and out of the beehive huts, not talking much. All the way up the stone steps, I had been remembering my first visit to Skelligs, with my father, when I was six. I had very vivid memories of the day. The weather had been bad for days and it was too wild to go out to sea. A trip to Skelligs had been promised and every day I watched the waves on the sea and unhappily counted down the days before our August holiday ended. Finally, one morning, when I had returned from my daily errand of fetching the milk from a farmhouse up the road, I had been told the trip was on. I was so excited all I wanted was to get to Béaltrá pier as fast as possible before the weather changed again, or my father changed his mind about taking me with him. And then, our Bunavalla neighbour Sean O'Shea's boat, the *l'oursin* out from Béaltrá, the wind and how cold it was on the boat; being handed onto the little harbour by Sean O'; the steepness of the steps and the number of them; the clustered stone huts at the top and my father explaining to me inside one of them that monks had once lived there. I had been dumb-founded at the notion of these cheerless stone places being homes. But I never forgot the place and thought often of that day as the years passed.

As the three of us wandered round the huts, I thought back

again to that first trip. I went into the hut in which my father had first told me about monks living there. I thought again about the stone steps on the way up. Something was puzzling me, and I couldn't work out what it was. Then I realised suddenly that when I had first come to Skelligs as a child, it had not yet been discovered that I was appallingly short-sighted. I hadn't had my glasses then. Everything I remembered was as if in a dream, since everything was a blur unless I looked closely at it, such as the steps under my feet or the stones in the beehive huts. That was partly why my memories of the place were so intense and also so odd: I remembered clearly the lovely, strange shape of Skelligs from far out at sea and how it still seemed the same even when we were almost in the harbour. I couldn't see it properly, so it remained throughout a magnificent, arcane blur. *I tell you the thing does not belong to any world that you and I have lived and worked in: it is part of our dream world.*

As we descended from the huts, I discovered that Arthur had fibbed about something in our joint letter to the Commissioners of Irish Lights. *Regarding practicalities, I have a head for heights ...* He did not. As he said later, "Most pilgrims go up on their knees. I came down on my arse."

We stopped about two-thirds of the way down and sat on the steps. It was around 7.30 p.m., and the sky was just beginning to darken slightly. We looked out to sea in a companionable silence. The lads smoked. At first, we didn't notice the birds. After all, Skelligs is alive with birds, and neighbouring Small Skelligs is an internationally famous gannet colony. There are birds everywhere, constantly calling and screeching and swooping. Then I looked up at the sky and stared hard, not understanding what was happening. I finally realised. "Look," I said, "the birds are coming home for the night."

We all looked up together. The sky was now dark with hundreds of birds flying in from the ocean after their day at sea. Most of them were puffins, their short distinctive wings beating like butterflies. They flew past us with no fear, so close their wings almost brushed our faces. Many of them stood outside their burrows, waiting for their mate to return also, and when the pair had landed, they disappeared together. We watched with amazement and delight.

There was a new moon that night. It shone in through my window. I fell asleep listening to the sound of the waves and woke up to the sound of the waves, far louder than they had been the night before.

There was a high wind. It was clear that David would not get off that day; Arthur and I had planned to stay for the two nights, but David needed to return to work. But there's no arguing with the weather at sea. Arthur went back up to the monastery with his camera. At base, I had noticed a path at the back of the lighthouse. Richard told us it led to the old lighthouse, higher up and out of sight from where we were. He offered to unlock the gate for us where the path started so we could go up and look at it. While Richard fetched oil for the salted-up lock, David and I examined the names carved on the wall adjacent to the lighthouse. Keepers have always carved their names at Skelligs, on this wall and elsewhere. *J. O'Connor 1833. L. Deasy 26. S.M. O'Donnell. D.P. Sullivan 1941. B.R. Jeffers 1888. J.B. Donovan 1874. W.J. Hamilton.* Some are very beautifully carved, deep and clear and as professional looking as if done by a stonemason. "I knew Hamilton," Richard said, as I scribbled the names in my notebook. "He was here in the 1930s. A great character. He made his own false teeth from the ivory handles of knives." Richard hasn't carved his own name into Skelligs yet, but he says he will before he retires.

It is a glorious, vertiginous walk along a narrow path blasted out of the rock to the old lighthouse. I soon discovered I had two brothers who had no head for heights. We were ankle-deep in the sea-campion that covers Skelligs. Although there was a high wind, the sky was blue and clear. The sea glittered far below us. We marvelled at how stones could have been carried for the building of the lighthouse along such a narrow path.

The old lighthouse and its adjacent building are now ruined, but it remains a wonderfully atmospheric place. The lighthouse itself is covered with slate tiles, and you can still see the original granite steps inside that led to the top: granite that came from Monaghan. The glass from the light lens and metal from the light at the top have fallen in and lie broken on the floor. Both David and myself took a small piece of glass each as a memento; the lens in the current lighthouse dates from 1909, and still functions perfectly well.

The keeper's house was built to the same plan as the new lighthouse, with a small boundary wall for shelter built on the side that faced the sea. The other side faced the solid slab of rocks from which the space to make the buildings had been blasted out by dynamite almost two hundred years ago. The more we looked around, the more impressive we realised the building and materials were for the time. The porticoes were cast-iron, the flagstones granite, the chimneys double-breasted. "It was a fine house. They had the best of materials," David declared, examining the stonework closely. Later, Richard told me that the builders lived in the beehive huts at the monastery when they were building both lighthouses. "If you look carefully, you can still see whitewash at the back of stones in the huts," he said. "They whitewashed the interiors of them all to make them brighter while they were living there."

On our way back, we diverted to walk along a path that led out to a headland and on which was a large rusted object we thought looked like a winch, but knew it couldn't be. We puzzled over it. It was too far up the rock for it to operate as a winch to a boat below. There was also a small stone building, like a phone-booth, in which we sheltered from a shower.

When we went back, Richard told us that this was where the lighthouse crew used to fire rockets during fog. Each man had a four-hour shift and had to fire a rocket to a timer every three minutes. Sometimes the fog lasted for days. "Many's the night I was out there," Richard recalled grimly. Irish Lights stopped using rockets when the Troubles started in the North, as it was thought that the lighthouse magazines would be potential targets for their detonators.

It would not have been the first time lighthouse supplies had been diverted to an armed struggle, as Richard told us. In the early 1920s, a keeper called King, who was the son of a Skelligs keeper, was discovered to be holding back some of the detonators from his rocket-firing shifts. He was suspected of selling them on to the Irish Republicans. He was arrested coming off a shift and taken in for questioning by the Royal Irish Constabulary in Cork. He indeed had smuggled detonators in his pocket, which the RIC discovered when King stood with his hands in his pockets too close to the fire, causing the detonators to go off, blasting some of his fingers away in the process. After he got out of hospital, he was called to a meeting in Dublin. The Irish Lights office used to be on O'Connell Bridge, where the old Harp building once was. The meeting was for 2 p.m. "Irish Lights were very pro-British," Richard explained. "It was clear he was going to be sacked." The head of Irish Lights at that time always went to the Gresham at 1 p.m. for lunch. As he walked over O'Connell Bridge that day, two men came up to him and put a gun in his ribs. "If you fire King at two," they told him, "you're dead by five." When King turned up at the office an hour later, the door opened a crack and the boss-man put his head out nervously. "King," he said, "go back to your station!" He remained in the employment of Irish Lights for the rest of his days.

The next day, Friday, the day we were all due to leave, a gale was blowing. Not only was it out of the question that a boat could land, Richard went to the heli-pad and declared the wind conditions too dangerous for the helicopter. We would have to stay a third night. In our little kitchen, we eyed our remaining provisions and listened to the Valentia coastguard weather forecast every three hours on David's VHF radio. It was possible that our already extended stay might be extended still further, should the wind not abate enough for us to have a window to get off. My brothers were untroubled by our dwindling stores: they told me gleefully that if they were stuck, well, they could always eat me.

I took my book and climbed up again to the monastery that afternoon. Although it was wild, and the sea was one huge angry swell, again it was blue and wonderfully hot. I read a few chapters and then lay down on the sea-campion and fell asleep. How often do you have a chance like that, to fall asleep under a hot sky among ninth-century beehive huts; to have the whole extraordinary place to yourself?

That evening, Arthur had finished the book he had brought out with him and was rereading for the fourth time a book he had given me, *The Forgotten Hermitage of Skellig Michael*, by Walter Horn, Jenny White Marshall and Grellan D. Rourke. It is a detailed and fascinating record of the time these archaeologists and conservation architects spent exploring the remains of a tiny hermitage on the South Peak of Skelligs. One monk left the other twelve and the abbot and went to live by himself as an anchorite high up on the other side of the rock. With the help of the Kerry Mountain Rescue Team, the archaeologists explored the near-inaccessible, self-contained site, which even had stone basins for collecting rainwater. From their findings, they were able to make a drawing of a reconstruction of the tiny hermitage. All three of us read the book when we were on Skelligs and all of us were astounded at the idea of one monk withdrawing even further from what was already a very remote and isolated monastery.

> From the oratory the climber doubles back to the trail that leads to the summit, an unusually wide and long dry-stone masonry traverse, 9 by 2 meters, that ends at the foot of the last perpendicular rock face. On the way up to this traverse one views with amazement a fragment of dry stone wall built by someone who must have been kneeling on clouds when he placed these stones in a narrow ledge that plummets into what appears to be eternity. Early in our investigations we believed that this wall once formed part of a beehive cell, the dwelling of the hermit ...

When I came back that evening from my nightly puffin-homecoming watch, I stood outside the lighthouse with the book, trying to work out from the photographs and maps where the hermitage had been located on the South Peak. The near-vertical wall of the South Peak overlooks the lighthouse. Close to the top were a few bits of scaffolding set against the rocks, put in place by the Office of Public Works and looking ludicrously fragile. Richard wasn't sure of the exact location of the hermitage, which is all but invisible from below in any case, but he pointed to the scaffolding and told me it was close by. Even to look at it made me feel dizzy. To have lived on such a tiny, precipitous shelf of stone, the anchorite must have had the soul of a bird.

Saturday morning was windless and flat calm. The inshore lifeboat returned for the lads. They went ashore first. I waited on the heli-pad with Richard while Mark and Paddy went ahead on the helicopter's first run to Castletownbere. For the first time that week, the weather was good enough for the tourist boats to come from Valentia. The passengers from the first two boatloads walked past us as we were waiting, saying hello in half-a-dozen different accents as they passed. I realised I was startled to see them, so used had we got to having the entire island to ourselves for those three unforgettable, extraordinary days.

Skellig Michael, Co. Kerry, 13–16 April 2005

~SLIGO~

LEGENDARY HILL OF THE "FAERIES"

"Are you in a fairy mood?" Melody Urquhart asked me, first thing, as I arrived at Gillighan's World, close to Knocknashee, on the day it re-opened for the season. I'm not sure how one answers that question. It was a new one on me, for sure. Was I in a "fairy mood"? What *is* a fairy mood?

Between Tubercurry and Ballynacarrow, there are signs on the main Sligo–Galway road that had intrigued me for months as I passed up and down. *Gillighan's World, Knocknashee, Legendary Hill of the Faeries, Faerie Park & Model Village*, they read. I had followed the signs the first time I had noticed them, the previous September. They led past the village of Lavagh to a site built into a hill opposite a chained-off car-park. I had looked through a locked gate that led through some sort of stone tunnel-like entrance but could see nothing. The fairy – *faerie* –

theme park had closed the previous week. I had determined to return when it re-opened on May Day.

The publicity flyer for Gillighan's World declares that it is:

> An idyllic mountain haven and heritage site set in beautiful botanical gardens with stone tunnels, dolmen and amphitheatre, the miniature model village's delightful "faerie habitats", enchanted glades, streams and secluded seating areas create a magical atmosphere, whilst a visit to the "faerie fort" offer spectacular panoramic views … Created by Melody, Baroness of Leyny Ph.D, to bring pleasure to people of all ages. This blessed mountain retreat reflects the true spirit of Ireland and its incomparable Celtic mythological past.

When I had called well ahead of visiting, Melody had agreed to an interview. But first, I wanted to have a good look round Gillighan's World on my own. She gave me a map of the site, which had a quiz on the back, and told me brightly I might like to fill out the answers to the quiz while on my wander round. I looked at the thirteen questions. They included: *How many mushrooms are there in Gillighan's World? Where do fairies get their sweets from? Where do fairies dance at night? Where can you find the hanging witch? Where can you buy your own fairy to take home with you?* What age did Melody think I was, I found myself wondering? Was she serious? Apparently, yes. She looked disappointed when I told her I would use the map and questions as a guide to what I might find, but that, no, I would not be completing the quiz.

The first thing you see when you come through the Newgrange-style stone entrance into Gillighan's World is a fake dolmen. I looked at it and wondered what it reminded me of. Not the Poulnabrone Dolmen of my home county in Clare, but the faux heritage installations that you sometimes see outside new housing estates: usually set there to emphasise the fact that the estate is called Dolmen this or Cromleach that.

The next thing you see is a rockery dominated by four large mushrooms painted purple. There is a little pink house squashed under the mushroom stalks. There is a fairy wind-chime. A squirrel. More fairies. A pair of legs disappearing into the gravel. Everything is on a different, mismatched scale to everything else and everything looks as if it is made of resin or some kind of toughened plastic.

There are several rockery-type installations of this kind throughout Gillighan's World, many of them with shops. Ye Olde Apothecary had a huge green frog alongside it. Stuck around the surrounding vivid red and yellow gravel was a plastic orange, which had sunglasses and a nose, a vegetable-creature with a smiley cabbage head and another one with the head of a smiley green pepper. I discovered where fairies dance at night. At Trumps Disco, in a stump of plastic log, with an eagle arching his wings on the roof over the entrance, perhaps to pounce on visiting fairy prey.

Hotel Le Posh had a Georgian door. Around Hotel Le Posh were: a pig dressed up as a policeman; a pig in a suit, holding a mobile phone; a frog on a plinth that said *Welcome*; a rabbit in a green jumper; two hedgehogs in formal clothes in a shooting brake being chauffeured by another hedgehog; a sofa; three plastic figurines of women in period costume.

There were quite a lot of other things in Gillighan's World. There was a row of three plaster frogs seeing, hearing and speaking no evil. There were plaques saying *Fairies Live in the Bottom of Our Garden* and *Froggie Land*. There were very many dressed-up pigs, rabbits and frogs. There was a farm, which contained, among other things, plastic ducks larger than the lions behind them and a Tellytubby, which may or may not have been the next meal for the lions. There was a church with an owl dressed as a preacher alongside a figure of the Sacred Heart. In the place for the belfry on the church, there were no bells: instead, there was a bridal couple, of the kind you usually see atop large wedding cakes. There was a shop that had *Hair by Heidi* painted on it. Outside Hair by Heidi were two rabbits, buried up to their torsos in sand, like Winnie and Willie in Beckett's *Happy Days*. If there had been a question on the

Gillighan's World questionnaire as to what your favourite bit of the village was, the Hair by Heidi installation would definitely have won my vote.

There were dressed-up badgers, frogs, foxes and rabbits behind barrow-planters of flowers. There was a blue Loch Ness Monster in the pond. There were a few (real) hens running round, two (real) goats and a (real) donkey braying in a nearby field. There were the Seven Dwarves, sharing an installation with four grumpy-looking traditional musicians with pints of Guinness. There was a terracotta figure of a small child holding her dress out by the hem and hanging her head coyly. *Little Po was placed on my favourite spot, to represent the "child within"*, Melody has written in her scrapbook detailing the building of Gillighan's World, which is available for the public to look through in the room alongside the Crock of Gold Gift Shop. There were also lots and lots and lots of fairies in various locations – behind bushes, hanging off trees, stuck here and there, seemingly at random, many of them in twee poses. One, by the stream, had her fingers to her lips registering mock-horror as she regarded the nearby bare bottom of a gnome with his trousers around his knees and his backside to the wind. There was, however, oddly, not a leprechaun in sight.

I ended my tour of Gillighan's World by walking up to the "faerie fort". It was a man-made circular ditch, with a gap left to enter it through. I didn't go inside. Instead, I stood on the adjacent picnic table, looking down over Gillighan's World and across Sligo, and discovered to my surprise that I felt strangely depressed.

Melody invited me into her comfortable mobile home, which is the daily base at Gillighan's World in summer for herself and the people who work with her, including her husband, David. Melody is originally from Blackpool, England. For many years, she choreographed, produced and directed variety shows in Britain and beyond. The shows she looked after travelled all over the world: on cruise ships; in hotels patronised by ex-pats; to British bases for overseas troops – Belize, Germany, the

Falklands. "And we were very, very, very successful. But the point is that I spent my life being paid to create other people's dreams, and I was getting pretty tired and there was something missing in my life. I needed to do some serious work on myself and find me again, and that was the reason I came here," she explained.

Melody came to Sligo in 1993 because she had bought her title, Baroness of Leyny, by then and wanted to explore the area the title had been associated with. She bought the title from a Lord de Freyne – she's not sure of his Christian name, "because I always called him Lord de Freyne", she explained. "The de Freynes were involved with Frenchpark and Roscommon as well. He was English with Irish connections, and the family had been here for a long time. And I happened to meet the gentleman, and I'm very, very interested in history, particularly in ancient documents. I already had a title in England; I was the Baroness of Eye." Melody had also bought that title.

"And why did you want to buy the title in Ireland?" I asked.

"It's nothing to do with the title," Melody insisted. "But you see, if people don't use them and get *involved* and that, they will just fade away and become dusty old things that people forget about. And that's sad. You need to live the title. The title isn't important. But it's what you can *do* with it that's important," she declared.

"I suppose, though, it's fair to say that Irish people don't hold any stock at all by titles?" I ventured.

"No, and neither do I. I mean, nobody calls me by my title. I mean, a lot of the locals will say, 'Oh, the Baroness is here!' But it's done with affection because I don't put on any pretences. I never use my title here."

Created by Melody, Baroness of Leyny Ph.D, to bring pleasure to people of all ages. "Apart from on the publicity for Gillighan's World?"

"We're not talking about why I wanted to buy a title," Melody said sharply. "We're talking about Gillighan's World."

I asked Melody what her Ph.D was in, since she had advertised the fact that she had one. I was not much wiser after the explanation. She spent three years studying the history of the Barony of Leyny by herself in her spare time. "When you read about the Tuatha De Danann and the Moytura Battles, it is almost like a classical ballet. It has every ingredient for a ballet. Which was my field!" But the Ph.D, she explained to me, had actually been given on an honorary basis for charity work in 1995 by an American university, the name of which I was unfamiliar with.

Two years after Melody had bought her Irish title, she came to Sligo to live permanently and set about creating the theme park. "I had lost the little girl in me. I had lost the magic." She bought the land from a local farmer. Gillighans had once lived on the farm, hence calling the park after the old family name. The park opened in 1998 for a month and since then opens six days a week, May Day through to 8 September. Entrance is €6 for adults and €5 for children. Melody's friends from the performing arts world with whom she used to work in England have come over to visit and told her that, in Gillighan's World, she has created a set for a ballet. "And this is where *I* dance now," she said. "And I am truly *happy*, for the first time in my life."

I asked Melody how she had planned the design and contents of Gillighan's World.

"Imagination. Heart. There were no master plans. So it was imagination and artistry really. No hard, cold plans." They collected up the fairies and other objects over time and commissioned someone to make the buildings, the shops and the village houses. The "dolmen" was created out of big stones that had emerged when clearing the site. Melody has never seen the real Poulnabrone Dolmen. "I haven't the time," she confessed.

"What about the frogs and the pigs and the rabbits? What do they have to do with fairies?"

"You see, a lot of people come in and they don't know how to imagine. They're coming in, they've got their mobiles with them, they've been rushing from work, they've been forced to bring their family out with them. We try to put every single thing to show that man, animal and nature can live in harmony and that we're all intrinsically linked to each other. And sometimes you need things to help people along. So there are little things in the park to help them smile!"

"Why aren't there any leprechauns in Gillighan's World?"

"You won't see any leprechauns out there," Melody agreed. "Leprechauns are cheap, plasticky, horrible *cheap* little things you buy as souvenirs!"

"But it would be true to say that a lot of the stuff you have out there would be plastic as well?"

"No, that's fairy-world, that's not plastic. They may be resin and that, and coated and that, but if it is, it's been carefully hidden," Melody insisted stoutly, and I left it at that.

The thing is, I had really been looking forward to visiting Gillighan's World. I get a tremendous kick out of kitsch, and I own quite a bit of it, between crockery, bric à brac, bags, the odd item of clothing and various other bits and pieces. One of my favourite things is a Barbie filofax, which I've used daily for years. My fondness for it sometimes mystifies my friends, but I am a big fan of kitsch simply because it makes me laugh. And if ever there was scope for kitsch in Ireland, it is in the area of leprechauns and rainbows and fairy gold and all that ridiculous, knowing blarney. Only the previous month, I had groaned at the sign outside the café at Moll's Gap in Kerry – a café much frequented by American tour buses in the summer. The sign, pointing across the road, has a cartoon drawing of a leprechaun on it and the words *Leprechaun Crossing*. It is awful, of course, but at least it is blatantly, knowingly, cute-hoor Oirishly awful.

Kitsch-lover as I am, the truth is I hated Gillighan's World. *This blessed mountain retreat reflects the true spirit of Ireland and its incomparable Celtic mythological past.* You cannot contrive or assemble the spirit of a country by throwing up a fake dolmen and sticking plastic fairies in trees and bushes and using diggers to construct a fake fairy fort. I had never consciously put my mind to the question of what I thought the "true spirit of Ireland" meant to me, but I did that day in Gillighan's World. I stood on the picnic table adjacent to the fake fairy fort looking out over Sligo and thought of places in Ireland I had visited over the years and experiences I had had that had truly meant something to me.

Growing up in Clare and scampering frequently as a child over the fissured limestone pavements of the Burren to visit the mysteriously satisfying solidity of the Poulnabrone Dolmen. Exploring the tombs at Oldcastle by candlelight. Visiting and revisiting the gold and silver treasures in the National Museum. Standing in the circle of standing stones in Kenmare. Climbing the spiral steps of ruined castles as a child. Lying on my back in the middle of a deserted Dun Eochla on Arainn one hot July afternoon. Seeing bright-yellow gorse laid on every doorstep outside Ballinasloe one early May Day morning. Hearing Martin Hayes and Dennis Cahill play their haunting, fluent music live for the first time in Kilkenny's Canice's Cathedral. Leaving Ireland to live abroad and missing the Atlantic, the horizons of the west of Ireland and its mercurial skies above all else. Talking to the farmer when walking the Kerry Way near Castlecove who showed me the carved stone concentric circles his great-grandfather had found on their land when he had finally come to the end of the turf bank that had always been fuel for the family and had hit stone: stone circles older than the ancient turf that had hidden them.

Dolmens, tombs, stone carvings, gold treasures, traditional music, the ocean, forts. Taken individually, my touchstones of what I understand the spirit of Ireland to be are all as hoary and clichéd an image of Ireland as the leprechauns and blarney and Guinness and "craic" are. Or as clichéd as a fake dolmen, a fake fairy fort and a crock of gold-painted stones outside the Gillighan's World shop. It is what you make of them that matters. The motivation behind Gillighan's World is completely admirable; *An idyllic mountain haven and heritage site* sounds terrific in theory. I just wish I hadn't hated what I found at Knocknashee so very, very much.

Gillighan's World, Knocknashee, Lavagh, Co. Sligo, May Day, 2005

~ LIMERICK ~

THE CAT WITH TWO TAILS

Browsing in a Limerick bookshop one day, I found a book called *The Limerick We Don't See: A Photographic Challenge to Find One Hundred Architectural Features in the Englishtown Precinct of King's Island*. I bought it and took it home with me. There are, in fact, two of these *The Limerick We Don't See* books, both published by Limerick Civic Trust. One, set in Newtown Pery, was published in 2002, and the King's Island one was published in 2004. The engaging idea behind the books was beautifully simple: photographer Michael Cowhey went out and about with Denis Leonard, director of Limerick Civic Trust, and photographed one hundred architectural details, some obvious, some obscure, on the streets and buildings of central Limerick. The public were invited to buy the book for €10 and identify all hundred images. The prize, put up by O'Mahony's Bookshop, was €1,000, with a second prize of €500, plus several other runner-up prizes in the form of book tokens.

When I was a child in 1979, there was a lot of excitement about a picture book called *Masquerade*, by Kit Williams. It was a book he had written and illustrated, and in the pictures he had hidden clues to find a treasure he had made and buried in a public space in Britain; a fantastic gold, turquoise, moonstone and ruby pendant in the shape of a hare, sealed in a specially made casket. I could not solve a single one of the cryptic coded clues in the book. But I loved my copy of *Masquerade* and loved the knowledge that there was a treasure buried out there somewhere, if one could only find it. Two million people worldwide bought the book and tried to locate the treasure; a huge sale for a picture book at that time. The puzzle was finally solved eighteen months after publication.

I thought of *Masquerade* when I looked at the Limerick books. How observant, patient and dedicated you would need to be to identify each of those visual images, some no more than tiny details, and how much local knowledge you would need to have to identify them. I went through both books, marking a score or so of images that I particularly liked and wanted to find out more about.

The idea for the books came from both Denis Leonard and David O'Mahony, a director of O'Mahony's bookshops. Denis had photographs taken from a Civic Trust history and folklore project and went to David to see how they could possibly be put into a book. David had seen a book in England, about Bradford-on-Avon in Bath, which was a similar idea: an architectural treasure hunt, although not using as many tiny details.

"We wanted to get people out of cars – looking up, looking down," Denis explained. "The whole thing was to develop an interest in the streets where we live. It was also important that everything wasn't old. It wasn't a knowledge quiz either. You didn't have to say if a certain fanlight was Victorian or Georgian, just identify where it was."

The first book focused on the city centre, Newtown Pery.

Denis, who is from Limerick city himself, walked the streets several times with the photographer. They took twice as many pictures as they needed and then sorted through them to select the most fiendish ones. The introduction to the book reads:

> In every city or town there are hundreds, if not thous-
> ands of little gems staring us in the eye. Some of which
> are centuries old and many are present day adornments
> subtly included in new developments ...

The first book sold out and attracted so much attention over its eigheen months that they did a second book, on King's Island. There will be a third, about Irishtown. So many people correctly identified all 101 images (including the tiebreaker) in the first book, on Newtown Pery, that the winner's name, Anne Cunningham, had to be drawn out of a hat at a public presen-tation of slides that showed where each image was located.

When she saw the Newtown Pery book first, although she has been living in Limerick city since 1976, Anne could only recognise about a quarter of the images right off. "It took three months to find the rest of them," she explained over coffee in the Bank café on O'Connell Street. "We worked as a team, my husband and son, Edward, who was sixteen at the time. He wasn't at all interested in the beginning, and then he really got into it – he identified the tie-breaker picture. It was a tiny piece of metal on the riser of a stair. I thought it was wonderful. It made you so observant, and I got to know the city so well. When we go to other cities now, we're always noticing things and saying, 'That would be a good one for a book.'"

Limerick Civic Trust has been around since 1983. In that time, they have done 106 projects involving the public. *The Limerick We Don't See* books have been, according to Denis, "by far the most successful project we have ever done. There was a huge feedback. We even got some letters in verse about it."

Denis and I set off one morning from the Civic Trust build-ings, at a brisk pace, on a customised walking tour of Limerick: he was going to bring me to the locations of some of the images from both books that I wanted to find out more about.

The Heart-Shaped Stone, Book 2, No. 69

Eejit romantic as I am, the image I selected first from the two books was an extraordinary photograph of a perfect heart-shaped stone set into the masonry of a stone wall, just as if it were part of the rest of the stones. At the bottom of the hill from the old Bishop's Palace in King's Island, there is a long high wall. Once, behind it lay the orchard for the Mercy nuns' convent. There are no fruit trees behind the wall any more, nor a convent, only a derelict site. Ivy trailed down from the top of the wall. Denis stood and waited patiently. I stared. Eventually, I saw it: the perfect heart, set high in the boundary wall on a lane called Googes Hill, a colloquial term that Denis doesn't know the origin of. The stone is as beautiful as it sounds, and all the more startling for being in the middle of nowhere, within a wall that now protects nothing. How, I asked Denis, had he found it? "A native told me about it," he admitted. What did it mean? He didn't know.

The Prince of Montenegro, Book 2, No. 63

In the Church of Ireland graveyard of St Mary's Cathedral, the oldest building in Limerick still in the original use for which it was built, is a small, simple headstone. It reads: *Milo Petrovic-Njegos, Prince of Montenegro, Born 1889–1978*. The Prince of Montenegro is not a person I would have associated with Limerick. But he lived here when he was exiled from Yugoslavia, dying in Barrington's Hospital, now closed. There is some talk of his body being taken home for reburial, but for the moment, his remains continue to lie in St Mary's graveyard.

The Gardener, Book 2, No. 58

Not far from the Prince of Montenegro's grave is a stone plaque on a wall overlooking a pretty flower-bed with bluebells and flowering shrubs, overhung by trees and close to the entrance of the church. The plaque reads:

> *The kiss of the sun for pardon*
> *The song of the bird for mirth*
> *One is nearer God's heart in a garden*

Than any place else on earth
In fond memory of
Katie (Cis) Smyth 1897–1995
Who as a labour of great love for
This cathedral at the age of 97 yrs
Still tended this flower bed
Having done so for more than fifty yrs

This was her flower-bed. For half a century, parishioner Cis would come and tend it regularly. She always hung her handbag on the same branch of a nearby tree, even later in life when people were less trustworthy. Twice, Cis had her handbag stolen from the tree as she gardened, but she refused to do as advised, to leave it in the church while she worked. She wanted to feel free and unrestricted by worry. She thought it was worth having her bag stolen occasionally in order to continue to enjoy that freedom.

The Horse Repository, Book 1, No. 94

Cut into the stone over an archway on Cecil Street are the words *Hartigans Horse Repository*. Underneath are the words *W.M.B. Fitt & Co MIAA Auctioneers*. A horse repository – something I had never heard of before – was exactly that: a place you left horses, a mart. "A horse car-park," Denis suggested. He knew the auctioneers next door to the archway, P. & W. O'Brien, and so we nipped in. Paul M. O'Brien was there. His grandfather inherited the Horse Repository from Hartigans. "It goes back to the 1850s," he explained. "It was like an auction yard, where people would buy and sell horses and where they were kept for a while. There was a Derby winner sold out of there once." Paul walked inside the old Horse Repository with us. The stables are derelict now, and many have been taken away altogether, but you can still see the large iron rings set into the walls that the horses would have been tethered to. There are cars parked now where once there were horses stabled.

The Stone Faces, Book 2, No. 49

I don't know how many times you would have to walk past the northern, right-hand end of Matthew Bridge before you would notice the stone faces. Hundreds? If I had not had Denis walking around with me as a guide, I would probably not have found more than one or two of the images from the books that fascinated me, but when I saw the stone faces, I knew that these would have eluded me completely. At the northern end of Matthew Bridge, there is a short piece of wall, three blocks high, between the end of the bridge and a black gate. Two of the stones in the limestone wall on the top row of blocks are carved. Each block has a primitive-looking face carved into it, a concave carving. One has a mouth slightly turned up, and the other slightly turned down. They stare out of the stones, quizzical, strange, unnerving. They are extraordinary. "Nobody knows who carved them," Denis said. He thinks they date from the 1800s. He explained that they had originally been facing the opposite way, directly overlooking the river itself, where they would not have been seen by the public at all. When the bridge was renovated, the blocks were swapped around, and now the two mysterious faces are there to be seen by sharp-eyed passers-by.

The Boat Club Boy, Book 2, No. 83

What struck me about the image of this little figure of a boy in formal cap and jacket with his right arm raised and hand outstretched was that something was missing. I wondered what he had been holding. The little figure is part of a battered, but still magnificent, Celtic-revival-type pair of gates, which lead into the Athlunkard Boat Club. Denis thinks the Boat Club is about 110 years old. The gates – locked the day we were there – are original. By any standards, they are both arresting and unique. About seven feet high, they are interspersed both with decorative Celtic images and images particular to Limerick. On top, there are images in metal of Limerick's Treaty Stone, alongside Limerick's Castle and a round tower. Two circular panels are filled with images of the Maid of Erin, with her harp and greyhound. There are also a spinning wheel, harps, shamrocks and decorated finials. Some of the pieces are missing or broken. At the very bottom is the figure of the boy, standing solemn, one arm crossed on his jacket, the other outstretched, hand upheld. Beyond the gates is the now-derelict original boat club (the new one is behind). In front of the old building is a painted Victorian-looking statue of a man in an old-fashioned bathing suit and knee-length shorts, holding an oar in his right hand, arm upheld. I crouched down and examined the small figure of the boy on the gate more closely. There is a flat piece of rounded metal beside his right foot that looks as if it once held something. I think it once supported an oar, which the boat club boy held until time or corrosion or vandals took it from him. His companion figure, on the other gate, is missing, so there is no way of knowing for sure now, unless anyone out there remembers what the gate looked like when it was still complete.

The Cat With Two Tails, Book 1, No. 23

The cat with two tails actually does have two tails. You can see them clearly. One tail arches over his back, and the other one across his back. He is painted black. Someone has picked the eyes out with white paint. The stone panel looks old, medieval. I'd have preferred to have seen the stone as it originally was, unpainted. It is partially obscured by a drainpipe and flanked on its other end by a rusted, empty neon sign, but it is lucky it's still there at all. The cat with two tails, according to Denis, is reputed to have come from Quin Abbey in Clare, in a job-lot of builders' stone. Nobody really knows how it ended up built into the gable-end of a shop in Limerick. The current owner of the shop has had it written into the deeds of the property that the stone is to be protected. "It's up there as long as I remember," Denis says. And where exactly is the cat with two tails? It's there, on a gable wall in the centre of Limerick city, there to be seen by all who look up, go searching, open their eyes.

Limerick City, Co. Limerick, 3 May 2005

~ ROSCOMMON ~

CREX-CREX

My mother remembers them. So too do my father, my aunts and everyone of a certain generation in Ireland who spent time in the countryside in summer. The corncrakes kept my mother and my aunts awake on summer nights on their farm in north Galway, so loud they sounded as if they were right outside the bedroom window.

Corncrakes used to be common in Ireland. Tens of thousands of them arrived each April from Africa – from Zambia, Mozambique, Tanzania and Madagascar – to mate and nest in hay meadows and overgrown fields. Since the 1970s, the numbers started to decline, and decline rapidly. In 2004, there were only 145 calling males recorded in Ireland by BirdWatch Ireland: 90 in Donegal, 33 in West Connaught and 22 in the Shannon Callows. The reason their numbers have dropped so drastically is almost entirely because of changed methods of farming.

"The change from hay to silage is the main reason for the decimation of numbers," says Brian Caffrey, Corncrake Project Officer with BirdWatch Ireland. We're in his car, on our way from his office in Banagher to the Roscommon part of the Shannon Callows, to an area known formally as Clonburren, but locally as Fahns and Mathers, not far from Shannonbridge. Corncrakes are secretive birds who nest on the ground, under cover. Their habitats are the long-grassed meadows and hedgerows at the edges of fields. With the early cutting of the cover for silage, the birds do not get a chance to raise their brood of chicks, nor does the method allow them an escape route to the outer edges of the field.

The Shannon Callows are one of only three areas in Ireland that corncrakes still return to each year. Callows are low-lying riverside meadows that become submerged in winter. In summer, they grow lush and high. "There is very little fertiliser used there, and since the land is so wet most of the year, the trend has always been towards cutting later in the year, as you couldn't get machinery onto them earlier," Brian explains. "Corncrakes need meadow. And the thing about meadow is that it's not a natural habitat; it has to be managed. If it isn't looked after, it becomes rank – matted, the vegetation falls over and it becomes flat."

Male corncrakes are about the size of a thrush; game-shaped birds, with brown speckles and a white-speckled breast. They arrive from Africa first, usually from 25 April onwards – always returning to where they mated the previous year – and call to attract a mate. They only start calling at dusk, and then continue all night. Once they have found a mate, they stop calling. Until later in the summer, when they mate again. Thus, with luck, the corncrakes will hatch two broods each summer. The female lays one egg per day, and a clutch is usually between eight and twelve eggs. "The corncrake's life-span is only about two years, so they need all the help they can get to regenerate themselves."

Every year, from 20 May until 20 July, on nights it is not raining, BirdWatch Ireland employees go out between midnight and 3 a.m. in designated areas to listen for corncrakes; a task for which there is no extra pay and hours which are on top of a normal working day. Brian and his colleagues are uncomplaining and philosophical about the situation, but to me, it seems a prime example of state underfunding and trading too heavily on individual goodwill. BirdWatch Ireland, by the way, don't go out during rainy nights because the birds don't call in those conditions – not because they'll get wet.

As corncrakes are so secretive, the only way of counting the birds is to listen for them. The only time Brian has ever seen a corncrake nest – a shallow, rough, basin-like thing of tumbled grass – was when he discovered ones ruined by mowing. The females are very rarely seen, and they do not call at all. Since they don't call, their numbers cannot be accurately recorded, and the figures are based only on the males of the species. There is a Corncrake Hotline number that the public are encouraged to call if they hear a corncrake, which is listed at www.birdwatchireland.ie.

We reached the entrance to the Callows, and I hopped in and out of the car twice to open and shut gates. The Callows, like a turbary bog, have few markers on them to show who owns what. At intervals, there may be a willow planted along the path or a pile of weighted fertiliser bags to roughly mark out the boundary strips of callow, but mostly, Brian says, everyone just knows where their bit of land ends and another farmer's begins.

If a corncrake is heard on your land, a circle corresponding to 250 metres in diameter is drawn on a map around the general area, since the birds are territorial and nest within 250 metres of where they call. The farmer who owns the land is then approached and asked if he would like to participate in corncrake-friendly methods of harvesting his land. For instance, mowing later in the season so the birds can raise two broods. And mowing from the inside out so that the birds can move outwards in the field and shelter in the long grass of the uncut margins. While most birds will simply fly away when in danger, corncrakes do not. They will not break cover, and thus remain hiding in the meadow, which is why so many of them have died in the mowing machines in the past. The payment a farmer receives depends on the date he mows his land: it ranges from €250 to €450 per hectare, and virtually everyone co-operates, since it is deemed to be an honour to have a corncrake on your land these days.

The corncrake belongs to our collective national memory. "The corncrake is the one bird in Ireland people remember. It's emotive: people would associate it with the start of summer. It's also a symbol, maybe, of how much things have changed. It's part of our heritage, and we've already lost so much of our heritage. We have to try and keep it from belonging to the past," Brian says.

Only a few days before I came to Roscommon, the government had announced that the controversial route of the M3 motorway would indeed cut through the land near Tara. The reason being given for their hotly debated decision was that it would make the traffic flow more easily in the surrounding towns. I thought about this as we got out of the car, hoping to hear one of the three corncrakes Brian knew were already in this callow.

It was about 9.30 in the evening of a beautiful blue day. Driving down to Roscommon, I had kept thinking of the first two lines of Larkin's poem "The Trees": *The trees are coming into leaf/ Like something almost being said*. Everywhere I looked, there was greenness, trees opening like green haloes, hedgerows glowing; everything was full of possibility and change. The Callows that we were walking through were almost ridiculously picturesque. Drowned in winter with Shannon flood-waters, in mid-May the meadows were starting to grow to their waist-high level. Among the sedge and grasses and reeds were lattices of flag-irises, marsh-marigolds, meadowsweet, buttercups, horse-tails, lady's smock, dandelions. It smelt clean and fresh and of something I couldn't identify; something vague, like a half-recalled memory. Meadow pippets and swallows dipped and darted. We walked a mile through the meadows towards the river. Swans lifted off in the distance, the sound of their beating wings carrying clearly across the water. The sky was red, then pink, then mother-of-pearl. There was a half-moon in the sky, sharp as a snapped disc.

Brian asked me if I had ever heard a corncrake calling. I had been wondering this myself for a long time. I didn't know, was the answer. It was possible I could have heard one as a child, while visiting my aunt and uncle's farm in north Galway; the same one where my mother and other aunt had grown up and been kept awake in the summers. But I wasn't sure. Nor did I know what they sounded like, although I thought perhaps if I heard one now, I might remember if I had once heard the call in the past.

"The call is so loud, people think it's a massive bird. Or that they are very close by, when they are usually about three hundred yards away," Brian explained. "And once it gets dark, they really get going. They'll call all night."

The light began to play that trick it does on an early summer evening in Ireland: when you could look at a photograph of a landscape and not know whether the image was taken when the light was fading, at dusk, or when the light was growing, at dawn; that mysterious in-between penumbra place of brightness and shade, the equivalent of the time spent between waking and sleeping, when you are not yet sure whether the day is beginning or ending; when you are not yet sure which is the dream and which the reality.

Then we heard them. *Crex-crex, crex-crex, crex-crex*, sounding just the same as their onomatopoeic Latin name. First one, on one side of the callow, and then the other two, on the opposite side. They called loudly, clearly, distinctively. Listening, I knew then that I had not heard them before. We slowly walked the mile back towards Brian's car, stopping now and then to listen. It sounded as if the meadow itself was calling, as if it had voices. *Summer has arrived*, I thought. I stood listening, transfixed, happy. It was only when I was driving back to Dublin later that night that I realised I had completely forgotten to turn on my tape-recorder. It didn't matter: I didn't need a recording; I already had the sounds in my head. I stood there in the Callows and listened to the corncrakes calling, as the moon rose, and the meadows faded to palest green, and the river gleamed.

What began it all was the bright bone of a dream I could hardly hold onto. I knew I would always remember hearing those corncrakes on that evening: the perfect ending to the year I had just spent navigating my way through thirty-two counties, charting my own secret map of Ireland.

The Shannon Callow at Clonburren (Fahns and Mathers),
Co. Roscommon, 16 May 2005

ACKNOWLEDGMENTS

Very many people helped me in various ways during the year it took to research and write this book. I literally would have got nowhere without the assistance I was so generously given. A huge thank you to all mentioned below.

Galway
My sister Cáitríona, niece Lucy and nephew Luke for accompanying me to Monivea at the start of the year's adventure, and encouraging me onwards after my first county's research. Mary O'Malley for the bed at unforgettable Fort Lorenzo.

Kilkenny
Helen Comerford and David Lambert, who first alerted me to the Raggedy Bush, and for the bed at Burnchurch. Mary Flood and Edward Law at the Kilkenny Archaeological Society, Rothe House. Journalist John Fitzgerald for permission to quote from his article.

Leitrim
Aoife Demel of the National Museum at Kildare Street, who helped me with contacts. Brian Harding of the Natural History Museum, who sent me literature on Parke. Mary O'Doherty, archivist at Mercer's Library, the Royal College of Surgeons, who showed me their Parke archive and who made Parke's diaries and papers available to me. Dora Murphy at Textile Conservation in the Conservation Department of Collins Barracks for showing me those items of Parke's held by the Museum. Dermot MacNabb of the Carrick-on-Shannon and District Historial Society, who sent me their commemorative pamphlet on Parke. Brian Leyden and Carmel Jennings for the bed at Dromahair and for introducing me to the marvel cure that is Kilcullen's Seaweed Baths.

Antrim
Bernard and Madeline MacLaverty, who first showed me the Fuldiew Stone some years ago, going miles out of their way to do so, and who later sent me literature on it. Bernie Delargy of the Glens of Antrim Historical Society for contacts. Malachy and Brigid McSparran at Knocknacarry for sharing their theories with me.

Armagh
Robert Brown of Tayto Northern Ireland for telling me about Tayto's operations in Northern Ireland. Emily Cox of Slattery PR for liaising with Tayto Dublin.

Wicklow
Gerry Egan of Coillte for finding out for me what is planted in the Avonmore plot at Ballygannon Wood.

Cork
Dena O'Donovan of O'Donovan's Hotel in Clonakilty for showing me where *T'aint-a-Bird* landed and where Tojo is buried (twice over), and for putting me in contact with people who remember the event. Hannah Coakley, Mattie Teehan and Paddy Hart for taking the time to talk to me. Elayne Devlin for putting me in contact with her uncle, Paddy Hart. Ian Kilroy and Isabelle Dussert for the bed at Blackrock in Cork, despite the fact they were still unpacking their Boston boxes.

Fermanagh
James Gallagher and Lorraine McGrath of Pettigo and Tullyhommon for taking time out from post-office duties to talk to me. Carmel Jennings for her brainwave.

Donegal
Colm Faherty of Met Éireann at Glasnevin for contacts and meteorological information. Paddy Delaney at Malin Head Met Station for talking to me.

Tyrone
Adrian Beattie at Gray's Printing Museum in Strabane for his enthusiastic help. Billy Dunbar at Omagh for telling me about his life's collectings and showing me his old Bygones museum.

Derry
Brian Rippey of the School of Environmental Sciences at the University of Ulster for his contacts. Brian Wood for sharing his extensive knowledge of Lough Neagh with me. Michael Savage of the River Bann and Lough Neagh Association for showing me the weir at Toombebridge. Caroline Marshall of the Lough Neagh advisory committee for her help.

Dublin
Emer Ní Cheallaigh of the Irish Folklore Department at UCD for helping me locate my aunt's contribution to the Schools Folklore Scheme. Máine for translating her contributions.

Mayo
The islanders of Inishlyre for making us so welcome. Tom Gibbons for ferrying us back and forth from Rosmoney pier. Rhoda Twombly, Sheila Keeley and John Gibbons of Inishlyre and Sean Jeffers of Inishgort for talking to me about their island lives. Brian McIntyre for accompanying me to Inishlyre, doing all the driving and playing the piano so magnificently at Delphi House. And I'm sorry *County Bounty* got lost along the way!

Clare
Máine, for giving up relaxing by a fire on St Stephen's Day to keep me company in my freezing, about-to-be-banjaxed car as we drove round west Clare.

Laois
Ciara Higgins and her father, Kevin Higgins, for their pictures of Morrissey's.

Meath
Ger Clark for giving up a day to show me around Dalgan Park and for telling me so many extraordinary stories. Father Pat Raleigh for facilitating my visit there. Michael O'Sullivan for his time. At the Columban's house in Donaghamede, Father Pat Crowley for his kindness in allowing me full access to the archives held there.

Kildare
Dennis O'Driscoll, who was concerned that his adopted county of residence get due attention and who went out of his way to provide me with possible leads. Colin and Bridget Doyle, who first told me about Donnelly's Arm over Christmas drinks in Ennis. Des Byrne, who owns Donnelly's Arm and who talked to me in Kilcullen and showed me the famous arm.

Cavan
Derek Evans, angling correspondent of *The Irish Times*, for his help and contacts. Margaret Sheridan, who fielded my many calls to the Derragarra Inn in Butlersbridge. Paul and Niall Sheridan for talking to me.

Louth
Hilary Fannin and Giles Newington, who first told me about Greenore Port. Vanessa and Nuala Price for talking to me. Mark Price, who gave me the text of the note that his grandfather had written to his great-grandfather in 1916.

Waterford
Seamus Heaney, for his kind permission to use lines from "St Kevin and the Blackbird", which is published in his collection, *The Spirit Level*.

Tipperary
Sarah Gillespie, curator at the Clonmel Museum, for her contacts. Esther Murnane in *The Irish Times* library for helping

me locate the Derrynaflan archive photographs. Michael Webb and Mona Croom-Carroll for taking me to where the Derrynaflan hoard was discovered on Littleton Bog.

Carlow
David and Moira Durdin-Robertson for taking the time to show me around Huntington Castle and the Temple of Isis.

Wexford
Father Denis Doyle of Kilmore parish for taking my many phone calls and being so helpful. Liam Sheil of the Kilmore Carollers for talking – and singing – to me. Dixie Devereux for his time.

Monaghan
Johnny, Lucy and Fred Madden for talking to me about their family history and showing me round their house and garden, and for being so welcoming – even if they *had* forgotten I was coming!

Down
Albert Colman, who showed me the site of Ballyvaston's lost village and who shared his knowledge of it with me.

Kerry
An especially grateful "thank you" to David Bedlow at the Commissioners of Irish Lights, who fielded my e-mails, letters and phone calls over three months with patience and humour and who facilitated not just myself, but also my two brothers to stay in the lighthouse in Skelligs. The Society of Authors in London, on behalf of the Bernard Shaw estate, to quote from Shaw's letter to Frederick Jackson (1832–1915), solicitor and political journalist. The Attendant at Skelligs, Richard Foran, who shared some of his astonishing stories with me and who was so helpful throughout the time we were on the Rock. Donie Holland at the heli-pad at Castletownbere. Mick Connelley for

piloting me out and back from Valentia. Michael Donnelly, Jerry Clifford, Brian Sullivan and Helen Wilson of the Derrynane Inshore Rescue Boat. My brothers, Arthur and David, whose company made this special journey even more so. And my sister-in-law, Annie, for providing us with such fine quantities of her curry, thus saving me from being put on the menu during our unscheduled third night on the Rock.

Sligo
Melody Urquhart for taking the time to talk to me on the first day of the season at Gillighan's World.

Limerick
Liam Burke of Press 22 for his suggestions and contacts. Denis Leonard of the Limerick Civic Trust for taking a morning to walk me around Limerick and for sharing his considerable knowledge of the city with me. David O'Mahony and Anne Cunningham for their time.

Roscommon
BirdWatch Ireland, in general, for all the information, and Brian Caffrey, in particular, for giving up an evening to take me to the Shannon Callows.

Thank you also to:
   The team at New Island, particularly Joseph Hoban, who was wonderfully enthusiastic and supportive about this book from the day I pitched the idea to him. Colm Tóibín, who read a draft of the manuscript. My friends and colleagues Belinda McKeon and Frank Miller: Belinda, who read a draft of the introduction and made spot-on, perceptive suggestions for changes; Frank, who went back to Monivea with me to photograph the key to Robert Percy ffrench's mausoleum for the cover. Sheila Pratschke and all the amazing women who work at the sanctuary and paradise that is the Tyrone Guthrie Centre at Annaghmakerrig, where half this book was written.

I also owe considerable gratitude to my friends Declan Jones, Oliver Comerford and Madeleine Moore. Although they may not have realised it, through their various projects – in Egypt at the new Museum of Antiquities in Cairo, and at sun-up and sun-down throughout Ireland on the film *Distance* – each played a crucial part in inspiring me to write this book. Similarly, an ad hoc post-interview conversation about travel and creativity in an Indian restaurant in Coventry a couple of years back with actor and director Mikel Murfi helped to kick-start me into thinking about this project, for which I am enormously grateful.

Thank you also to my great family and friends – particularly Brian McIntyre and Julie Cruickshank, two of the wisest people I know – who regularly inquired over the year this project took as to how things were going, and whose support kept me focused and motivated.

Finally, I am indebted to my employers, *The Irish Times*, who gave me sabbatical leave of four weeks to complete the research I needed to do; and to my features editor, Sheila Wayman, for facilitating me to take up the leave at short notice.